Teaching Children

Other *Child Light* books
published by Crossway Books

For the Children's Sake by Susan Schaeffer Macaulay

Books Children Love by Elizabeth Wilson

Teaching Children

A Curriculum Guide to What Children Need to Know at Each Level Through Grade Six

Diane D. Lopez

Subject Overviews by Elizabeth Wilson

Crossway Books • Wheaton, Illinois
A DIVISION OF GOOD NEWS PUBLISHERS

Teaching Children. Copyright © 1988 by Diane Lopez. Published by Crossway Books, a division of Good News Publishers, 1300 Crescent Street, Wheaton, Illinois 60187.

Cover and book design by K. L. Mulder.
Cover photographs by Karen Holsinger Mullen.

Eighth printing, 1994

Printed in the United States of America.

Library of Congress Catalog Card Number 87-71895

ISBN 0-89107-489-9

*This book
is dedicated to my wonderful children,
Jim and Beti, Tim and Rowena,
Clifford and Felicity;
Dorothy Kennedy, a dear friend and great proofreader;
and to all the boys and girls
who will benefit from the Child Light
approach to learning.*

Table of Contents

Introduction

The child of today inherits a society which has confused, opposite ideas of what education is all about. We have swung like the proverbial pendulum from structure to total freedom with as few boundaries as possible and then back again. We have sought for the child more play experience, and then earlier skills. (Teach a baby to read.) In the search for the best education confused parents and teachers have prodded or left children to develop at their own rate. More school time has been tried, as has no school at all. The Japanese look longingly at the creative and individual development in the West while we wring our hands governmentally at the fact of falling literacy rates.

Education! It encompasses our view of who the person is, and what life is all about! The very word assumes that the child has had his basic needs met and enjoys a secure background of home care. The child has been loved, fed, given place to run, explore, play imaginatively, have friendships. He or she has had plenty of conversational experience, and has enjoyed books from the comfort of lap or fireside. This child has two mature giving parents, and the home is within a community. The child knows right from wrong and has the self-knowledge of using his or her own conscience as everyday moral choices are made. The child says, "I ought to do this (or that). . . . and I will (even though I feel like doing something else)."

This is the child who traditionally wended his or her way to the little one-room schoolhouse, or to Public School No. 234. The teacher didn't have to do the groundwork. He or she could get on with the basics of the 3 R's.

We now live in a different world, a different age. Teachers bemoan the state of the children coming to them. More fundamental questions must be asked. And we can't find answers without a worldview.

□ *ix*

What is life all about? It there objective morality? Depending on what we believe, our answers will be very different.

This is no matter for casual, muddled thinking. It is of great importance to get our thinking straight from the groundwork up. And where shall we turn for guidance? One unchangeable principle is to assess the fruit of a system . . . and then go back and examine the infrastructure that produced that fruit.

About fifteen years ago, my husband and I were urgently seeking answers for our own children. We had a worldview, we believed that reality is as given in the Biblical teaching. That is, the Judeo-Christian teaching of a God who is actually there, who is righteous and also love, who created the person separate from Himself, and who provided salvation through Christ's free work and grace when our first human parents fell by their own choice.

As we sought for a satisfactory school for our own children, we sometimes felt despair. What was provided seemed so unacceptably far from any ideal, or even anything reasonable. And then, we stumbled over a product: a small one-room private school in the back of a cottage in southern England. Two of our children attended, and we saw fruit all right. It was like watching a desert that had had the first rain in ten years. Our children were very clearly onto a good thing. A very good thing indeed. Eagerly we sought the *what* and the *why*. The ideas practiced came from an educator named Charlotte Mason. We sent for her books and devoured them. Here was someone who had worked at the turn of the century who had produced in her students the excellent fruit we had longed for in our own children. "It's just what we've always wanted," we said to each other.

And then, we realized that not only were the C. Mason books out of print, but as a society we had so changed our homes, our communities, and our aims that her methods could not be implemented in small changes. If anybody else was interested, they'd have to go back to the beginning and think everything through again.

Many other young couples pressed us for just such guidance. Scores of teachers asked for "magic clues" to providing the fruit of this excellent educational philosophy. In answer to these pleas, I wrote a book called, *For the Children's Sake*. In it, essential family groundwork and then educational practice is described. We called the whole approach "Child Light."

Now this is the second of two books that has grown out of that original one, which must be read first! These two further books are for the hundreds of parents, teachers and schools who started inundating us with urgent pleas for further guidance. "It's just what I've always longed for," wrote one mother, "but *please, please* could you tell me what books I should read with the family?"

"You're right," wrote another, a teacher in an urban school. "The reading skill workbooks I'm given bore the kids stiff. But I wasn't brought up myself enjoying books, and I don't know which are alive, interesting, well-written.

"We're starting a grade school; we ourselves have a Christian worldview. Your book made us eager for a school based on Charlotte Mason's ideas. But we need guidance for that. Is there any chance that we could get some specific guidelines we could use?"

Three of us have pooled our resources so as to make the ideas written about in *For the Children's Sake* usable and practical at home and at school. Some of the ideas can be used by an individual teacher in a classroom, while others are able to implement them in an entire grade school program. Home schooling families also will find guidance and much to use, while the hurried parent whose child is in school and a day-care program will be guided to wonderful books to read aloud in the precious moments that *do* exist for the family together.

The basic ideas, philosophy and way of life of the Child Light program for home and school are explained in the book *For the Children's Sake* by Susan Schaeffer Macaulay. You'll need that book in order to use these curriculum guides.

This applies to parents, single parents, teachers, schools, and all working in children's programs, etc. It has to do with public school, private school, home school . . . it has to do with children's lives.

However, this brings us book number two—*Books Children Love* by Elizabeth Wilson. One of the central ideas in the Child Light program is introducing children to excellent books, living books. Elizabeth, a lifetime of book-oriented life and work behind her, gave us all a year of her time in her search for a core of these living books. If you want to use this book of curriculum guides, you'll also have to get *her* book, as it is referred to all the time by its title. Why do we need such a guide? Really good alive books aren't just there for the taking. You have to sort books out! There is plenty of shoddy work; dull, of poor quality. Then there are more and more children's books which are unacceptable from a Christian viewpoint. For instance, some assume that there are no acceptable moral standards or promote occultism. On the other side of the market, the school textbook markets, there are books put together in dry textbook ways which treat the child as if he were a bloodless automaton. Children should have truly good books and a wide variety of them, too.

We actually believe in seeking the best that we can find. The books do not all assume one basic viewpoint, but we sought what was good, worthwhile, interesting and lasting.

This, the third book in the basic Child Light package, takes the whole concept one step further. Our production team is now joined by a third participant, Diane Lopez. In this book we want to bridge the gap between Charlotte Mason writing for teachers and parents sixty years ago, and using her ideas in the late twentieth century—*today*. This is for people who want to use the ideas *now* in any educational setting. Diane is well qualified to make the whole thing practically applicable. She has had professional experience as a teacher and administrator both in public schools and private Christian schools. She also founded and directed a school for missionary children. The three of us have worked together writing these guides.

Although particularly aware of the system and requirements in the United States, these guides should be useful to anyone in the English-speaking world. This is especially true as they truly are *guides*, so that for example where American History is scheduled you'd merely substitute a living narrative Canadian or Australian history, etc. Literary works are, of course, applicable to all English-speaking children. They all share the same cultural heritage, although local enrichment should always be included. In the same way, all Western children need to be in touch with the historical flow that produced our culture. They must see the flow from Mesopotamia, the Jewish people, Greece, Rome, the coming of Christianity, the Middle Ages, the Renaissance, the Enlightenment, the growth of democracy, etc.

We believe that children must also have a good basic core education. They must be good readers and writers, and have a sound understanding of mathematical principles. Their minds should be capable, disciplined, alert and enthusiastic with many broad interests. In order to allow for differences both in the child and in materials available, the guides give a sequence of skills to be developed. This allows for much freedom in book choices, and yet ensures that the child isn't cheated of a carefully thought out learning sequence. Therefore, you can make up an actual program for a particular child or class that includes these steps, but uses varied material.

As this is a guide only, it opens the possibility for individual teachers or schools to be creative, to use what seems best for them. However, the guides make full suggestions combining appropriate selections from *Books Children Love,* plus enough actual book and textbook selections so that the entire curriculum can be made up of the texts chosen as examples by Child Light. There is enough direct guidance here to get the books needed for teaching reading in first grade or sixth graders' math requirements.

A last confusion will trouble some first-time inquirers into this Charlotte Mason or Child Light educational philosophy and practice. "If you believe in the revealed truth given in the Bible, if you are

Christians believing that the whole of Christianity is actually what is *real* in the universe, why don't you choose only Christian books?"

In the last decade, in response to an increasingly secularized society, Christian textbooks and materials and full school curriculums have mushroomed into production. In fact, in a way, these three Child Light books form part of that response! As in any area of human production, these "Christian books" are of varying excellence. Any textbook should be judged on its depth, quality and excellence of writing, and content. Textbook writers need to have personally developed a love and enthusiasm for good writing, a knowledge of what is excellent, and an understanding of learning for its own interest.

The Bible tells us that children are to be brought up in the real world as it is. As Christian parents and teachers, our first responsibility is spontaneously answering the endless questions children ply us with, from a Christian perspective. So when my three-year-old one night said to me, "Open your eyes. You're silly, there isn't Jesus there, only the ceiling," she was asking a deep important question that demanded a good answer (Quick! And understandable to a three-year-old!) *right then*. It is not good to think, "She'll study this in sixth grade."

Children constantly amaze me, even though I've been bringing up six of them over the last twenty-six years (and still have a five-year-old to shake me up) and have taught scores more. The parent or teacher remains the most important resource to the inquiring child. Therefore, it is *we* who must do our own homework! If you mean business, *you* have to be prepared to meet the clear honest question with a good answer. Therefore, perhaps one of the most important or key chapters in this book is "Developing a Christian Mind and Christian Worldview." I'm not saying there aren't Christian books that can also act as resources. We merely recognize that in normal life the child is in contact with many people, their books, their magazines, their conversations, their acts, and we *must* be able to relate to and understand what is being said from a Biblical Christian perspective.

For instance, a boy who is now an alert, clear-thinking young man would often pore over *National Geographic* magazines and maps with his father when he was a little boy, say six to ten years of age. In the endless interest, verbal exchanges, and companionship, far more was achieved in his personal growth as a young Christian in response to the world as it is than through reading in one grade a "Christian" geography series.

Many of the treasures in books of all kinds were published in the English language before the 1950s. Until then, children were used to verbal and literary communication and conversation. There was a

Christian memory in standards, character, morality. Also, the educational standards were still stable. We will sometimes find what we're looking for in these books. However, there have been many beautiful and valuable books produced recently too, and some of the older books are drab or dry. It isn't as easy as it might at first seem!

Jesus is Lord of all of life! Study to be in a living relationship with Him, and you grow in firm understanding of all that is around us. We discern the evil, shun darkness, but as children of the light we can walk through the real world. Let us take our children's hands and be their companions in this walk of faith and life.

Susan Schaeffer Macaulay

Further Information—
Child Light

T his guide is for schools and persons who are trying to provide a Christian education and life for children. Three of us have contributed to it, and we're aware that any such guide will need further work, input, and development. Education, the world, life . . . all are changing. Only the Lord is the same forever! However, we are attempting to offer educational perspectives from a Christian worldview. Gems of great value come from the simple word! We offer, therefore, a *Newsletter*, attempting to present ideas, books available, etc., for those who are concerned about children. If you've written to Child Light (formerly Child Life) in the past and heard nothing, please try again! Because of new, capable volunteer staffing offers, and the royalties from these books, we now hope to do a lot better!

We also would like to hear from you: What helped you? What worked? Did you use any new ideas, books . . . anything . . . with children, that could be a help to others? At home, in schools both public and private, in camps, day-care centers? With disturbed children? The Lordship of the Christ of the Bible extends over all of life. Can you share your findings with others?

Write to: Child Light
P.O. Box 2035
430 Boyd Circle
Michigan City, IN 46360 USA

A newsletter will be available three times a year.

May our lives, our every thought and action come under the direction of our Lord, and be acceptable to Him. Thanks to Him who gave us Jesus, as we fall so short!

☐1 The Child Light Curriculum Guide: Philosophy and Use

W hat is education? The answer given to this question will affect how the process of educating a child takes place. Charlotte Mason believed education to be an atmosphere where there is respect and understanding; a discipline of habits of mind and body; a life that includes intellectual, moral, and physical sustenance, and where the mind feeds on ideas; and a science of relationships where a child has natural relations with a vast number of things and thoughts, and is exposed to living books, nature, science, art, music, drama, physical exercises, and handicrafts. For a discussion of these areas see *For the Children's Sake* by Susan Schaeffer Macaulay.[1]

The aim of such education is to prepare children to live in contemporary society; to develop their relationship with God, His world, and people; and to cultivate an appreciation of culture and ideas. This includes the necessity of being able to ask questions, to draw their own conclusions, and to become independent thinkers.

Child Light views education as a means of stimulating a child's growth in knowledge and developing a love for learning. It is not viewed as utilitarian, where children are taught to parrot responses or where they are viewed as robots to be programmed to take their places as cogs in the wheel of society, but as a means of presenting facts and informing ideas. Children are seen as persons created in God's image and therefore of great worth and value. Each child has been given talents and abilities by the Creator and education should aid them in developing these for God's honor and glory. A child should not simply move through a system which causes him or her to become that which society thinks is important and meaningful.

What is curriculum? To many, curriculum means a written document, programmed material, or a textbook. In the Child Light context, it is all the experiences a child encounters in the learning process.

The purpose of a planned curriculum is to provide a framework, guidelines, and continuity in learning experiences. It is not a list of rigid content to cover or rigid requirements to be met, but a logical sequence of skills and experiences. The goals and objectives are known, but the experiences that will take place in order to reach them are unknown.

Provision is also made for the individual personality, creativity, and talents of the teacher and for flexibility which will allow for the individual differences, abilities, and interests of the students. It is always kept in mind that children and not textbooks, programs, or documents are being taught.

Knowledge and truth are acknowledged to have their source in God. The child is to be put in touch with this fount of knowledge as he or she takes in the revelation given in God's Word, the Bible. An interest in and an understanding of the knowledge of reality needs to be established—the world all about us, creation and structure. It is also essential to understand other people, their culture, ideas and history, and their creativity. The sum of these relationships to God, the universe about us and other people is understood to be the product of education.

Change in an individual and society is brought about by personal choice. These choices are made on the basis of worldview or the understanding of what is right and wrong, what is important and true, etc. It is of vital importance that the child understands the infrastructure of truth as revealed in the Bible. He or she also will need a personal relationship to Christ our Lord as only He, and the work of the Holy Spirit, gives us personal life-changing strength to implement the choices we see are right. Right choices come out of right ideas. These ideas must be understood. Right living comes from obedience to God and is a lifetime's challenge, only possible as we understand the Lordship of Christ over all of life, and over our own personal lives, too, in each aspect.

The Child Light curriculum guide is broad-based in scope and applies a literary, written, and verbal approach to teaching. Provision is made for the developmental readiness, uniqueness, and needs of each individual child. Critical-thinking and problem-solving skills are an integral part of the total program. Each child is guided in learning to think Christianly and in developing a Christian worldview. The natural integration of Biblical principles into the total learning experience is seen as fundamental, since Christian education includes the whole realm of human experience without separation between secular and spiritual.

Each subject guide presents a logical, sequential order of skills, concepts, and content. For convenience they are divided into grade levels. Learning a new skill is often dependent on knowledge of a previously learned skill. A skill learned at one time will be expanded and applied in different ways at another time. Skills are viewed as tools for learning and not as an end in themselves. Content areas and concepts allow for greater flexibility, but a sequential plan assures that a broad spectrum of general information, background material, relevant applications, and ideas will be presented.

The individual differences of children must always be kept in mind. Children grasp skills, concepts, and content at differing rates. Interests and talents also vary. It is essential to make provisions for reinforcing or enriching what is being learned and to utilize interest areas in the process. A child should not feel inferior or superior due to the pace at which he or she is acquiring skills, concepts, or content or the depth at which these are being applied. Each child should feel special and loved because of who he or she is and not because of how he or she performs. No child should ever feel that his or her acceptance by others or that any individual's worth and value are based on how that person performs in any area of life.

It is not the intent of this guide to be an exhaustive "how to" book. For specific ideas on how to teach skills, concepts and strategies, the selective use of teacher's guides will prove helpful.

2 Narration

Charlotte Mason used retelling, which she called narration, in a much broader sense than it is generally used by educators. Miss Mason observed that narration was not just a process for factual learning, but that it also engaged the mind and imagination of the children in the learning process. She believed that children retained more when they narrated since they put a part of themselves into the retelling and therefore became active participants. They seemed to absorb a sense of the whole and not just isolated incidents. The material was read aloud or silently and then was narrated by the children. Tests at the end of each term were narrations of selected portions of the term's work. Thus the narration became the means by which children learned. A person of any age likes to tell, or narrate events or stories that are important to him/her because something has stirred his/her interest, imagination or emotions. Charlotte Mason took this natural and spontaneous communication and used it as an important tool in education. When a child is narrating, vague ideas must be organized and verbalized. This process insures that thinking has gone on! Once having put a story into words somehow this remains part of the person far, far more permanently than it would have by merely hearing the story.

Listening *only* can be shallow and vague if not developed. Children used to only TV viewing may never develop listening skills. Listening with concentration is a discipline. If the child knows he/she is to be asked to "tell me the story" after listening, that listening will be far more concentrated!

Charlotte Mason knew that if a dry, uninteresting textbook-like portion was chosen and read, the child might not have taken anything in. And so, the secret of developing this invaluable skill and discipline lies in the initial choice of the story. It should be well-written, and not depend on pictures for the story to unfold. The story should hold plenty of interest for the child; it should stir the imagination, be alive.

Basically, narration in this Masonian sense begins with the tiny child who, on his/her mother's lap, has listened entranced to a short story read straight through. "Now you tell *me* the story." As the child tells back the story the mother doesn't interrupt. At the end she responds, "That was good. Wasn't it funny that the cow fell in the ditch? But tell me, what else do you remember . . . tell me about the plank the farmer's boy brought out . . ." This will jog the memory of a whole section left out without giving a sense of failure. However, in following Mason's educational method, the mother will not press for every detail she thinks is important. Mason believed the child's perception and response should be respected. After all, it is the child's response that matters.

A child who had learned to narrate a story would, in the Mason schools, tell back long sections of history by the age of six and seven. This wasn't a textbook recitation of facts, it was a story retold.

By nine or ten a child can begin to narrate in writing. At twenty-two he or she may be narrating a dissertation for a graduate course, in fact, the same process. Having read many books on a theme that has grabbed his or her interest and imagination, our "child" is "telling back." But by now this has become a complicated process of interrelating facts, bringing in relevant data and drawing conclusions.

The guidelines Mason advocated are recommended by Child Light. Until a child reaches the age of six, narration should generally be spontaneous, oral responses to what has been heard, experienced, or observed. Therefore, "Tell me about your vacation," is actually asking for a narration. So is, "Let's play a game. I'll sit here under the tree and you run to the top of the hill, look hard at the view and come back and tell me what you've seen so I can imagine I've seen it!"

From six to nine, narration can be used throughout the week in the structured study schedule. The actual process of retelling, or narration, is important. Literature, Biblical stories, history stories, travel descriptions, a person's story (biography), anything that has the children listening or reading eagerly is suitable for retelling in the child's own words.

When the child has mastered fluent writing skills, the average age being about nine, telling back, or narrating, in writing can begin. For instance, "Write all you can about Abraham Lincoln's life," after a narrative story of his life has been read with the class, should inspire a good bit of written material from the child used to telling a complete story orally. One accepts that this will be shorter than the oral telling since writing is more time-consuming.

From then on, both written and oral narrations are used. Oral narration often is a springboard for its cousin, the discussion of ideas. Time should always be left for this.

Narration is not parroting or memorization. Parroting is simply repeating by rote and is usually a mechanical, unthinking repetition of the material. Memorization is repeating over and over what is being memorized until it has been learned. Memorization has its place in the learning process, but should not be confused with narration. Poetry, Bible passages, and multiplication tables are examples of things that should be committed to memory. The procedure in the Bible section for memorizing Bible passages is the recommended process to follow when anything is memorized.

The use of narration is advised throughout the Child Light curriculum guide. The selection to be narrated should be read only once. Children will need to learn to read carefully and listen accurately. Most children will pay close attention to what is being read and as a result will develop good listening and retention skills, if they know that the passage will be read only once and that they will then be asked to narrate. The narration should be a point-by-point and not word-for-word account of the reading. In narrating, the child recalls the proper sequence of events or arguments, the main points of the selection, and items that were of particular interest. During an oral narration there should be no interruptions allowed. When the narration is completed the teacher can, by questions and discussion, draw from the class any corrections, clarifications, or additions. Written narration should be read by the teacher. Correct handwriting, grammar, and spelling should be encouraged ahead of time, but only the content considered when checking the narration.

The portion being read can be paragraph by paragraph, two or three pages, or a chapter. The breakdown will depend on what is being read (a literature book lends itself to the reading of a longer portion), the age of the children, and the difficulty of the material. The review of a selection will include the whole section that was read, while the narration following the reading will be only of the portion just read.

The basic procedure to follow when narrating is:

1. Introduce the new selection or book, or review what was read previously.

2. Motivate the children to want to listen by enthusiastically and interestingly introducing the new lesson.

3. Introduce new vocabulary, background information, and items such as dates and geography when applicable.

4. Read the selected portion. The portion is read by the teacher or students and is read only *once*.

5. Narrate the portion read.

6. Engage in follow-up activites such as pictures being shown, diagrams drawn, or moral points and questions discussed.

This process allows the individual to read and think and therefore become actively involved in the learning process.

Although written and oral narration will be the approaches most often used, the following are also good variations to include in the narration process.

Six- to Eight-Year-Olds

• Record the oral narration on cassette.

• Create a mural—individual or group.

• Draw sequence pictures—beginning, middle, end.

• Dictating the narration. (The teacher writes it down exactly as the child gives it.)

• Dramatize the selection.

• Draw a picture about the selection.

Nine Years and Up

• Write a narrative summary of the material.

• Create a mural, diorama, shadow box, TV program, 3-D poster, collage, or scene to illustrate a part of the story.

• Dramatize the selection.

• Record the dramatization on cassette.

• Record the oral narration on cassette.

• Record the written narration on cassette.

• Draw an illustration of the selection.

Written, oral, or any of the variations of narration can be used with an individual child or with any size class. It is advisable to keep the reading portions short if oral narration is being used with a large class so that more children have an opportunity to participate. Proper courtesy and listening skills should be stressed when oral narration is used.

Charlotte Mason's original program was used very successfully in the large public school classes. These often had sixty children of varying ages to one teacher! She would divide the large number into small reading groups. An older pupil would be in charge of a small group. Either choosing one reader, or reading in turns, the selection would be read aloud. Following the reading, children would take turns narrating orally to each other. The older pupil would listen.

Parents, grandparents and friends will often provide a listening ear for narrations. Another useful contribution for these helpers is the taking of dictation. A child narrates to the adult, who writes down each sentence. It is astounding to see the length, language skill and content of the narrations of young children. In Mason schools, the children had a rich selection of books read to them. There would be weekly narrating, and at the end of the semester, narration would be used to help them "give back" material read weeks or months previously without any review at all.

However, in narration the questions should not ask for a specific answer to be given. Essay questions often ask the child to *write* an answer rather than choose the correct multiple choice, matching, or True/False answer. Written narration is a type of essay response. The child is given a broad, open-ended question and then writes what he or she recalls and feels about the topic or selection.

Narration Question Examples

• Tell about the play that was read.

• Pretend that you live in Japan. Write to a friend in the United States and tell him or her about holiday customs in your country.

• What do you think about the way Thomas Jefferson reacted to the problems he faced?

• Write a newspaper article about an event which took place during the battle of Gettysburg.

• Tell the story of *As You Like It*.

When using narration for testing, children should be instructed to write all they remember and to include any feelings or reactions they have.

A child who learns to narrate from the beginning of his or her school experience will benefit greatly, as it allows for freedom to learn without tenseness or hesitancy to respond because the answer might be wrong. Narration is also a valuable aid in the retention of knowledge. In addition, telling back what has been read or heard allows the teacher to ascertain what the child has really appropriated.

A child may feel anxious when asked to narrate if narration is a new concept. This will probably be due to fear that the answer will receive a "No, that's wrong." Confidence will be gained and the fear of answering will lessen and finally disappear if the child is given open-ended questions, ones to which there is no right or wrong answer.

Examples of Open-ended Questions and Activities

• How would you have felt?

• If you had been there what would you have seen?

• Whom would you have liked to be and why would you have liked to be that person?

• What do you think?

• You are a newspaper reporter during the time of the westward movement. What would your newspaper article say?

• You are part of the first trip into space. How would you describe it in a letter to a friend?

• Why do you think some people don't believe Christianity is true?

Narration variations should be combined with oral and written narration when introducing an older child to narration.

^{3} Language Arts Overview

T he overview which follows is not intended to outline the specific scope and sequence of language arts objectives for the curriculum. It is, rather, a comment on our approach to the teaching of elementary language arts. We believe it is in harmony both with the Child Light philosophy of education, and with attitudes and methods already being practiced by many dedicated teachers. Because we anticipate that our curriculum may be used by beginning as well as experienced teachers and by parents, we have gone into some specific details that would not be necessary for many of you who will be reading this material.

It is almost impossible to overestimate the importance of a competent grasp of language arts skills, both written and oral. This is true not only in direct relation to education, but also to the whole of life. An ability to read intelligently and to write and speak clearly and coherently is the foundation upon which all the rest of children's academic education is undisputedly based. In addition, it is the key to a broader experience in the nonacademic aspects of education.

For example, it would be ideal if all children could have the opportunity to learn a variety of handicrafts and of mechanical and outdoor skills directly from adults who were proficient in such skills, and who also had the gift of being able to pass their knowledge on to the young. Unfortunately, this is frequently not possible. But for children who are at home with written and oral language, it is possible to learn many skills by reading about them, or by contacting information sources orally and obtaining helpful answers to clearly worded questions.

As for the whole of life, it is almost unnecessary to mention the ongoing significance of language skills in every imaginable area. A few moments of thoughtful contemplation provide the emphasis as to the universal value of the following: a ready understanding and/or enjoyment of written material; a confident ability to write an opinion, instruction, report, or an effective expression of love, sympathy or apology; an ability to communicate to one or more people the same kinds of things just listed, but orally, rather than in writing, and to be able to do so without undue self-consciousness or paralyzing fear. Beyond these basic applications of language skills there are, of course, a wide range of vocations and avocations in which highly developed abilities in writing or public speaking are indispensable requisites.

Education should be for living, for every part of life, and for all of life. As in every other aspect of the Child Light program, the approach to language arts is from this broad perspective.

Reading

Several texts have been recommended to allow for some variation in approach, but all are designed to be used in a strong basic reading program in which children learn to deal happily and confidently with well-written material. Because competence in reading is so crucial, a lack of this skill can have a profoundly damaging effect on a child's academic progress, and even more importantly, on his or her self-image. This fact should not, however, be felt by either parents or children as a grim, threatening burden. One of the chief elements in reading readiness should be an early, pleasurable relationship with books and words. The child who enters school with a background of having been extensively conversed with and read to for all of his or her life, has received the best possible preparation for language skills.

A parent (very young child on lap) turns the pages of a picture book, reading the brief text and always allowing the child time to ask questions, point out things that catch his or her interest, etc. Responses will differ from child to child. Some may soon become restless at first. The child should be able to jump down at will and terminate the story session at any point without receiving any subtle messages of impatience or disappointment on the part of the parent. But the very brief sessions should continue each day, always guided by the child's response. (Occasionally this may mean waiting a few weeks before making a new start.) Another child may rapidly develop an ever-increasing attention span and level of comprehension and request frequent story or poem sessions. Other children will fall somewhere between the two extremes.

Most children are ready at six to start formal reading instruction in a warm, supportive environment, with a teacher or parent who uses appropriate methods and who is sensitive to individual needs of the child. This matter of responsiveness to the specific child is extremely important, for there are some children who may benefit from not starting such instruction until age seven. Or, in rare cases, at an even older age.[1] Children themselves can provide the guidelines, but as suggested above, they need to be offered the *opportunity* to respond to books at a very early age. During such early story time sessions over a period of several years, the countless parental answers to children's questions about what they see and hear in relation to books give them a splendid store of reading readiness information. More than that, the children develop a sense of wonder, joy and anticipation in relation to books and reading.

But what about school-age children who have not yet had this sort of preparation? The Child Light program is designed to provide reading instruction that will involve children, parents and teachers in the same kind of positive relationship with books and reading that was outlined above.

Because the importance of a positive attitude toward books and reading has been so strongly emphasized, it might be appropriate to add a clarifying note. Child Light is strongly convinced not only of the importance of reading competence, but also of the lifelong benefits a friendship with books can offer a child. Its program is *not*, however, aimed only at children who have a particularly strong affinity for books and reading. There is a realistic awareness of the great diversity in interests and natural propensities among children—an awareness that playing competitive games, observing the natural world, building and making things, training a dog or a horse, planting a garden or any one of dozens of other worthwhile activities may be so stronly preferred by some children that they have little or no time for reading other than in their schoolwork.

Such children will benefit greatly from the Child Light program with its broad-spectrum approach and its appreciation of nonacademic as well as academic activities. At the same time, they will be given the reading skills and the positive attitudes about what books have to offer that are of great practical as well as aesthetic value. On the other hand, the book-oriented child will find enrichment, encouragement and an opportunity to fully develop his or her literary tastes and skills.

The Child Light reading program places an emphasis on several important overall objectives:

1. Establishment and maintenance of a pleasurable, enthusiastic atmosphere in relation to books and to the processes of reading instruction.

2. Use of especially well-written literature to be read aloud to early graders (material above their own reading level) or assigned to be read by more experienced readers.

3. Encouragement and development of both factual comprehension and a response to imaginative, creative ideas in material read by students.

4. Encouragement of questions and logical reasoning on the part of students in relation to material read.

5. Inclusion of contemporary as well as classic literature, and of biographical, historical, etc., reading with a wide variety of settings, characters, and living conditions.

6. Instruction which not only enables students to read controlled-vocabulary material, but which also prepares them to decode unfamiliar words and to move ahead in their reading as rapidly as they are able.

7. Thorough mastery on an individual basis of each sequenced skill in a specific area before moving on to the next concept.

8. Development of listening skills (accuracy and comprehension) in relation both to materials read aloud and to oral instruction.

9. Development of reading-related oral skills in a variety of contexts and at appropriate grade levels: narrating to the teacher and class a story that has previously been listened to or read (see item 2); reading aloud to the teacher and class from a reading text or selected piece of children's literature; presenting an oral book report. (Other oral skills will be outlined in the discussion of English.)

10. Inclusion of a "story time" period at all grade levels in which a wide variety of especially appealing books or poems are read aloud, just for enjoyment. (No assignments or testing to be done on this material.)

Handwriting

In addition to the guidance on letter formation offered in reading and spelling texts, a specific handwriting program is needed in the early grades. Texts have been recommended which follow a traditional manuscript-to-cursive instructional pattern.

Many children have started writing at least some of the letters of the alphabet before they start school. In a majority of cases, they are not forming the parts of the letters in the correct order (starting downstrokes at the wrong point, etc.). They also tend in some cases to confuse their capital and small letters. Unless they have been specifically and carefully taught, most children have developed an approach to writing which must be gently unlearned as they are taught how to form letters correctly.

It is of real importance that the correct formation, first of manuscript, and then of cursive letters becomes an established writing habit, for a failure to deal with the problem initially simply means repeated difficulties with writing through the years. Guided proofreading and self-correction help to fix the correct process in a student's mind—and fingers.

The goal should be clear, readable writing, produced with enough ease so that, for example, a third or fourth grader's ability to write an in-class paragraph or more in a given period of time is not hindered by lingering problems with the formation and joining of letters.

Since beautiful, endlessly practiced handwriting is rarely perceived today as an eminently practical goal, most schools feel that once cursive writing is well established, there is no longer a need for a specific handwriting program. Students' writing problems that arise are dealt with on an individual basis. Whether or not a formal program is continued through the elementary grades students should be helped to see the importance of conveying information or ideas in a form that can be readily deciphered by the reader, and to take personal satisfaction in neat, legible writing.

As in every part of the Child Light program, it is of great importance that the individual needs and responses of each child are sensitively monitored. It is sometimes in the area of learning to form letters that vision or coordination problems, which need to be immediately investigated and cared for, surface.

Spelling

Child Light is recommending strong, traditional spelling texts for those who wish to use such a series. Some schools prefer to use spelling lists they have developed themselves. Whichever choice is made, it is of great importance that as much relevance as possible be maintained between the words assigned in spelling and other classwork being done.

It is quite true that for most people the actual spelling of a word is primarily a visual identification skill. However, students (particularly in the higher grades) are often learning the *meaning* of a word at the same time they are fixing the spelling in their minds. Virtually the only way that a new word can be effectively added to students' vocabularies is for the word to be used, to be associated with an idea or fact that gives the word relevance and causes it to be retained in the students' memories.

A teacher or parent should not hesitate to include an adequate amount of skills practice in spelling. As in laying a foundation of skills in all the basic academic subjects, a certain amount of drill and rote practice in spelling (always done in as positive and constructive a manner as possible) is indispensable. Accurate spelling should not be considered an optional skill. Students should not only be monitored on their spelling, but should also early acquire the lifelong habit of *seeing* how the letters of a word new to their spelling vocabulary are sequenced. They should also learn to routinely look up in a dictionary or word book any spelling about which they are in doubt.

English

This final segment of the language arts programs covers material taught in the subject area usually labeled English: grammar (including usage, etc.), composition, speech, literature, and study skills including using a dictionary, other reference and general library use, the history of the English language and word origins. Texts that offer a strong, well-rounded approach have been recommended and a broad range of literature and books on language are offered in *Books Children Love*.

Grammar

Grammar, the first subject-component on the list, is another of the basic skills areas that needs to be seen from a broad perspective. The focus should never be merely on the bare-bones rules governing the structure of language; instead it should be on the larger view of demonstrating how language functions and explaining what the rules mean in speaking and writing that realistically involve the student. The subject guide for English describes ways in which this approach is used, starting with the earliest grades. Some memorization, exercises and specific techniques such as the diagramming of sentences are included, but in a way that helps the student to understand their purpose, and not as dominant elements.

Composition

In the teaching of composition it is even more important to maintain an effective balance between the mechanical and the creative than it is in relation to grammar. Writing, the fashioning of a story, poem or factual report from the substance of imagination, memory, impression or raw data is a highly personal endeavor. When students are asked to write, they are asked to commit something of themselves, of that which has been previously within, unformed and unseen, to the scrutiny of a teacher and perhaps to classmates as well. Thus the initial response of the teacher to student writing should be made with great sensitivity, considering both the vulnerability of the student and the personal risk he or she has taken in putting thoughts on paper. A perceptive, specific response should also be made to each evidence of the writer's observation, insight, imagination, humor and enthusiasm.

With this in view, the correction of errors in grammar, usage, etc., in a composition should be kept in perspective. Some of it needs to be done, but it should never be made preeminently important. The writer with a spark of life, the timid beginnings of a true expression of thought and imagination may be gently guided into correct usage. If the correction of errors, however, becomes the dominant part of the teacher's response, the spark is easily quenched and writing becomes a hated and dreaded task. As much as possible, students themselves should find and remedy such errors through proofreading under judicious guidance from the teacher.

It is not only overemphasis on the correction of usage errors that often discourages student writing. When the teaching of composition is related almost exclusively to a patterned form—endless outlining, topic sentences, rigidly controlled development and neat, pat conclusions—much that is joyful, spontaneous, creative and real may be quenched. Obviously, students do need to learn how to organize material, to write with unity and coherence, but such matters are only a framework, not the real substance. Having something to *say*, some product of the mind and imagination to share with others, is the significant aspect of composition, one that should never be lost sight of.

How, then, should problems in organization, emphasis, etc., be remedied? Again, as with the correction of errors involving the mechanics of writing, children need to become true *writers* from the start. This simply means that they take in hand what they have written, feel a sense of control over it, and revise and reshape it to make clearer what they are trying to say, bringing out more effectively the aspects that have more significance. Well-phrased questions from the teacher, along with a deft suggestion here and there, can serve to help the student writer see more clearly how he or she needs to organize the material of a composition, or to state something more effectively.

The rewriting and reshaping referred to is done of course, in connection with assigned compositions. On the other hand, the written narration done for tests or as the immediate response to materials read in various classes is written just once and evaluated on that basis.

Thus, the entire Child Light program, with its emphasis on listening, reading and narration, encourages and develops composition which has purpose, meaning and content. The organization of material develops readily and naturally. Minimize the need for rigid structure and the kind of imposed form that results in each student's paper being like the other—and all equally dull and lifeless.

Speaking

The ability to speak with at least a modest degree of effectiveness is not as overwhelmingly related to academic achievement as are reading and writing, but it is nonetheless of very real importance in elementary education. Not only does it give children some of the personal confidence that is so valuable during their school years, but it may also be practically applied in a wide variety of situations throughout life. Effective speech, for example, enables a person to clearly articulate opinions, wishes, encouragement, grievances or requests to others; to make informal presentations in classes or other groups; to engage in formal debates or make formal speeches in classes or meetings and, finally, for some students, to function eventually as professionals in the fields of law, the ministry, teaching, communications and a variety of other callings.

Because the uses of trained oral communication are generally more obvious in higher education and in adult walks of life, oral skills are often neglected in the education of children. Like so many skills, however, oral communication is far easier to master when the foundations are laid at an early age. Children who are involved in conversation all of their lives, who are encouraged in the home to repeat their favorite poems or songs, and who have been taught how to meet and talk with their parents' adult friends are already on the way to competence in oral communication.

The Child Light program emphasizes oral skills in all grades in a variety of contexts related to the grade levels: making an oral response to a specific question or direction of the teacher; reciting poems or other materials both individually and in chorus with other students: telling the teacher and class an original story, or the account of a personal experience; orally narrating a story that has previously been listened to or read; presenting a variety of oral reports and speeches and participating in skits and drama; engaging in formal debates.

Effective oral presentations may be listened to on tapes or records, and speeches may be read and analyzed. Students may be assigned to listen to a current television speech or other specific talk or lecture appropriate to their grade level or individual capacity.

Throughout all the grades, methods and techniques for improving students' oral skills are dealt with as an ongoing emphasis. In addition, such procedures as making general introductions of one person to another (or others) or of introducing someone who is going to speak to the class are practiced until the skills become habitual.

In harmony with all areas of the Child Light program, the perspective is of the broad-spectrum uses of oral language. The practical application of skills is implemented through involving the students in actually using the skills on a day-to-day basis so that they become an integral part of their experience and personal abilities.

Literature

Whatever else it may be in children's experience, literature should be, first, last and always full of wonder and delight. (The "whatever elses" will be spoken of later.) It should be eluding Mr. McGregor with Peter Rabbit, and sharing lessons in friendship with Frog and Toad; slipping into another wonderfully imagined world with the children of the Narnia tales; watching Rikki Tikki Tavi conquer the cobra; striving suspensefully for right and justice with Miss Bianca; sailing with the Swallows and Amazons; and gazing in amazement with Aladdin at heaps of treasure. It should be racing for the silver skates, hiding in the greenwood with Robin, watching the secret garden come to life, rescuing a fair maiden as a knight of King Arthur, finding the footprint on Crusoe's lonely island, and escaping the Cyclops with Odysseus: high adventure and cozy corners, exotic sights and sounds and the imagined taste of a piece of newly baked bread; other lands and other worlds—and a fresh view of the warmth and security of a home.

It was the response of wonder and delight that Charlotte Mason saw as an open channel into children's minds and imaginations. Through this channel, important truths about themselves as people, about how life should be lived, about God and His world, would be received in a natural, unforced manner. These truths would be observed and, when acted upon by the will of a child, would be made a part of his or her own being. It is in harmony with this view that Child Light places great importance on the use of literature throughout its program and especially so in the area of language arts.

Before enlarging upon this concept, it may be important just now to make some distinctions and define terms in relation to literature. The handful of stories specifically alluded to above were deliberately chosen from among classic tales (either traditional or modern) so that most readers would recognize the new, which fully qualify as literature in its more specific sense. The literature section of *Books Children Love* includes these books, along with a number of other excellent stories and poems which may not meet every criterion as literature in the strict sense of the word, but which are well worth reading. For use in English classes, however, it is preferable to select books from the list which do meet high literary standards. Knowing where the line should be drawn between literature in the specific sense, and books which are one step down the scale, is far from being a totally objective exercise in judgment. At the close of this overview, however, is a list of questions which may be applied in determining something about a book's literary level.

Returning to the concept that fine literature provides an open channel into the consciousness of children, it is clear that what is being discussed is not some form of indoctrination. It is, rather, a matter of providing children with the kind of material Charlotte Mason referred to as "living books." Such books, whether they are fantasies, or historical or contemporary realism, embody in the characterization and the events that which is true to the human heart, that which is emotionally and spiritually real.

This basic truth in the fabric of the writing reveals itself in an intrinsic support of Judeo-Christian values: honesty, integrity, courage, loyalty, faithfulness, compassion, etc. Not only that, but because there is truth at the core of the writer's thinking, situations arise in the books which display dishonesty, hypocrisy, cowardice, betrayal, fickleness, harshness and the like. Often the situations are somewhat complex, and as children read, they must think, question, evaluate, and bore their way through to the real issues. As they identify with a character, they are unconsciously making choices with him or her, seeing how cause and effect work, and learning about consequences.

Book by book, the readers are feeling the lift of spirit that comes as they identify with characters who demonstrate courage, self-sacrifice, generosity, etc. As they observe struggles between good and evil, readers also learn much about human nature. The characters of fine literature are portrayed with truth and keen perception, not as flat, cardboard people, moved about by a writer simply to implement a catchy plot. And while mediocre stories are essentially the same no matter where they are set, literature opens the windows and doors of the world and takes its readers into the surroundings, the thoughts, the realities of life in places the reader may never see. A gifted writer unfolds the character of someone who is part of a faraway culture—or someone just "around the corner" whose life is different because of a handicap, tragic home circumstances, or racial background—the reader can to some extent understand the lives of others.

Beyond the growing awareness of other people and places, other ways of life, that develops during the thoughtful reading of literature, questions about a variety of social and moral issues may also be generated by the historical background or specific circumstances of a story: Mark Twain's *The Prince and the Pauper,* for example, or Erik Christian Haugaard's *The Little Fishes.*

In every case, it is important for the teacher simply to bring the literature and the students together. Let the one communicate to the other without constantly intervening in overt efforts to "point out the moral values of the story." Skillful questions, when appropriate, will help the students themselves to identify, discuss and ask their own questions about issues and values.

Narration (telling back orally or in writing) is used extensively with literature in the Child Light program. This practice not only aids students in their retention of what they have read, but also provides the opportunity for them to raise questions and discuss the stories and poems.

Literature-related classwork in English should also focus strongly on each book or poem as a piece of writing. At appropriate levels, consideration should be given to the ways in which the writer achieves certain purposes. In discussing fiction topics would include: how he or she tells the story (as a third person outside the story, as a first person narrator, etc.), what level of language is used, what the overall tone of the book is (humorous, dramatic, warmly human, etc.), how description is used, and how characters are developed. In connection with poetry, attention appropriate to specific grade levels should be given to: the form of the poem, the use (or absence of) rhyme, the effect of the sounds of the words chosen, the vividness or subtlety of the visual images, the intensity of meaning created by the spareness and compression of poetry in contrast with the greater openness and expansiveness of prose. Such matters will be discussed in detail in the subject guides for English.

The wonders and delights of the worlds upon worlds encompassed in literature are not only of intrinsic value in themselves. They also encourage children to move more readily out of the small, "me-centered" world in which they begin their experience. Far vistas, different people, interesting words and phrases, and fresh ideas expand their horizons and provide from another angle that broad, panoramic view of life and of the world that is such an important goal of the Child Light program.

Some questions to use in evaluating the literary quality of a book:

• Does the story catch and hold the interest of a reader?

• Is the story timeless, in the sense that regardless of when it was written it can still be enjoyed and related to today and, presumably, could continue to be so?

• Is the story credible? Allowing a reasonable amount of latitude for fictional invention, do the people speak and behave the way people in the particular place and time of the story would be likely to speak and act? Are the emotions and reactions of the characters true to the reality of human experience?

- Are the setting, culture and any factual background events depicted with reasonable depth and accuracy?

- Are the characters well rounded and do they develop as the story goes on, changing in response to events, insights they have gained, etc.?

- Are the overall language use, vocabulary and writing style excellent and in harmony with the book as a whole?

- Are the values, truths or "lessons" which might be drawn from the story an integral, natural part of the whole? Does the reader simply see and infer them on his own without the tacking on of sermons or heavy-handed moralizing?

In this connection it is important to realize that just because a book's purpose is to emphasize Christian standards, or even to evangelize readers, this does not make it a good book in the literary sense. Literary artists create literature; highly competent craftspeople create good, worthwhile books; good intentions without other qualifications only result in dreadful books.

$\boxed{4}$ Reading

S uccess in education depends on the ability to read. Reading is a complex activity that involves more than just reading words. It includes word attack skills, getting meaning from the printed page, understanding what is being read, grasping the main idea, drawing conclusions, making inferences, arriving at generalizations, and reading critically.

A vital part of the Child Light program is the reading and narration of "living books"[1] at all levels. Suggestions of books to be read to and by children are listed for each grade level. These books should be read in their entirety.

> It was Charlotte Mason's conviction that the child should work steadily through a complete book. Little snippets of information here and there just don't hang together. Our generation is prone to amuse itself with fragmentary information and resources. We flip on the TV for brief programs, and then we think we know about the subjects they dealt with. A few paragraphs in a magazine, and we think we've formed an opinion. What is happening so often is that we are merely forming a habit of amusing our interest, and then forgetting the fragments . . .
> Because they've tackled a complete book, they [children] become acquainted with its flow and its use of language. They are students of another person—the author. Further, they are allowed to notice the content themselves. As they aren't forced to memorize facts, they are free to react to the writing themselves. They are the ones who decide what parts they consider important. It becomes an active experience of the mind, personality, and language.[2]

The listed books are also applicable for story time reading. For additional books, see the Child Light book list, *Books Children Love* by Elizabeth Wilson.

Child Light also recommends the use of a basal reading series. Although the emphasis of each series may differ, a balanced, sequential approach with variety in reading material and provision for individual differences are included. Which basal series to use will depend on the reading approach that has been selected.[3]

A basal series will include selections from literature and content areas. Additional emphasis should be given to reading in the content areas—social studies, science, math, English, Bible, spelling, physical education and fine arts. Literature selections should be treated as an introduction to the entire book.

The skills in this curriculum are not necessarily listed in the sequence in which they should be taught, but there should be progression from the easier skills to the more complicated ones. Many of them will be taught simultaneously. The teacher's edition of the basal reading series will suggest a sequence, give suggestions on how to approach teaching the skills, and ideas for reinforcement and enrichment. Teachers' editions should be viewed as guides. The teacher will need to choose what to use and what to delete and how to adapt the material for the individual needs of the children being taught. Remember, it is not a book that is being taught, but children.

Great care should be taken to assure the establishment of a relaxed atmosphere in which no stigma is attached to reading at a lower level or at a slower pace than someone else. Ample enrichment should be provided for the child who is reading above the level of the class, and no child should be asked to "learn" a skill that is already known.

Readiness for Reading

Before formal reading instruction begins, a child should have a varied background of experience: visiting zoos, museums, airports, historical sites, parks; cooking, setting the table and other household chores; creative play and other creative activities; caring for a pet; being read to; listening to the radio and viewing movies and television; Sunday school and other group activity participation; and being encouraged to take initiative and to develop independence. All these experiences help prepare a child for reading success.

Some indications of readiness for formal reading include: being able to distinguish between likenesses and differences (pictures, objects, forms, colors, letters, words); the ability to tell a story from looking at pictures; distinguishing rhyming words and words that begin or end with the same sound; recognizing and naming letters and associating the letter sound with its symbol; sequencing a story or an event; developing an attention span of no less than ten minutes; left to right and top to bottom orientation; and a speaking vocabulary that enables ideas to be expressed clearly. There are tests available to help in determining a child's proficiency in these areas.

However, teacher observation is the most important determining factor. Some children will be ready for reading but will not test well due to fear, not understanding the directions, an unfamiliar format, poor physical coordination, or other factors. Test results should never take the place of a teacher's careful observation of the physical, emotional, mental, and social development of a child. Formal testing is usually unnecessary and should be administered only when it will be a helpful tool in deciding a child's readiness.

If teacher observation and any tests used do not indicate readiness, the child should be given opportunity to engage in readiness activities, with formal reading to be started only when the child is ready. On the other hand, a child who is already reading should not be held back but allowed to read at an appropriate level while developing any weak skill areas.

Reading Readiness Tests

> Metropolitan Readiness Tests
> > Harcourt Brace Jovanovich, Inc.
> > 757 Third Ave.
> > New York, NY 10017

> Gates-MacGinitie Readiness Skills Test
> > Teachers College Press
> > 1234 Amsterdam Ave.
> > New York, NY 10027

> American School Reading Readiness Test
> > California Test Bureau/McGraw-Hill
> > Del Monte Research Park
> > Monterey, CA 93940

> Lee-Clark Reading Readiness Test
> > California Test Bureau/McGraw-Hill
> > Del Monte Research Park
> > Monterey, CA 93940

> Harrison-Stroud Reading Readiness Profiles
> > Houghton Mifflin Co.
> > 110 Tremont St.
> > Boston, MA 02107

> Basal reading series readiness tests

First Grade Reading

First grade reading provides for a thorough introduction of the basic reading skills. Opportunity is provided for vocabulary enrichment and development through basal readers, literature, and content areas. Word attack and comprehension skills and application are presented. Reading orally with expression and meaning is emphasized, and beginning study skills are introduced. Children are exposed to "living books" and given opportunities to verbalize their feelings and reactions through narration.

Curriculum

1. Chart Stories. The story content is based on something the children have experienced, plan to experience or are experiencing. A theme is chosen and the children dictate the story while the teacher writes it on the chalkboard. Then a title is chosen. Later the story should be copied in a chart tablet or on a large piece of paper (24" x 36" or 18" x 24"). Key words and phrases should be written on cards (one word or phrase per card) and each sentence should be written on a sentence strip.

   Generally the story will consist of five to eight sentences. Repetition of words is desirable since this is a prereading activity. Pictures can be drawn to illustrate the story.

   After writing the story on the chalkboard the teacher reads it to the class and then the children read it in unison with the teacher. A marker (paper strip or the teacher's hand) should be used when reading the story. The marker is moved along under each sentence as it is read as an aid in establishing left to right orientation and to assure that the correct word is being looked at during the reading.

   The following day the story is again read aloud by the class. Children can then be asked to point to different words and to match a word on the chart with a word card, a phrase with a phrase card, and a sentence with a sentence strip. Individual children can volunteer to read the story to the class.
2. Ability to recognize and write in correct manuscript form all upper- and lower-case letters. (See handwriting curriculum.)
3. Recognition of the symbol and the long and short sound each vowel stands for.
   a. Look at the symbol and give the sound it stands for.
   b. Listen to the sound and write the symbol that stands for the sound heard.
      Single letter—ā ă ē ĕ ī ĭ ō ŏ ū ŭ
      Beginning of a word—<u>a</u>n <u>i</u>t <u>o</u>at

End of a word—be so
Medial—sit huge
4. Recognize the symbol and the sound each consonant stands for.
   a. Look at the symbol and give the sound it stands for.
   b. Listen to the sound and write the symbol that stands for the sound heard.
      Single letter—b c d f g h j k l m n p q r s t v w x y z
      Beginning of a word—fall tick
      End of a word—mat on
      Medial—batter cabin
5. Recognize the symbols and sounds that consonant blends and consonant digraphs stand for.
   Blend—two or three consonants blended together but each keeping the sound it stands for.
      bl br cl cr dr fl fr gl gr pl pr sc scr sk sl sm sn sp spl spr squ st str sw tr tw
   Digraph—two consonants that stand for one sound.
      ch ck ng ph sh th wh
   a. Look at the symbols and give the sound they stand for.
   b. Listen to the sound and write the symbols that stand for the sound heard.
      Beginning of a word—drive prize ship
      End of a word—past tusk dish
6. Develop the ability to sound out one-syllable words.
   a. Two vowels together—usually the first vowel stands for its long sound and the second vowel is silent. meat sail
   b. Word ending in e preceded by a single consonant—the final e is silent and the single vowel preceding the consonant usually stands for its long sound. cake kite
   c. Consonant-vowel-consonant or vowel-consonant—in a one-syllable word a single vowel followed by a consonant usually stands for its short sound. hot pin an
   d. Vowel at the end of a one-syllable word when it is the only vowel—usually stands for its long sound. so be
   e. When a y comes at the end of a word and there is no vowel—the y stands for the same sound long i stands for. sky by

Note: When sounding out words it is important to give pure sounds. Consonants should not have the sound uh attached—buh, huh, muh. Cat should be c-a-t, cat and not cuh-a-tuh, cuhatuh.

7. Sight vocabulary—words that do not follow the phonetic rules that have been learned and other sight words that are used fre-

quently. Sight words should be presented to the students in context and then drilled and reviewed (as creatively as possible) until the words are instantly recognized. "Dolch sight vocabulary" is named after the educator who first developed the list. These are frequently used list of sight sight words.

a. Dolch List

Preprimer Level

a	find	is	one	three
and	for	it	play	to
away	funny	jump	look	two
big	go	little	red	up
blue	help	make	run	we
can	here	me	said	there
come	I	my	see	you
down	in	not	the	where

Primer Level

all	do	new	saw	under
am	eat	no	say	want
are	four	now	she	was
at	get	on	so	well
ate	good	our	soon	went
be	have	out	tail	what
black	he	please	there	white
brown	into	pretty	they	who
but	like	ran	this	will
came	must	ride	too	with
did				

First Grade Reader Level

after	fly	his	old	take
again	from	how	once	thank
an	give	just	open	them
any	going	know	over	then
as	had	let	put	think
ask	has	live	round	walk
by	her	may	some	were
could	him	of	stop	when
every				

b. Basal reading series—any words not on the Dolch list that are presented in the basal readers as sight words.

8. Vowel and consonant variations.

a. y as a vowel—baby   my

b. Hard and soft c—soft sound when followed by e, i, or y.
   cent city cycle   came cut cot
c. Hard and soft g—usually soft sound when followed by e, i, or y.
   gem giant gym   good game gun
d. Effect of r and w on vowels—a single vowel followed by r or w is usually controlled by the r or w and the vowel does not stand for either the long or the short sound.
   er ir ur—her fir purple   ar—car far
   or—born world   w—saw dawn
e. ow stands for two sounds—shown bow   plow town
f. a followed by l—ball walk
g. ph stands for the same sound f stands for—phone elephant

9. Other word attack skills.
   a. Context clues—a very important skill. Making a wild guess is not the same as considering what makes sense in the context and using the word length and beginning and ending sounds as clues in decoding the word. This skill is particularly helpful when dealing with sight words.
   b. Structural analysis noted but not stressed at this level—a valuable skill. However, this should not be overemphasized during the reading of a selection or comprehension may be affected.
      Structures to note—root words, suffixes, prefixes, possession('s), contractions, compound words, hyphenated words.
   c. Word families (phonograms)—word families should not be confused with "finding little words in big words." Word families seldom vary in pronunciation, while "little words in big words" vary greatly depending on the letters that precede and follow them—like the "little words" on and at in congratulation. Adding a consonant, consonant blend, or consonant digraph to a word family does not change the pronunciation of the word family. For example, the word family at—bat cat that flat sat
      Word families—ike an all en and ake am old et ay ink in at ate ack ide ell ight ill it

10. Dividing words into syllables.
    a. Each syllable must contain a vowel.
    b. While saying the word, clap hands to indicate each syllable.
    c. Divide words into syllables between two consonants that are alike— ap ple fel low; after the consonant that follows a vowel if the vowel stands for its short sound—pil grim ob ject; and after the first vowel if the vowel stands for its long sound—Bi ble   la dy.

11. An introduction to antonyms, synonyms, homoyms, and homophones.
    a. Antonyms—words that have opposite meanings—hot and cold, day and night
    b. Synonyms—words that have nearly the same meaning—little and small, loud and noisy
    c. Homonyms—words that are spelled alike but have different meanings—trip (journey) and trip (stumble), game (sport) and game (animal)
    d. Homophones—words that are pronounced alike but spelled differently and have different meanings—to too two, hear and here
12. Comprehension skills—recognition of individual words is useless unless meaning is derived from what is written. Even though a breakdown of comprehension skills is given, there is a high degree of correlation between them.
    a. Vocabulary development—recognizing words and knowing what they mean, understanding meaning change of individual words when reading phrases (on the other hand, down to earth), and perceiving sentences as complete thought units.
    b. Real and make-believe—enjoying make-believe but differentiating it from fact.
    c. Main idea—learning to distinguish a detail from a major point (seeing the detail as supporting the main idea).
    d. Making inferences—learning to predict the outcome.
    e. Sequencing—arranging events in the order in which they happen.
    f. Drawing conclusions—predicting the outcome and learning to generalize on the basis of what is stated.
    g. Critical reading/thinking—distinguishing fact from opinion and evaluating information in light of what is already known from other reading, from television, and from personal observation.
    h. Narration—recall of information with verbalization of feelings and reactions. Narration involves all the comprehension skills mentioned here. (See Chapter 2.)
13. Parts of a book—becoming familiar with the way a book is put together.
    a. Title page
    b. Table of contents
    c. Body
    d. Glossary
    e. Index

14. Alphabetizing—writing words in alphabetical order according to the beginning letter.
15. Oral reading proficiency—reading with expression, clarity, good intonation, and fluency.
16. Listening skills—listening to a story being read only once and then narrating it using any of the various narration activities. (See Chapter 2.)
17. Study skills.
    a. Using the table of contents in the reader to locate a story.
    b. Understanding the function of an index—comparing a table of contents and an index.
    c. Finding the meaning of a word in the glossary of the reader.
    d. Understanding that a dictionary helps with understanding word meaning and that an encyclopedia and other reference materials give information on particular subjects.
    e. Learning to skim a page to find desired information—at this stage it will usually be to find an answer to a question.
    f. Introduction to using the library.
18. Literature for pleasure reading and story time.
    a. Reading for narration should be from new material and read only once before narrating. However, story-time reading should include favorite stories that are read and enjoyed again and again.
    b. The interest areas of first grade children include pretend stories (especially those that have talking animals), fairy tales, stories with rhyming words, realistic stories about children their own age, community helpers, different occupations, and space and non-space travel, and vehicles.
    c. Recommended books.

    ✓ *The Story of Babar*   Jean De Brunhoff

    ✓ *Mike Mulligan and His Steam Shovel*   Virginia Lee Burton

    ✓ *The Little House*   Virginia Lee Burton

    ✓ *The Story About Ping*   Marjorie Flack

    The Snowy Day   Ezra Jack Keats

    ✓ *Make Way for Ducklings*   Robert McCloskey

    ✓ *One Morning in Maine*   Robert McCloskey

    ✓ *And to Think I Saw It on Mulberry Street*   Dr. Seuss

    The Biggest Bear   Lynd D. Ward

    Marshmallow   Clare T. Newberry

The New Pet Clare T. Newberry

Angus and the Ducks Marjorie Flack

Any *Arch Book*

Use more books from *Books Children Love* by Elizabeth Wilson, part of this Child Light package. Refer also to lists in:

Honey for a Child's Heart by Gladys Hunt (Zondervan)

How to Grow a Young Reader by John and Kay Lindskoog (David C. Cook)

Five to Eight by Dorothy Butler (London: The Bodley Head).
Warm, including many aspects of living, playing and growing, this book is about children from five to eight. It is about their books, their lives, and *reading*. Parents and teachers will learn a lot here and be guided to important books, and their use.

Note: These extra lists can relate to every grade in the curriculum.

Second Grade Reading

Second grade reading includes a review and expansion of the skills begun in first grade. Emphasis focuses on analysis of compound words, plural and possessive forms of nouns, verb variants, recognition of the feelings and corresponding behavior of the characters in stories, sequencing of events, and finding main ideas and supporting details.

Curriculum

1. Sight vocabulary—words that do not follow the phonetic rules that have been learned and other sight words that are used frequently. Sight words should be instantly recognized.
   a. Dolch List
      Second Grade Level

always	cold	green	sing	use
around	does	its	sit	very
because	don't	made	sleep	wash
been	fast	many	tell	which
before	first	off	their	why
best	five	or	these	wish
both	found	pull	those	work
buy	gave	read	upon	would
call	goes	right	us	write

b. Basal reading series—any words not on the Dolch list that are presented in the second grade basal readers as sight words.

2. Application of phonetic skills to decode new vocabulary words.
   a. Beginning and ending sound—identifying the sounds a single consonant, consonant blends, and consonant digraphs stand for. (See first grade, numbers 4 and 5.)
   b. Identifying the sound a vowel stands for in a one-syllable word. (See first grade, numbers 3 and 6.)
   c. Identifying the sound a vowel stands for in a word of more than one syllable.
   Closed syllable—short vowel followed by a consonant at the end of the syllable. cab in win ter
   Open syllable—long vowel at the end of the syllable. pa per ba by
   d. Application of knowledge of vowel and consonant variations. (See first grade, number 8.)
3. Application of other decoding skills (See first grade, number 10.)
4. Prefixes and suffixes recognizing those commonly used.
   a. Prefixes—dis- in- mis- non- pre- re- un-
   b. Suffixes—er -or -ment -ness -able -ible -ful -ous -ish -ly -ed -s -ing -es
5. Silent letters—recognizing letter combinations that contain silent letters and knowing the sound the letters stand for. gn kn ight igh wr
6. Ability to alphabetize to the second letter—if able to the third letter.
   a. Second letter—bake bean bib blow boat brown
   b. Third letter—back bad bag bake ball basket bat
7. Applying comprehension skills in both oral and silent reading. (See first grade, number 12.)
8. Study skills
   a. Continue developing the skills taught in first grade. (See first grade, number 17.)
   b. Dictionary skills should include looking up words for meaning and spelling. Entry and guide words should be introduced and used.
   c. Develop the ability to distinguish which person is speaking in the story being read.
   d. Recognize paragraph divisions.
9. Continue developing the ability to recognize and use antonyms, synonyms, homonyms, and homophones. (See first grade, number 11.)
10. Dividing words into syllables. (See first grade, number 10.)

    a. Divide between two consonants—cam pus   har bor
    b. Divide between the two words in a compound word—use only those in which each word has only one syllable. snow man bird house
11. Listening skills—continue to develop the ability to narrate after only one exposure to the material. (See Chapter 2.)
12. Oral reading—be sure to tell the child any word not known.
    a. Understand the use of punctuation as a clue for correct intonation.
    b. Read with expression—thinking about how the person talking in the story would sound and reading aloud in that manner.
    c. Understand what one is reading so that others will get the meaning from the selection as it is read aloud.
    d. Avoid "round robin" reading (having the children read one after the other until the entire selection is read). Have one child be the narrator and other children take the part of the speakers in the story, or have the oral reading be reading the sentence that answers a question or gives the main idea or helps in predicting the outcome.

Note: Oral reading also helps in diagnosing reading difficulties—omitting, inserting or substituting words, phrases or letters; omitting suffixes; letter or word reversals; repetition of words, phrases or sentences; or failure to regard punctuation. Specific remediation procedures are beyond the scope of this book.

13. Literature for pleasure reading and story time.
    a. Reading for narration should be from new material and read only once before narrating. However, story-time reading should include favorite stories that are read and enjoyed again and again. Books read for pleasure and story time can be narrated if the child desires to do so. Literature narration is included in the English section. Books listed in the reading section can be read by an individual child or they can be read to the children.
    b. Second graders can read a book themselves by applying reading skills in a non-basal situation. A book may be read to find information in an interest area or just for personal enjoyment.
    c. Interest areas generally include realistic pretend stories, fairy tales, myths, legends, all types of transportation, mysteries, sports, recreation, and stories about people in other countries.

d. Recommended books.

Mary Poppins   Pamela L. Travers

✓ *Charlotte's Web*   E. B. White

Mei Li   Thomas Handforth

✓ *The Tale of Peter Rabbit* and any of the other twenty-two volumes by Beatrix Potter

April's Kittens   Clare T. Newberry

Yonie Wondernose   Marguerite De Angeli

✓ *The 500 Hats of Bartholomew Cubbins*   Dr. Seuss

✓ *Alexander and the Terrible, Horrible, No Good, Very Bad Day* J. Viorst

Paddle-to-the-Sea   C. Holling

Homer Price   Robert McCloskey

The Mouse and the Motorcycle   Beverly Cleary

Jungle Doctor's Monkey Tales   Dr. Paul White[4]

Jungle Doctor Fables   Dr. Paul White[5]

Third Grade Reading

Third grade reading emphasizes the application of the skills begun in first and second grade. Vocabulary development is continued and the cause and effect principle is introduced.

Curriculum

1. Sight vocabulary—words that do not follow the phonetic rules that have been learned and other sight words that are used frequently. Sight words should be instantly recognized.

✓ a. Dolch List
Third Grade Level

about	eight	hurt	myself	six
better	fall	if	never	small
bring	far	keep	only	start
carry	full	king	own	ten
clean	got	laugh	pick	today
cut	grow	light	seven	together
done	hold	long	shall	try
draw	hot	much	show	warm
drink				

b. Basal reading series—any words not on the Dolch list that are presented in the third grade basal readers as sight words.

2. Application of all decoding skills
   a. Mastery of the skills introduced in first and second grades. (See first grade, numbers 3, 4, 5, 6, 8, 9, 10 and second grade, numbers 2c, 4, 5.)
   b. The le ending—recognizing it, knowing the sound it represents, and including the consonant preceding le with it when dividing a word into syllables—ta ble   pad dle   waf fle gur gle   peo ple   tur tle

3. Continued development of the ability to recognize and use antonyms, synonyms, homonyms, and homophones. (See first grade, number 11.)

4. Singular and plural
   a. Expanding the ability to recognize the plural form of nouns (adding s or es) churches boats
   b. Recognizing irregular noun plurals—feet mice

5. Alphabetizing to the third and fourth letter.
   a. Third letter—mail make man matter may
   b. Fourth letter—snag snail snake snare

6. Begin developing an understanding of the cause and effect principle.
   a. Cause—the reason something happens.
   b. Effect—what happens.

7. Comprehension skills
   a. Mastery of the skills introduced in first grade. (See first grade, number 12.)
   b. Fiction and nonfiction—distinguishing what is imagined from what is about real people, animals, things, or events.
   c. Develop the ability to handle fiction and nonfiction information differently.
   d. Critical thinking—distinguish if the actions of the characters are justified or are wrong; understand why they are or are not wrong; discerning if the qualities of the characters are true-to-life.

8. Study skills
   a. Mastery of the skills introduced in first grade. (See first grade, number 17.)
   b. Skimming and scanning
   Skimming—getting the main idea of a paragraph or short selection by quickly glancing at the material and not reading it word by word.
   Scanning—finding specific information by quickly glancing

at a paragraph that contains it. Looking for key words (not word-by-word reading).

9. Syllabication principles
   a. Review of open and closed syllables. (See second grade, number 2c.)
   b. VC/CV—when two consonants are between two vowels usually the word is divided between the two consonants. fab ric   don key
   c. V/CV or VC/V—when one consonant is between two vowels the consonant can go with either vowel. First try putting it with the second consonant (V/CV). After applying the rules for pronunciation, if the word is unknown then put the consonant with the first vowel (VC/V) and see if it forms a known word when pronunciation rules are applied. căb ĭn (not cā bin) bā sic (not băs ĭc) sī lō (not sĭl ō)
   d. Consonant plus le—when a consonant precedes le, the consonant le combination usually forms a syllable. fa ble ti tle
   e. Double consonants—when two consonants are the same the word is divided between the two consonants. ap ple   yel low

10. Oral and silent reading (See first grade, number 15 and second grade, number 12.)
    a. Oral—the material should first be read silently. The reader needs to understand what is being read in order to convey meaning to the listeners. Expression, intonation, clarity, and fluency should not be emphasized to the detriment of comprehension.
    b. Silent—most content area reading that a student does will be silent reading and, therefore, silent reading ability is extremely important. Ability to read silently to find an answer, the main idea, specific information, or to narrate should be increased at this grade level.

11. Prefixes and suffixes (See second grade, number 4.)

12. Reading rate—developing an understanding that the proper rate for reading depends on what is being read. Reading for pleasure can be at a faster rate than when noting details, locating the main idea, or following step-by-step directions.

13. Listening skills (See Chapter 2.)
    a. Continued development of the ability to use various narration forms after listening to the material being read only once.
    b. Ability to follow directions after hearing them only once.

14. Literature for pleasure reading and story time
    a. Reading for narration should be from new material and read only once before narrating. However, story-time reading should include favorite stories that are read and enjoyed again and again.
    b. Third grade children generally enjoy stories that have factual information about people and places in other countries, fairy tales, mysteries, adventure, biography, animal stories, stories about family life, sports, and events of the past.
    c. Recommended books.

   Pippi Longstocking   Astrid Lindgren

   Mr. Popper's Penguins   Richard & Florence Atwarer

   The Secret Garden   Frances Hodgson Burnett

   The Courage of Sarah Noble   Alice Dalgliesh

   Beezus and Ramona   Beverly Cleary

   Encyclopedia Brown, Boy Detective   D. Sobol

   Bread and Butter Indian   A. Cone

   Parsifal Rides the Time Wave   N. Chenault

   And Then What Happened, Paul Revere?   Jean Fritz

   From the Mixed-up Files of Mrs. Basil Frankweiler
   E. L. Konigsburg

   Jungle Doctor   Dr. Paul White[6]

   Jungle Doctor on Safari   Dr. Paul White[7]

Fourth Grade Reading

The skills begun in the first three grades should now be mastered. Any child having problems in any area should be given individual help. Care needs to taken so that no child feels superior or inferior. The attitude of the teacher will be "caught" by the children.

Curriculum

1. Sight vocabulary—words that do not follow the phonetic rules that have been learned and other sight words that are used frequently. Sight words should be instantly recognized.
    a. Increase the number of words recognized by sight—words taken from reading and content areas.
    b. Develop the ability to use sight words correctly.

2. Silent reading rate—recognizing that the rate should vary according to the reader's purpose and the difficulty and type of material being read.
    a. Slow—a new area of information and/or details and specific information are needed, or the material contains difficult vocabulary and concepts.
    b. Moderate—magazines, some fiction, and material where there is some familiarity with the topic but some details are desired.
    c. Fast—when just the most important facts and ideas are needed and for some fiction.
    d. Very fast—newspaper, light fiction, skimming, and scanning.
3. Study skills—continue reviewing and developing previously studied skills. (See first grade, number 17, and third grade, number 8.)
    a. Apply alphabetizing skills in using an index, dictionary, glossary, or thesaurus.
    b. Use a dictionary, glossary, or thesaurus to find word meanings.
    c. Organizing—when reading the material note the use of center and side headings and words like first, second, or third. Make a simple outline using these as guides.
    d. Learn how to use a telephone directory.
    e. Develop the ability to interpret graphs and maps.
    f. Locate and use reference materials.
4. Oral reading—an important aid in communicating ideas and providing enjoyment for others. Any selection read orally should first be read silently. The use of word emphasis, expression, intonation, and punctuation to help convey meaning should be developed. When reading orally a child should be told any word that is not recognized.
5. Syllabication principles
    a. Review and application of previously studied principles. (See first grade, number 10 and third grade, number 9.)
    b. Compound words—divide between the words and then between the syllables in each word. table cloth   ta ble cloth
    c. Consonant blends and diagraphs should usually be treated as single letters. se <u>cr</u>et   ja<u>ck</u> et
    d. Prefixes and suffixes usually form a separate syllable. <u>re</u> turn   play <u>ing</u>
6. Prefixes and Suffixes—introduce meanings.
    a. Review of those already studied. (See second grade, number 4.)

b.

Prefix	Meaning	Example
dis-	not, apart, away from	disconnect dislike
in-	in, into	inactive indoors
mis-	wrongly	miscue misplace
non-	not	nonsense nonpaying
pre-	before	prepaid preheat
re-	again, back	repeat return
un-	not	uncertain uneven
en-	in, to make, put into	encode enclose
de-	from, away	dethrone debrief
sub-	under	subhead subplot
ex-	out, from	exile export

c. Suffix meanings.
   To form nouns

-er and -or	a person who	farmer exhibitor
-ment	real result	payment improvement
-ness	quality	goodness politeness

   To form adjectives

-able and -ible	capable, worthy	passable responsible
-y	characterized by	dirty thrifty
-ful	fills	armful houseful
-ous	full, having	poisonous famous
-ish	bit, like, nationality	foolish British

   To form adverbs

-ly	manner, point of view	quickly theologically

   To form different tense of a verb

-ed	past tense	played lifted
-s and -es	present tense third person singular	plays lifts goes
-ing	present participle	playing lifting

   To form plurals

-s and -es		books dishes

7. Content area reading
   a. Develop a vocabulary for each subject area.
   b. Decide on the purpose of the reading.
   c. Choose the proper reading rate for the material and purpose.
8. Cause and effect principle (See third grade, number 6.)
   a. Increase the ability to understand how one event causes another.
   b. Develop an awareness of any changes that might have occurred if an event had not happened as it did.

9. Comprehension skills (See first grade, number 12 and third grade, number 7.)
   a. Making generalizations—forming a generalization on the basis of stated facts and developing the ability to distinguish specifics from general information. After arriving at a generalization, pictures can be drawn for a "TV program," or a mural can be made to illustrate the points that led to the generalization.
   b. Developing the ability to distinguish between a fact, a fact stated in a slanted manner, and opinion. Develop the ability to distinguish between material that is presented as an emotional appeal from that which is presented as unbiased fact. Compare two or more articles on the same subject and note the main idea and supporting details. Discern if the information is presented as pure fact, fact slanted to influence the conclusion to be made by the reader, fact and the writer's opinion, or the writer's opinion only.
   c. Recalling information in the content area of social studies by the extensive use of all aspects of narration.
   d. Vocabulary development—deriving word meaning from the context or from the dictionary when encountering new vocabulary in the content areas and applying vocabulary development skills to words that are beyond the understanding vocabulary when reading for pleasure.
   e. Recognizing the meaning of idiomatic expressions.
10. Listening skills—continue development of previously studied skills. (See Chapter 2 and third grade, number 13.)
11. Narration (See Chapter 2.)
   a. Applying oral narration skills to content area material.
   b. Increasing the ability to apply written narration skills in the content areas.
   c. Using narration for book reports—both oral and written.
12. Literature for pleasure reading and story time
   a. Recognizing the difference between a biography and an autobiography.
   Biography—life story of a person written by another person.
   Autobiography—life story written by the person the story is about.
   b. Interest areas generally include tall tales and myths, biography, history, adventure, different cultures, mysteries, romance, sports, everyday events, science, and hero stories. Girls and boys tend to differ more in their preferences at this age.
   c. Recommended books.

A Wrinkle in Time Madeleine L'Engle

Little Women Louisa May Alcott

Little Men Louisa May Alcott

Wheel on the School Meindert De Jong

Mrs. Frisby and the Rats of NIMH R. O'Brian

Captains Courageous Rudyard Kipling

Lassie Come Home Eric Knight

Men of Iron Howard Pyle

Heidi Johanna Spyri

The Saturdays Elizabeth Enright

Where the Lilies Bloom V. Cleaver

Hurry Home Candy Meindert DeJong

Black Beauty Anna Sewell

Wheel on the School Meindert DeJong

Pursuit in the French Alps P. J. Bonzon

Born Free J. Adamson

Jungle Doctor's Enemies Dr. Paul White[8]

Jungle Doctor Attacks Witchcraft Dr. Paul White[9]

Fifth Grade Reading

The fifth grade reading program emphasizes the application of reading skills in the content areas. A combination of a basal reader and literature which utilizes different categories—historical, scientific, science fiction, adventure, mystery, poetry, etc.—may be used, or reading skill development can be continued by using literature and content area material only.

Curriculum

1. Vocabulary development
   a. Expand sight vocabulary—words that do not follow the phonetic rules that have been learned and other sight words that are used frequently.
   b. Expand reading and speaking vocabulary through literature and content area materials.

2. Content area reading—social studies, mathematics, spelling, English, science, Bible, and fine arts.
   a. Continue the development of previously studied skills. (See fourth grade, number 7.)
   b. Apply study skills to locate information.
   c. Develop the ability to read and use charts, graphs, and diagrams.
   d. Apply comprehension skills to content area reading. (See fourth grade, number 9.)
   e. Apply critical thinking skills to content area reading. (See first grade, number 12g, third grade, number 7d and fourth grade, number 9b.) Developing the ability to distinguish when information presented is fact, when it is slanted to reflect the author's view, when it is opinion, or when it is written to appeal to the emotions. Distinguishing the main ideas and supporting details and not confusing generalizations with supporting details. Learning to evaluate details to ascertain if they are important or unimportant, relevant or irrelevant. Understanding that generalizations are applicable to new situations.
3. Reading and developing an understanding of the different types of literature—fiction, nonfiction, fantasy, folk tales, fables, myths, prose, poetry, and realistic and historical fiction.
4. Singular and plural nouns
   a. Review of irregular noun plurals. (See third grade, number 4.)
   b. Learning special plural forms—four-year-olds   mothers-in-law
5. Oral reading—selections to be read orally should be read silently first. Most reading is not oral, but oral reading is an important communicative tool. Children should consider any oral reading done in school as having a purpose and being worthwhile. Oral reading should include: reading to younger children, reading to prove a point, reading the part of a character in a play, and reading poetry.
6. Silent reading—continuation of the ability to select and use the proper reading rate. (See fourth grade, number 2.)
7. Study skills—refining of previous skills. (See first grade, number 17, third grade, number 8 and fourth grade, number 3.)
   a. Note taking—listening to a selection which is read by paragraphs or by sections (or to a short tape) and writing the main idea of each paragraph or section.
   b. Learn to summarize material in the content areas using both oral and written narration.

   c. Use the library—becoming familiar with the different sections: fiction, nonfiction, reference, card catalog, and computer. Learning to use the card catalog and computer to locate books, and learning to locate and use reference materials.

   d. Develop proficiency in skimming and scanning skills. (See third grade, number 8b.)

   e. Develop the ability to use an almanac to find information.

8. Comprehension skills

   a. Continue development of previously studied skills. (See first grade, number 12, third grade, number 7, and fourth grade, number 9.)

   b. Learning to recognize and use the writer's style as an aid to comprehension. Styles to note: states facts, shows cause and effect, makes comparisons, uses analogy.

   c. Comprehending and recalling information in the content areas of science, studies and math. These methods should be useful: narration: listing the main idea and supporting details of a paragraph, selection, or problem without confusing generalizations with supporting details; selecting details that deal with the subject or problem and illustrating them in a mural; conducting a science experiment; evaluating details to ascertain if they are important or unimportant, relevant or irrelevant; explaining a mathematical process.

   d. Drawing conclusions—checking a conclusion or generalization with the facts to see if it has validity, drawing pictures for a "TV program" that illustrate the points that led to the conclusion, and distinguishing general information from specific details.

   e. Distinguish between fact, a fact slanted to the author's position and opinion by comparing two articles on the same subject. The main ideas and supporting ideas should be noted and analyzed to see if the information presented is fact, fact slanted to influence the conclusion to be made by the reader, fact combined with the author's opinion, or the author's opinion. It should also be noted if the author's writing is an appeal to the emotions.

   f. Develop the ability to distinguish if the actions of the characters are justified or are wrong; discern if the qualities of the characters are true-to-life.

   g. Understand that generalizations are applicable to new situations.

9. Prefixes and suffixes—continuation of skills begun previously. (See second grade, number 4 and fourth grade, number 6.)

10. Narration—increasing the ability to interject personal emotions, feelings, and reactions into what is being read or heard. (See Chapter 2.)

11. Listening skills (See third grade, number 13 and fourth grade, number 10.)

    a. Become aware of personal thoughts, feelings, emotions, and reactions while listening to a selection.

    b. Visualize what is being heard—how the characters look, the setting, etc.

    c. Develop the ability to note the effect of the reader's gestures, intonation, and word emphasis on the listener's reaction to a selection.

12. Book reports—using oral and written narration and other narration techniques.

13. Literature for pleasure reading and story time

    a. Fifth graders are generally interested in history, geography, biography, personal adventure, humor, romance, fantasy, historical nonfiction, geographical nonfiction (other cultures), and animal stories.

    b. Recommended books:

    Otto of the Silver Hand   Howard Pyle

    Henry Reed, Inc.   Keith Robertson

    Crystal Mountain   Belle D. Rugh

    The Good Master   Kate Seredy

    Kidnapped   Robert Louis Stevenson

    Tom Sawyer   Mark Twain

    The Swiss Family Robinson   Johann David Wyss

    Big Red   Jim Kjelgaard

    The Winged Watchman   Hilda Van Stockum

    The Incredible Journey   Shelia Burnford

    Jungle Doctor to the Rescue   Dr. Paul White[10]

    Eyes on Jungle Doctor   Dr. Paul White[11]

    Dirk's Dog Bello   Meindert DeJong

    The House of Many Fathers   Meindert DeJong

    The Four-Story Mistake   Elizabeth Enright

    The Load of Unicorn   Cynthia Harnett

The Queen Elizabeth Story   Rosemary Sutcliff (Oxford)

Bridge to Terabithia   Katherine Paterson

Sixth Grade Reading

The sixth grade reading program provides for developing proficiency in any skills not yet mastered as well as expanding skill development in all areas. Reading at this level can be approached through the use of a basal reader and literature or through literature and content area materials only.

Curriculum

1. Vocabulary development—continued expansion of reading and speaking vocabulary.
2. Comprehension skills
    a. Mastery of all previously studied skills.
    b. Learn to use the writer's style as an aid to comprehension. (See fifth grade, number 8b.) Additional styles to note: use of narration, presentation of details, use of description, persuasive/argumentative style, and other styles encountered in reading materials being used.
    c. Fact or opinion. (See fifth grade, number 8e.) Additional skills: checking additional sources to confirm or refute the generalization or conclusion drawn, making generalizations and drawing conclusions based on the stated facts and not on a previous idea or conclusion, discerning if the author is qualified to write on the subject, deciding if the author's background is influencing the presentation of the material, recognizing the difference between factual statements and the author's opinion or interpretation, understanding the author's purpose in writing the material, and checking the copyright date to ascertain if some of the information may be out-of-date and comparing any out-of-date information with a source with a recent copyright.
    d. Propaganda—developing the ability to recognize words that cause an emotional response: humanism, fair play, communist, home, parents; recognizing relevant and irrelevant statements; recognizing inconsistencies; recognizing when facts are presented in such a manner that an incorrect impression is given; recognizing propaganda techniques such as name calling, the bandwagon approach, or testimonials; recognizing the omission of facts and/or the use of generalizations so that the information presented is slanted to one position.

3. Study skills
   a. Mastery of all previously studied skills.
   b. Critical thinking—knowing the author's background, qualifications, and position on the topic; deciding what the author's purpose is in writing; analyzing material on the same topic written by two different qualified authors with different backgrounds, and deciding how this has influenced the positions represented; looking at the qualifications of several authors and deciding what subjects they would be qualified to write about; developing an understanding that familiarity with the subject and a good reputation as a writer and person are important qualifications.
   c. Note taking—listening to a selection and writing the main idea and supporting details.
   d. Skimming and scanning (See third grade, number 8b.)
   Skimming—look at the table of contents, skim a chapter or article to learn the author's position, skim the material to see if it contains the desired information and recognize if all or only part of the material needs to be read to obtain the desired information.
   Scanning—look quickly at the material in order to locate a date, number, or to locate an answer to a question. Use chapter titles and headings as guides to the contents, and decide if the desired information will be found in the material.
   e. Library skills—continuation of the skills begun in fifth grade (See fifth grade, number 7c); learning the Dewey decimal system, Library of Congress, or other classification system used; learning to locate audiovisual materials; learn to use the *Reader's Guide to Periodical Literature*.
4. Oral reading—(See third grade, number 10, fourth grade, number 4 and fifth grade, number 5.)
   a. Mastery of previously studied skills.
   b. Sight reading development—read a passage that has not previously been read silently. At this age sight reading should be done by volunteers or by an individual reading only to the teacher.
   c. Include reading to younger children, reading to prove a point, reading the part of a character in a play, and reading poetry.
5. Silent Reading (See third grade, number 10 and fourth grade, number 2.)
   a. Mastery of previously studied skills.
   b. Application of skills in all content areas.

6. Content areas—social studies, science, mathematics, English, spelling, Bible, fine arts. (See fourth grade, number 7 and fifth grade, number 2.)
   a. Mastery of previously studied skills.
   b. Application of skills to reading in the content areas—vocabulary development, following directions, critical thinking, making inferences, drawing conclusions, generalizations, indepenent thinking, and observing the author's style and purpose.
7. Listening skills—(See third grade, number 13, fourth grade, number 10 and fifth grade, number 11.)
   a. Mastery of previously studied skills.
   b. Continue developing the ability to narrate after listening to a selection only once.
   c. Listen to old radio programs on tape and then narrate, both written and oral, after listening only once.
   d. Apply listening/narrating skills in the content areas.
8. Prefixes and suffixes—(See fourth grade, number 6.)
   a. Review of previously studied skills.
   b. Increase the ability to use, recognize, and know the meaning of commonly used suffixes and prefixes.
9. Independent thinking—being able to deal with an idea or an issue and form one's own opinion is vital if an individual is to become a thinking person who exerts a positive influence on society. The ability to apply all skills learned throughout the elementary grades is essential. Special emphasis should be given to word meaning and usage; critical reading and thinking; making inferences; drawing conclusions; making generalizations; discerning if the material is fact, opinion, or propaganda; establishing the credibility of the author; and the use of reference materials. The sixth grade teacher should endeavor to see that each child is equipped with the tools for independent thinking.
10. Types of literature—(See fourth grade, number 12 and fifth grade, number 3.)
    a. Biography and autobiography—distinguishing a balanced approach from one that undervalues the characters or presents them as almost infallible.
    b. Review of other types of literature.
11. Book reports
    a. Reporting by using written and oral narration. (See Chapter 2.)
    b. Review books using the author's style and the type of literature skills as a basis. (See fifth grade, numbers 3 and 8b.)
12. Literature for pleasure reading and story time

a. Sixth grade reading preferences will vary, but interest areas include historical fiction, romance, adventure, mystery, science fiction, careers, geographical fiction and nonfiction (other cultures), humor, biographies, fantasy, history, and animal stories.

b. Recommended books:

All Creatures Great and Small   James Herriot

Carry on Mr. Bowditch   Jean Lee Latham

The Eagle of the Ninth   Rosemary Sutcliff (Puffin)

Adam of the Road   Elizabeth Janet Gray

The Ark   Margot Benary-Isbert

Treasure Island   Robert Louis Stevenson

The Adventures of Huckleberry Finn   Mark Twain

Jane Eyre   Charlotte Bronte

Winston Churchill & the Story of Two World Wars   Olivia Coolidge

Robinson Crusoe   Daniel Defoe

The Count of Monte Cristo   Alexandre Dumas

David Copperfield   Charles Dickens

The Diary of a Young Girl   Anne Frank

Ramona   Helen Hunt Jackson

L'Abri   Edith Schaeffer

Across Five Aprils   I. Hunt

Doctor of Tanganyika   Dr. Paul White[12]

5 Handwriting

andwriting is not an end in itself, but a communication tool. Legible, neat handwriting should be an integral part of all written work. The integration of handwriting skills into all content area written work is essential. It is recommended that handwriting practice be with words and/or sentences rather than with individual letters.

When making letter shapes children should start at the correct point and move in the proper direction. Letters should be well formed with correct height and width and there should be correct spacing between letters and between words. Although perfection is not the goal, each child should produce a finished product that is the result of his/her best effort. A distinction should be made between careless work and work that is not perfect.

Formal handwriting lessons should be between ten and fifteen minutes in length. In order to achieve the best results, children should adhere to the following guidelines:

1. Sit up straight with feet on the floor.
2. Position the paper correctly—right-handed children should slant the paper to the left and left-handed children should slant the paper to the right.
3. Pencil—held loosely between the end of the middle and index finger and the thumb. It should rest at the point between where the index finger and thumb join the hand. The pencil should be held loosely enough so that it can easily be pulled from the fingers.
4. The lower arm and hand (not just the hand) should move across the paper when writing.
5. During writing the paper should be moved up so that the lower arm always rests on the writing surface.

First Grade Handwriting

Manuscript is recommended for first grade. Emphasis is placed on correct letter formation, spacing between letters and words, width and height of letters, neat and legible work, and proper position of paper, pencil, and body. Fine and gross motor development will vary; therefore, expectations will be on an individual basis. Each child will be expected to work at his/her ability level and encouraged to improve during the year.

Procedure

1. Teacher writes the letter or word on the chalkboard while the children watch.
2. The teacher and children write the letter or word in the air, keeping the elbow straight.
3. Teacher again demonstrates the correct formation on the chalkboard.
4. Children write the letter or word on the paper while the teacher gives oral directions—where to start, direction to move, and spacing.
5. Copying over dots should be used for those experiencing difficulty.
6. Use primary pencils, primary crayons, or large felt markers during the first semester and longer if indicated by individual motor development.
7. Use first grade writing tablets or paper.
8. Work can be copied directly from the chalkboard or written from dictation when the child is able to form the letters correctly.

Second Grade Handwriting

Manuscript is recommended for all written work in second grade and for handwriting instruction during the first semester. The introduction of cursive writing should begin during the second semester. Correct hand and body position, formation of the letters, and legibility should be emphasized for both manuscript and cursive writing. When introducing cursive, the same procedure should be followed as for the introduction of manuscript. (See first grade.) Second grade writing tablets or paper should be used.

Third Grade Handwriting

Cursive writing should be emphasized in third grade. Attention should be given to correct shape of the letters, letter size, proper slant of the letters, and spacing between letters and words. During the first semester a transition should be made from the use of manuscript to the use of cursive in all written work. Third grade writing tablets or paper should be used.

Fourth Grade Handwriting

All work in fourth grade should be done in cursive writing. The use of ink should be introduced and emphasis should continue to be placed on correct letter shape, size, slant, and spacing. Manuscript should also be practiced periodically for use on posters, maps, graphs, charts, and for labeling. Fourth grade tablets or writing paper should be used with a transition made to notebook paper in the second semester.

Fifth and Sixth Grade Handwriting

Generally formalized instruction in handwriting is not necessary at the fifth and sixth grade levels. Individual needs should be identified and corrected. Freedom to develop an individual style should be allowed, but emphasis should continue to be placed on legibility and neatness in all work.

6 Spelling

S pelling is an important communication tool and can be taught by using an individualized approach that takes words from reading, literature, and creative writing or by using a systematic program. There is a close correlation between spelling, reading, handwriting, and English; the skills from these areas need to be applied when spelling words. Children also learn to spell informally from such things as cereal boxes, TV, books, computer games, etcetera. During a school day, spelling is used in many areas other than a formal spelling situation; therefore, spelling should be an integral part of the whole school program.

An individualized approach can be one that a teacher or school develops. Spelling words can come from a list of words that have been misspelled or whose spelling was unknown when doing written work. In the latter case each child should keep a list of words that were misspelled or unknown. In an individualized program words can also be taken from reading and literature.

A developmental program plans for a systematic development of skills and the application of those skills. A developmental program needs to be supplemented with words from reading, literature, and other content areas.

Weekly Plan for All Approaches

1. The introduction of the words—pronunciation and meaning.
2. The development and application of a skill area.
3. Learning to correctly spell the words.
4. Writing the words from dictation.
5. Learning any words that were misspelled on the dictation.

□ 71

Charlotte Mason's Approach—Dictation

In addition to the spelling approach selected, Child Light recommends using Charlotte Mason's method as a supplement to the primary approach. In first, second, and third grades once a week is recommended, while once every two weeks is suggested for fourth, fifth, and sixth grades. Each child should be supplied with a copy of the selection to be learned for dictation. The material selected for dictation can be lengthened as the children progress in ability, but care should be taken that the selection length never becomes excessive. The study process should take about ten minutes, but more time may be needed for one- or two-page selections. This approach is applicable for selections from reading, literature, and other content areas.

Procedure

First and Second Grades
1. Use words from reading—short poems and verses can be used for those that indicate readiness for passages.
2. Each word is looked at—in poems and verses only those words not known are studied.
3. The eyes are closed and the word is visualized. Words should not be written, only visualized.
4. The eyes are opened and the word visualized is checked with the written word for accuracy.
5. If the word was not visualized correctly the process is repeated.
6. The words are dictated to the child in sentence form and the child writes the entire sentence. Poems and verses are dictated by phrases. Each sentence or phrase is dictated only once.
7. Any misspelled words should be looked at, visualized, checked for accuracy, and then written correctly.

Third, Fourth, Fifth, and Sixth Grades
1. Third and fourth grades use paragraphs, poems, or verses; fifth and sixth grades use one- or two-page selections.
2. The child looks at the selection and notes words that will need special attention.
3. The teacher points out any additional words that may need attention.
4. Each word is then looked at, one at a time, and visualized with the eyes closed.
5. The eyes are opened and the visualized word is checked with the written word for accuracy.

6. The teacher writes any words on the chalkboard that the child is still uncertain of.
7. The child looks at the word until it can be visualized and then erases it.
8. If desired, the child writes the word on the chalkboard while the teacher watches and erases any incorrect letter immediately.
9. The child then writes the word correctly.
10. The teacher gives the dictation, clause by clause with each clause repeated only once.
11. Incorrectly spelled words are marked out with a magic marker.
12. The child studies the incorrectly spelled words following the original procedure, and then writes them correctly above the marked out words.

Note: With short selections the dictation immediately follows the study period. Longer selections may call for a longer preparation time—short study periods repeated for two to four days before the dictation.

First Grade Spelling

Spelling should not be emphasized as a separate subject until the second half of the first grade. However, creative writing and handwriting will necessitate the correct spelling of words. Children should be shown or told how to spell any desired word when doing creative writing. Many words will be incidentally learned through the study of reading skills such as word families. Correct spelling should be encouraged without pressure being placed on the child. Words dictated for formal spelling lessons should be in short sentences. The child should write the sentence and not an isolated word.

Curriculum

1. Word families
   Introduce formalized spelling through the use of word families.
   Examples: <u>at</u> family—bat cat fat hat mat pat rat sat
2. Phonetic and structural analysis principles
   Base a lesson on a principle that correlates with a reading skill.
   Example: Final <u>e</u>—bake came dime fine gate mile
3. Sight words
   Use words from the Dolch list and the basal reader.
4. Number and color words
   Number words from one to ten and basic color words—red blue green yellow black white brown orange purple

5. Calendar-related words
   Days of the week, months of the year, and seasonal words—fall winter spring summer
6. Creative writing
   Use words misspelled or not known from creative writing.
7. Charlotte Mason approach supplement—once per week
   Short poems, such as "Mix a Pancake" by Christina Rossetti and "Down! Down!" by Eleanor Farjeon, or Bible verses are appropriate.

Second Grade Spelling

Each second grader should develop the desire to spell words accurately in all written work. Skills from reading should be seen as applying to spelling also.

Curriculum

1. Phonetic and structural analysis principles
   Example: silent letter(s) "ight"—bright fight light might night right sight tight
2. Content areas
   Words from the content areas should be used to supplement the regular word list.
3. Sight words
   Use words from the Dolch list and the basal reader.
4. Calendar-related words
   Review the days of the week, months of the year, and seasonal words.
5. Holiday words
   Thanksgiving Christmas New Year's Day Valentine's Day Easter
6. Creative writing
   Use words misspelled or not known from creative writing.
7. Charlotte Mason approach supplement—once per week
   Short poems such as "Fog" by Carl Sandburg and "The Night Will Never Stay" by Eleanor Farjeon, or Bible verses are appropriate.

Third Grade Spelling

Third grade spelling continues to instill within the child a desire to spell words accurately in all written work. Word meaning and usage is also introduced.

Curriculum

1. Calendar-related words
   Review the days of the week and months of the year and learn their abbreviations.
2. Content areas
   Regular spelling should be supplemented with words from the content areas.
3. Sight words
   Use words from the Dolch list and the basal reader.
4. Structural analysis
   Example. consonant plus le—table title Bible people
5. Other skill areas
   Regular and irregular plurals, possessives, and contractions.
6. Creative writing
   Use words misspelled or not known from creative writing.
7. Verbs
   Regular and irregular verbs—present and past tense.
8. Charlotte Mason approach supplement—once per week
   Short poems, Bible verses, or short passages.

Fourth Grade Spelling

Fourth grade spelling provides for the individual to become a self-correcting speller while providing for continuation of skill development. Correct spelling in all written work is emphasized.

Curriculum

1. Structural analysis
   Application of skills from reading.
     Example: spelling root words to which prefixes or suffixes have been added.
2. Irregular word spellings
   Verbs
     Example: run/ran sing/sang
   Noun plurals
     Examples: deer/deer mouse/mice foot/feet
3. Supplementary words
   Content area words, sight words, and misspelled words.
4. Compound words
   Correctly spelling compound words.
5. Other skill areas
   Correctly spelling antonyms, synonyms, homonyms, and homophones.

6. Dictionary
   Locating words to check spelling, meaning, plural form, and usage.
7. Creative writing, narrations, book reports
   Emphasis on correct spelling of all words used.
8. Charlotte Mason approach supplement—once every two weeks
   Poems, Bible passages, or one-page selections.

Fifth Grade Spelling

Fifth grade spelling provides for reinforcement of phonetic and structural analysis skills and further development of word usage and meaning. Syllabication should be introduced as an aid in spelling words correctly. Spelling words correctly in written work and self-correction of all written work should continue to be encouraged.

Curriculum

1. Review of previously presented areas
   Phonetic and structural analysis skills; regular and irregular plurals of nouns and verbs; compound words; calendar-related words; prefixes and suffixes.
2. Syllabication
   Apply syllabication skills as an aid to spelling words.
3. Supplementary words
   Content area words, sight words, and misspelled words from written work.
4. Other skill areas
   Correct spelling of antonyms, synonyms, homonyms, homophones.
5. Dictionary
   Locate words for spelling, meaning, plural forms, usage, and syllabication.
6. Correct spelling in all work
   Creative writing, narration, book reports, outlines, and research papers.
7. Charlotte Mason approach supplement—once every two weeks
   Poems, Bible passages, or one- to two-page selections.

Sixth Grade Spelling

Sixth grade spelling builds on phonetic and structural analysis skills, other word attack skills, and spelling generalizations. Using the dictionary to check spelling, meaning, and usage is stressed as a means to assure correct spelling and usage in written work. Self-correction skills are emphasized.

Curriculum

1. Application and review of all previously presented skills.
2. Supplementary words
   Content area words, sight words, and words misspelled in written work.
3. Individual problem words
   Individualized spelling for an individual's problem words.
4. Correct spelling in all work
   Creative writing, narration, book reports, outlines, summaries, and research papers.
5. Self-correction
   Emphasis on becoming a self-correcting speller with special stress placed on the use of the dictionary as an aid in self-correction.
6. Charlotte Mason approach supplement—once every two weeks or once a month for exceptional spellers.
   Poems, Bible passages, or one- to two-page selections.

7 English

English grammar and composition need to be a natural outgrowth of normal classroom activities. Interesting, relevant material presented in a challenging, exciting manner can be a motivational tool. On the other hand, irrelevant material and an emphasis on drills can destroy any interest in the study of oral and written English.

Provision should be made for group interaction with meaningful discussions where ideas, reactions, emotions, evaluations, and critical thinking are evidenced. Child Light recommends oral narration as an aid in developing the ability to speak freely and to listen and observe accurately.

Written narration is also recommended because it fosters the development of good listening and writing skills as well as the expression of feelings, emotions, reactions, evaluations, and critical thinking. In addition, emphasis is placed on creative writing as a means of skill development and of expressing ideas in a clear, concise manner.

Poetry and literature are important areas of the English program. An appreciation for and enjoyment of poetry and literature is developed through reading or listening to living books.

> In literature, we have the opportunity of developing a series of relationships with other persons, places, and historical times in a direct way. Perhaps this is the best place for mind to meet mind. We all realize the deep influence our companions have upon our thinking and behavior. In literature, a child is introduced to persons who think deeply and sensitively, and who express themselves well.[1]

Literature presented in English studies should be followed by oral or written narration, while story time literature should be solely for enjoyment with no narration following the reading unless the child desires to narrate.

The classroom should have a relaxed atmosphere that stimulates the pupils to observe accurately; to see *richness* in their experiences; to express ideas, emotions, and feelings; to enlarge their vocabulary; to experience group interaction; and to master the mechanics of writing. In the first three grades there should be provision made for more oral than written work. In all grades any drill lessons should stem from significant speaking and writing situations and not be drill for drill's sake.

Note: Books recommended for use at each grade level are found within this curriculum. For additional suggestions see *Books Children Love*.

First Grade English

First grade English is correlated with reading, spelling, and handwriting. Oral communication skills are emphasized and developed through the use of narration. The use of capitals and correct punctuation are observed in reading and applied in spelling, handwriting, and creative writing. Most first grade English skills are taught as a part of the reading program. Dramatic play, choral speaking, literature, and poetry are also important parts of the first grade program.

Curriculum

1. Writing
   a. Dictated, copied, and original sentences
   b. Original stories and poems (second semester)—emphasis on creativity with the mechanics of writing (punctuation and capitalization) minimized so that creativity is not stifled by the fear of making a mistake.
   c. Self-correction—checking to see if each sentence is started with a capital letter and ended with a punctuation mark.
   d. Writing the alphabet—upper- and lowercase.
   e. Alphabetizing by the first letter—<u>b</u>oy <u>c</u>ome <u>h</u>at <u>p</u>an
2. Expressing ideas
   a. Through chart stories (See first grade reading, number 1.)
   b. Through narration
   c. By sharing observations
   d. By sharing experiences
3. Oral communication
   a. Through narration
   b. Through group interaction

    c. Dramatic play—role playing, puppets, acting out a story, and pantomime

    d. Choral speaking

    e. Reciting poetry and Bible passages

    f. Using the telephone

    g. Storytelling

4. Listening

    a. Listening to and following directions

    b. Listening as a means of learning and identifying

    c. Becoming a good listener when interacting in a group situation

5. Grammar

    a. Capitals and punctuation—noted in reading and applied in writing

    b. Understanding that some words name (nouns)—mother house

    c. Understanding that naming words can be singular or plural— dog dogs

    d. Understanding that some words tell what happens (action verbs)— play work sing

    e. Understanding that words that tell what happens can be present—walk sit, past—walked sat, or future—will walk will sit

    f. Understanding that some words describe (adjectives)— *green* house *small* boy

    g. Understanding the function of a subject pronoun, an object pronoun, and possessive pronouns and being able to use them in a sentence. (A pronoun takes the place of a noun.) Subject pronouns—I you he she it we they; object pronouns—me you him her it us them; possessive pronouns—my your his her its our their

    h. Recognizing and using antonyms and synonyms

Note: The grammatical terms can be used by the teacher, and some children will pick them up and use them. Using the term should not be a requirement.

6. Study skills

    a. Locating and using the parts of a book—table of contents, index, and glossary.

    b. Understanding that information can be obtained in encyclopedias, in books, and in an atlas.

    c. Skimming and scanning to answer questions about what has been read.

Skimming—quickly glancing at the material to recall the main ideas

Scanning—quickly glancing at the material to find a specific answer

7. Poetry—listening to and memorizing
   a. Promote a feeling for language usage to express ideas, feelings and emotions.
   b. Vocabulary enrichment
   c. Develop familiarity with the nursery rhymes
   d. Memorize two or more poems per semester
   e. Some suggestions for memorization (let the child choose). Follow same procedure as for Bible memorization. (See Bible curriculum.)

   "The Animal Store"   Rachel Field

   "Bed in Summer"   Robert Louis Stevenson

   "Boats"   Rowena Bastin Bennett

   "The Cupboard"   Walter de la Mare

   "Ferry Boats"   James S. Tippett

   "The Ice Cream Man"   Rachel Field

   "Indian Children"   Annette Wynne

   "A Little Bird"   Alison Fischer

   "The Little Turtle"   Rachel Lindsay

   "Mice"   Rose Fyleman

   "Sh!"   James S. Tippett

   "Someone"   Walter de la Mare

   Nursery Rhymes

   "The Swing"   Robert Louis Stevenson

   "Traffic"   Jane Lear Talley

   "What Does Little Birdie Say"   Alfred Lord Tennyson

   f. Suggested books for reading aloud:

   Nibble, Nibble   Margaret Wise Brown

   I Can't Said the Ant   P. Cameron

   Now We Are Six   A. A. Milne

   Mother Goose

Old Nursery Rhymes   illustrated by Kate Greenaway

Book of Nursery and Mother Goose Rhymes   Marguerite De Angeli

Once Upon a Rhyme: 101 Poems for Young Children   Sara and Stephen Corrin, eds. (Faber/Puffin paperback)

8. Literature—to be read aloud to the children
   a. Develop an appreciation of literature through living books.
   b. Promote a feeling for language usage and richness.
   c. Distinguish between real and make-believe stories.
   d. Suggested books to be read aloud and narrated:

      Just So Stories   Rudyard Kipling

      Rip Van Winkle and the Legend of Sleepy Hollow   Maud & Miska Petersham

      Winne the Pooh and the House at Pooh Corner   A. A. Milne

      Little Old Mrs. Pepperpot   Alf Proysen

      The New Golden Land Anthology   Judith Elkin, ed. (Viking/Kestrel Puffin paperback)

      Favorite Fairy Tales Told in England   Virginia Haviland, ed. (Bodley Head)

      Tell Them Again Tales   Margaret Baker (Hodder and Stoughton)

      The Fairy Tale Treasury   Raymond Briggs (Puffin) (See also first grade reading, number 18c.)

Second Grade English

Second grade English is closely correlated with reading, handwriting, and spelling. There is continued emphasis on oral communication through the use of narration, choral speaking, and dramatic play. Written communication is developed through creative writing, simple narrations, and letters and original cards. Grammar is approached in a relaxed, natural manner that utilizes relevant non-drill materials. Developing an appreciation for poetry and living books is also an important part of second grade English.

Curriculum

1. Writing
   a. Simple narration for those that show readiness for written narration

     b. Original stories and poems with emphasis on creativity. Grammar mechanics should be minimized in order to allow freedom to express ideas without fear of failing to do it correctly.

     c. Paragraph—noted in reading and applied in written work

     d. Simple friendly letters and cards

     e. Self-editing and revision—checking to see that capital letters and punctuation marks are used where needed, that paragraphs are indented, that words are spelled correctly, and that unnecessary sentences are deleted

2. Expressing ideas, emotions, feelings
   a. Through narration
   b. By sharing observations and reactions
   c. By sharing experiences

3. Oral communication
   a. Through narration
   b. Through group interaction
   c. Dramatic play—role playing, pantomime, puppets, plays
   d. Choral speaking
   e. Reading or reciting poetry and Bible passages
   f. Using the telephone
   g. Storytelling

4. Listening
   a. Listening to and following directions
   b. Listening as a means of learning and identifying sounds
   c. Becoming a good listener when interacting in a group situation

5. Grammar—note usage in reading and apply in written work
   a. Capital letters—names of people, days of the week, months of the year, cities, states, countries, holidays, titles, abbreviations, beginning of a sentence
   b. Punctuation—at the end of a sentence, quotation marks, apostrophes, commas
   c. Parts of speech—identify and use words that name (nouns), words that tell what happens (verbs), words that describe (adjectives), words that take the place of a naming word.
   d. Recognize and use possessives and plurals.
   e. Differentiate between complete and incomplete sentences.
   f. Note the usage and structure of compound words.
   g. Recognize, construct, and use contractions.
   h. Recognize and use antonyms, synonyms, homonyms, and homophones.
   i. Recognize and use prefixes and suffixes. (See second grade reading, number 4.)

6. Study skills
   a. Alphabetizing to the second letter— came cent city coat
   b. Using entry words and guide words in the dictionary
   c. Recognizing and using the parts of a book—table of contents, index, glossary
   d. Learning to use the library
   e. Skimming and scanning to answer questions about what has been read. (See first grade, number 6c.)
7. Poetry—listening to and memorizing
   a. Recognizing rhyming words
   b. Developing an appreciation for and enjoyment of poetry
   c. Vocabulary enrichment
   d. Memorize two or more poems per semester
   e. Some suggestions for memorization (let the child choose):

      "Bedtime" Eleanor Farjeon

      "Cat" Dorothy Baruch

      "The Christening" A. A. Milne

      "The Door at the End of Our Garden" Frederick E. Weatherly

      "Foreign Children" Robert Louis Stevenson

      "General Store" Rachel Field

      "A Good Play" Robert Louis Stevenson

      "A Kitten" Eleanor Farjeon

      "Marching Song" Robert Louis Stevenson

      "Missing" A. A. Milne

      "Monkey and the Crocodile" Laura E. Richards

      "Mumps" Elizabeth Maddox Roberts

      "Spring Prayer" Ralph W. Emerson

      "Where Go the Boats" Robert Louis Stevenson

      "Talents Differ" Laura E. Richards

      "Barefoot Days" Rachel Field

   f. Suggested books for reading aloud:

      The Little Bookworm Eleanor Farjeon

      When We Were Very Young A. A. Milne

      A Child's Garden of Verses Robert Louis Stevenson

Rhymes and Verses Walter de la Mare

Poems of Childhood Eugene Field

8. Literature—to be read aloud to the children and narrated
    a. Develop an appreciation of literature through living books.
    b. Promote a feeling for language usage and richness.
    c. Distinguish between real and make-believe stories.
    d. Suggested books to be read aloud and narrated:

    Jungle Book Rudyard Kipling

    Wizard of Oz Lyman Frank Baum

    Velveteen Rabbit Margery Williams

    Adventures of the Little Wooden Horse Ursula Maray Williams

    Puppy Summer Meindert DeJong

    The Cricket in Times Square George Seldon

(See also second grade reading, number 13.)

Third Grade English

Third grade English continues to develop and reinforce previous skills by correlating English with reading, handwriting, and spelling. Narration promotes oral and written communication skills and the expression of emotions, feelings, reactions, and independent and critical thinking. Appreciation and understanding of drama, poetry, and literature is extended.

Curriculum

1. Writing
    a. Narration of living books
    b. Creative writing—original stories, poems, and plays with emphasis on creativity and not mechanics of grammar
    c. Friendly letters, invitations, thank-you cards, get-well cards, and envelopes
    d. Learning editing marks and applying them in self-correction of written work— ⟰ capital letter, ⊙ add period, ⋏ add comma, ⋏ add word, ℯ take out
    e. Self-editing, revising, and proofreading—check for correct use of capital letters and punctuation, indenting paragraphs, and spelling. Remove any unnecessary sentences.
2. Expressing ideas, emotions, feelings, reactions
    a. Through narration
    b. By applying critical thinking skills

    c. By sharing observations

    d. By sharing experiences

3. Oral communication
   a. Through narration
   b. Through group interaction
   c. Drama—plays, choral speaking, pantomime, role playing
   d. Interviewing and being interviewed
   e. Using the telephone

4. Grammar
   a. Recognizing nouns, proper nouns, pronouns, and verbs, and identifying and using them in sentences. Also developing the ability to understand the grammatical terms.
   b. Recognizing verb tenses and using the correct tense in sentences
   c. Using correct capitalization
   d. Identifying and using compound words, contractions, and possessives
   e. Using correct punctuation—in sentences, contractions, possessives and abbreviations
   f. Identifying and using antonyms, synonyms, homonyms, and homophones
   g. Identifying and using prefixes and suffixes correctly
   h. Identify the subject and predicate of a sentence
   i. Recognizing and writing different sentence forms—noun/verb (n/v), Dogs run; noun/linking verb/adjective (n/v/a), Apples are red; noun/linking verb/noun (n/v/n), Apples are fruit; verb/noun (v/n), Play ball!
   j. Recognizing and using singular and plural nouns and verbs—regular and irregular
   k. Diagramming sentences—noun and verb

5. Study skills
   a. Using an index, dictionary, glossary, and thesaurus
   b. Using a dictionary, glossary, and thesaurus for word meanings
   c. Organizing material
   d. Using a telephone directory
   e. Alphabetizing to the third and fourth letter— knave knee knife; outing outlaw output
   f. Skimming and scanning (See third grade reading, number 8b.)
   g. Using the library

6. Poetry—listening to and memorizing
   a. Expanding an appreciation for and understanding of poetry
   b. Vocabulary enrichment
   c. Memorize two or more poems per semester

d. Some suggestions for memorization—let the child choose

"An Introduction to Dogs"   Ogden Nash

"Animal Crackers"   Christopher Morley

"The Creation"   Cecil Frances Alexander

"Hiding"   Dorothy Aldis

"Jack in the Pulpit"   Rowena Bastin Bennett

"Jonathan Bing"   B. Curtis Brown

"The Land of Storybooks"   Robert Louis Stevenson

"My Shadow"   Robert Louis Stevenson

"Puppy and I"   A. A. Milne

"A Sea Song from the Shore"   James Whitcomb Riley

"Us Two"   A. A. Milne

"The Umbrella Brigade"   Laura E. Richards

"Vespers"   A. A. Milne

"Eletelephony"   Laura E. Richards

"The Wind"   Robert Louis Stevenson

"Yesderday in Oxford Street"   Rose Fyleman

"Halfway Down"   A. A. Milne

e. Suggested books to be read aloud:

Girls Are Silly   Ogden Nash

A Boy Is a Boy   Ogden Nash

Then There Were Three   Eleanor Farjeon

A Book of Americans   Rosemary & Stephen Vincent Benét

7. Literature—to be read aloud to the children and narrated
   a. Develop an appreciation of literature through living books.
   b. Develop good listening skills.
   c. Vocabulary enrichment and developing an understanding of the use of language as a tool for expressing ideas
   d. Learning from literature
   e. Suggested books to be read aloud and narrated:

   Peter Pan   Sir James M. Barrie

   The Wind in the Willows   Kenneth Grahame

Treasures of the Snow   Patricia St. John

The Lion, the Witch and the Wardrobe   C. S. Lewis

Pilgrim's Progress   (John Bunyan). A shortened edition may be used.

Roller Skates   Ruth Sawyer

Fourth Grade English

In fourth grade English, written work is emphasized and the development of oral communication skills is continued. A more in-depth study of grammar and study skills is pursued and other skills studied previously are reviewed and expanded. Critical thinking is stressed and independent thinking is encouraged.

Curriculum

1. Writing
   a. Narration of living books
   b. Creative writing—using similes and metaphors in writing poems; stories; advertisements; book reports and reviews; and plays
      • A simile is a figure of speech that compares two unlike things that are similar in some special way, using *as* or *like*. nose like a cherry   sins washed white as snow
      • A metaphor is a figure of speech that compares two unlike things that are similar in some special way without using *as* or *like*. the sun is a flaming ball   Jesus is the Lily of the Valley
   c. Letters, cards, announcements, and envelopes
   d. Written reports
   e. Self-editing, revising, and proofreading—review editing signs and check for capitals, punctuation, spelling, words left out, unnecessary sentences, and indented paragraphs
2. Expressing ideas, emotions, feelings, reactions, conclusions, generalizations
   a. Through narration
   b. By sharing observations
   c. By sharing experiences
   d. By applying critical thinking skills

3. Oral communication
   a. Through narration
   b. By storytelling
   c. Giving directions

d. Giving reports
e. Through group discussions
f. By reading aloud
g. Using the telephone
h. By interviewing and being interviewed

4. Grammar
   a. Recognizing the parts of speech, identifying them in sentences, and using them correctly in sentences
   b. Applying correct punctuation and capitalization in written work
   c. Forming and using contractions, possessives, and abbreviations
   d. Sentences—ability to write complete sentences and recognize incomplete sentences
   e. Ability to identify and use prefixes and suffixes and know their meaning (See fourth grade reading, number 6.)
   f. Forming and using singular and plural nouns and verbs correctly—regular and irregular
   g. Review and use antonyms, synonyms, homonyms, and homophones correctly.
   h. Diagramming sentences—noun, verb, adjectives, adverbs

5. Study skills
   a. Dictionary—entry words, guide words, syllables, accent marks
   b. Parts of a book—ability to locate and use a table of contents, index, and glossary
   c. Ability to locate and use reference materials
   d. Library skills
   e. Making an outline of material heard or read
   f. Skimming and scanning (See first grade, number 6c.)

6. Poetry—listening to, reading, and memorizing
   a. Appreciating, understanding, and enjoying poetry
   b. Identifying different styles
      • limerick—a poem of five lines in which lines 1, 2, and 5 rhyme with each other and lines 3 and 4 rhyme with each other
      • haiku—a Japanese nature poem of three lines which do not rhyme. Lines 1 and 3 have five syllables; line 2 has seven.
      • tanka—a Japanese poem of five lines which deals with nature or the seasons of the year. Lines 1 and 3 have five syllables; lines 2, 4, and 5 have seven syllables.
      • narrative—a poem which tells a story
      • tongue twisters—a sentence where all words begin with

the same sound. When said quickly, it is difficult to repeat the sentence correctly.

- lyric—a poem describing the writer's feeling regarding a topic
- sonnet—a lyric poem of fourteen lines in any of several fixed verse and rhyme schemes
- couplet—two successive lines of poetry which rhyme

c. Vocabulary enrichment
d. Memorize two poems per semester
e. Some suggestions for memorizing (let the child choose):

"A Child's Thought of God"   Elizabeth B. Browning

"The Duel"   Eugene Field

"Father William"   Lewis Carroll

"From a Railway Carriage"   Robert Louis Stevenson

"Godfrey Gordon Gustavus Gore"   William B. Rands

"If I Were a Pilgrim Child"   Rowena Bastin Bennett

"King's Breakfast"   A. A. Milne

"Little Boy Blue"   Eugene Field

"My Heart Is in the Highlands"   Robert Burns

"Sneezles"   A. A. Milne

"Stopping by the Woods on a Snowy Evening"   Robert Frost

"Whenever I say 'America' "   Nancy Byrd Turner

"Wynken, Blynken and Nod"   Eugene Field

"Thanksgiving Day"   Lydia Maria Child

"Casey Jones"   Wallace Saunders

f. Suggested books to read aloud:

Famous Poets for Young People   Laura Benét

The Rime of the Ancient Mariner   S. T. Coleridge

Poems   Ralph Waldo Emerson

7. Literature—to be read aloud to the children and narrated
   a. Vocabulary enrichment and development
   b. Appreciation for and understanding of the use of language to convey ideas and information

    c. Appreciating and enjoying literature through living books
    d. Expanding knowledge through literature
    e. Developing good listening skills
    f. Suggested books to be read aloud and narrated:

       Famous Modern Storytellers for Young People
       Norah Smaridge

       Prince Caspian   C. S. Lewis

       The Voyage of the Dawn Treader   C. S. Lewis

       Arabian Nights

       The Wool-Pack   Cynthia Harnett

       The Borrowers   Mary Norton

       A Midsummer Night's Dream   William Shakespeare

       The Comedy of Errors   William Shakespeare

       Tales from Shakespeare   Charles and Mary Lamb

Note: Please refer to Appendix V for notes on reading Shakespeare with children.

Fifth Grade English

Fifth grade English continues to build on previous skills in order to develop effective oral and written communication ability. Oral and written narration is continued with an emphasis placed on written work. Independent thinking skills are stressed and an appreciation for and enjoyment of poetry and literature is fostered. The skills necessary to do a research paper are developed and applied.

Curriculum

1. Writing
    a. Through narration of living books
    b. Creative writing—poems, stories, plays, descriptions, and advertisements with emphasis on creativity and not mechanics of grammar
    c. Business and friendly letters, cards, invitations, announcements and envelopes
    d. Self-editing, revision and proofreading—recognizing and using editing symbols: ⹀ capital ⋀ add comma ⋀ add word ℓ take out ⱽⱽ add quotation marks ⌒ spelling ¶ indent paragraph / lowercase letter ⊙ add a period.

Check for complete sentences, punctuation, capital letters where needed, spelling, and paragraph indentations.

2. Expressing ideas, emotions, feelings, reactions, conclusions, and generalizations
   a. Through narration
   b. By critical thinking
   c. By sharing observations
   d. By sharing experiences
   e. Through group interaction
3. Oral communication
   a. Through narration ⱪ
   b. By debating
   c. Through group discussions ⱪ
   d. By oral reading ⱪ
   e. By storytelling
   f. By using the telephone ⱪ
   g. Through drama
4. Grammar
   a. Identify and use the various parts of speech. ⱪ
   b. Identify and use the different tenses of verbs.
   c. Apply correct punctuation and capitals in written work. ⱪ
   d. Develop the ability to write quotations correctly in reports.
   e. Recognize and writing compound words.
   f. Recognize, use, and know the meaning of prefixes and suffixes.
   g. Diagramming sentences—using different sentence forms (See third grade, number 4.)
5. Study skills
   a. Review dictionary skills and expand the usage of the dictionary ⱪ
   b. Ability to locate and use various reference materials
   c. Library—ability to locate and use any materials in the library
   d. Understanding the function of, locating, and using the parts of a book—table of contents, index, glossary, title page, copyright, bibliography
   e. Outlining of material heard or read ⱪ
   f. Developing the ability to take notes ⱪ
   g. Writing summaries ⱪ
   h. Writing a research report ⱪ
   i. Using an almanac
   j. Skimming and scanning (See first grade, number 6c.)
6. Poetry—listening to, reading, memorizing
   a. Appreciating and enjoying poetry

b. Vocabulary development and developing a deeper understanding of word usage in expressing ideas

c. Recognizing, enjoying, and writing different styles of poetry
  • limerick, haiku, tanka, narrative, sonnet (See fourth grade, number 6b.)
  • cinquain—a poem of five lines. Line 1 is one word and is the title; line 2 is two words that describe the title; line 3 is three words that express action about the title; line 4 is four words that express feelings about the title; line 5 is one word that is a synonym for the title in line 1.
  • humorous—a nonsense poem of funny words
  • haikon—a haiku poem written around a picture that illustrates the poem
  • painted—the words or sentences are placed so that they look like or suggest the subject of the poem

d. Memorize two poems per semester.

e. Suggestions for memorizing (let the child choose):

"The American Flag"   Louise Abney

"Arithmetic"   Carl Sandburg

"Christopher Columbus"   Rosemary & Stephen Vincent Benét

"Clipper Ships and Captains"   Rosemary & Stephen Vincent Benét

"Forgiven"   A. A. Milne

"Grandpap's Spectacles"   Unknown

"I Saw God Wash the World"   William L. Stidger

"Western Wagons"   Rosemary & Stephen Vincent Benét

"Johnny Appleseed"   Rosemary & Stephen Vincent Benét

"The Liberty Bell"   George L. Kress

"The Night Wind"   Eugene Field

"The Tale of Custard the Dragon"   Ogden Nash

"A Wonderful Weaver"   George Cooper

"When Frost Is on the Punkin"   James Whitcomb Riley

"The Brook"   Alfred Lord Tennyson

f. Suggested books to read aloud:

Famous American Poets   Laura Benét

The Poems of Longfellow

The Complete Poetical Works of Oliver Wendell Holmes
Cambridge Edition

The Poetry of Robert Frost

The Road Not Taken   Robert Frost

7. Literature—to be read aloud to the children and narrated
   a. Enjoying and appreciating literature through living books
   b. Learning from literature
   c. Gaining an understanding of character development
   d. Vocabulary development and appreciating and understanding the use of language to convey ideas, information, and feelings
   e. Suggestions for listening, reading, and narrating:

   Famous Authors for Young People   Ramon Peyton Coffman

   Famous Modern American Novelists   John Cournos

   The Hobbit   J. R. R. Tolkien

   Call It Courage   Armstrong Sperry

   The Iliad   (Homer) Retold by Alfred J. Church

   The Iliad of Homer   Retold by Barbara L. Picard

   King Arthur and His Knights   Anthony Mockler (Oxford)

   An Introduction to Shakespeare   Marchette Chute

   As You Like It   William Shakespeare

   The Merry Wives of Windsor   William Shakespeare

   Hamlet   William Shakespeare

   Macbeth   William Shakespeare

   Tales from Shakespeare   Charles and Mary Lamb

Note: Please refer to Appendix V for notes on reading Shakespeare with children.

Sixth Grade English

Sixth grade English reviews previous skills and identifies individual areas of weakness. Written and oral narration, study skills, understanding and applying basic grammar skills, poetry, and literature are emphasized. Opportunity to do research and write a research paper is given. By the end of the sixth grade a child should be able to convey ideas, beliefs, and facts in a logical and coherent manner.

Curriculum

1. Writing
   a. Through narration of living books
   b. Friendly and business letters, invitations, announcements, cards, and envelopes
   c. Creative writing—plays, stories, poems, and advertisements with emphasis on creativity and not mechanics of grammar
   d. Expository writing
   e. Self-editing, revision, and proofreading—using editing symbols and checking for punctuation, capitalization, complete sentences, indented paragraphs, and spelling
2. Expressing ideas, emotions, feelings, reactions, conclusions, and generalizations
   a. Through narration
   b. By critical and independent thinking
   c. By sharing observations
   d. By sharing experiences
   e. From movies and TV
   f. By debating
3. Oral communication
   a. Through narration
   b. By group discussions
   c. By debating
   d. Through oral reading
   e. By storytelling
   f. Through extemporaneous speaking
   g. Through drama
   h. By using the telephone
4. Grammar
   a. Knowledge of and ability to use the parts of speech
   b. Diagramming sentences—nouns, verbs, adjectives, adverbs, conjunctions, prepositions, objects
   c. Using correct capitalization and punctuation
   d. Recognizing and using antonyms, synonyms, homonyms, and homophones
   e. Recognizing and correctly using noun and verb plurals—regular and irregular
   f. Recognizing and using the correct verb tense
5. Study skills
   a. Mastering dictionary and reference material skills

b. Ability to use all areas of the library and learning the classification system used

c. Outlining material

d. Taking notes—from oral and written material

e. Ability to do a research paper

f. Skimming and scanning (See first grade, number 6c.)

6. Poetry—listening to, reading, memorizing

    a. Enjoying, appreciating, and understanding poetry

    b. Vocabulary development and enrichment

    c. Identifying and enjoying different forms of poetry

- limericks, sonnets, narrative, haiku, tanka and cinquain (See fourth grade, number 6b and fifth grade, number 6c.)
- psalm—a sacred song or poem used in worship
- triangular triplet—three lines that rhyme, written in the form of a triangle. The poem can start with any of the three lines.
- senryu—a Japanese poem of three lines that do not rhyme. It can be written on any subject. Lines 1 and 3 have five syllables and line 2 has seven.
- ballad—a narrative poem suitable for singing

    d. Memorize two poems per semester.

    e. Suggestions for memorizing (let the child choose):

"Adventures of Isabel"   Ogden Nash

"The Ant and the Cricket"   Aesop

"The Children's Hour"   Henry W. Longfellow

"Christ and the Little Ones"   Julia Gill

"If"   Rudyard Kipling

"The Nose and the Eyes"   William Cowper

"Our Two Opinions"   Eugene Field

"A Psalm of Life"   Henry W. Longfellow

"The Runaway"   Robert Frost

"The Sugar-Plum Tree"   Eugene Field

"Seein' Things"   Eugene Field

"The Village Blacksmith"   Henry W. Longfellow

"Wilbur Wright and Orville Wright"   Rosemary & Stephen Vincent Benét

"The Duel"   Eugene Field

"Your Flag and My Flag"   Wilbur D. Nesbit

"Youssouf"   James R. Lowell

"The Table and the Chair"   Edward Lear

   f. Suggested books to read aloud:

Famous British Poets   John Cournos & Sybil Norton

The Complete Works of Alfred Lord Tennyson

Tales and Poems of Edgar Allan Poe

The Complete Poetical Works of Whittier   Cambridge Edition

7. Literature—to be read aloud to the children and narrated
   a. Enjoying, understanding, appreciating, and learning from living books
   b. Understanding and appreciating the language forms of Scripture—psalms, proverbs, epistles, and histories
   c. Recognizing and enjoying different types of literature
   d. Vocabulary development and appreciating and understanding the use of language to convey ideas, information, feelings, emotions, reactions, and opinions
   e. Suggestions for listening, reading, and narrating:

Note: Before listing sixth grade books, an important factor in their choice should be mentioned. By the sixth grade some children have been reading well for what seems like a lifetime. Others see books as work. Obviously, there will be big differences here. A child who has been read to, and who has progressed to reading alone the sort of books listed for the previous grades, will be able to enjoy *Jane Eyre* or *David Copperfield* read aloud to them. For the pupil new to this experience of literature, remember that the goal is to choose books that can be enjoyed. You'll find plenty of appealing choices for this age group from the previous grades' reading lists, and from *Books Children Love*. Never choose a book because it will impress an adult as being "hard" or "advanced." On the other hand, avoid the easy books our generation is churning out. This is a guide to enjoying truly excellent books; these will lead the reader into high standards of language and cultural awareness.

Famous British Novelists   John Cournos & Sybil Norton

Famous American Authors   Sarah K. Bolton

A Christmas Carol   Charles Dickens

Tale of Two Cities   Charles Dickens

The Pilgrim's Progress   John Bunyan

Don Quijote de la Mancha   Miguel de Cervantes Saavedra, retold by Judge Parry

Odyssey of Homer   retold by Alfred J. Church

Tales from Shakespeare   Charles and Mary Lamb

Shakespeare's Theater   Walter C. Hodges

Twelfth Night   William Shakespeare

Taming of the Shrew   William Shakespeare

Romeo and Juliet   William Shakespeare

Julius Caesar   William Shakespeare

Note: Please refer to Appendix V for notes on reading Shakespeare with children.

$\boxed{8}$ Mathematics Overview

T he overview which follows is not intended to outline the specific scope and sequence of mathematical skills objectives for the curriculum. It is, rather, a brief comment on our approach to the teaching of elementary mathematics. We believe it is in harmony both with the Child Light philosophy of education, and with attitudes and methods already being practiced by many dedicated teachers.

The Child Light mathematics program recommends texts that offer a clear, comprehensive program in a format designed to motivate students, to encourage them to apply the concepts they learn and to recognize the value and usefulness of mathematics.

It is of crucial importance that students thoroughly grasp the concepts on which each new mathematics skill is based. Simply because mathematics is one of a number of academic areas in which a certain amount of memorization and drill is essential, there is a very real danger that the students' whole approach to the subject will become unthinking and that they will lose sight of the meaning, the conceptual reality, of what they are doing.

On the one hand, nothing takes the place of the repeated practice in addition or subtraction (both written and oral) which results in the instant and automatic recognition that, for example, $3+2=5$, and later, that $9+8=17$; that $8-5=3$, and again later, that $16-7=9$, and so forth. As the student progresses, nothing takes the place of the kind of brisk, consistent drill that not only enables a student to quickly and accurately recite the "times tables," but that also ensures that the skill will be quite naturally applied in any practical situation that arises.

On the other hand, memorization and drill must never be perceived as ends in themselves. Children, like most of us, tend to slide into "easy way" patterns of behavior. It is not unusual, therefore, for a young mathematics student to learn only a mechanical, surface skill, to run smoothly through drills, fill in blanks, go through motions, appear to have learned a particular concept, whereas <u>in reality he or she has not yet thoroughly grasped and internalized the necessary concept.</u>

Constant efforts need to be made to relate a specific mathematical concept to practical reality. Even beginning students should be encouraged to make up their own problems relating to the concept being studied. Practicing problems given in the text or workbook is necessary, but assignments should never be confined to filling in blanks and putting numbers at the ends of columns of figures. Students should routinely be able to take down problems that are dictated to them, writing them on their papers in correct form; mental arithmetic should be practiced and encouraged; students should be able to write problems out in sentence form, and they should be asked routinely to apply the mathematics concepts they have learned, to the practical aspects of daily life.

How *do* we make sure the child relates the shorthand of the math book to real life? Daily life constantly includes applying number concepts. Many chores a child does include a need for accuracy in mathematical terms: setting the table for the family (*six* forks, *six* plates); setting for the family plus two visitors coming; how many will that make?; setting the table, but Dad is away—one less; counting steps up to the bridge; shopping, checking the change; measuring the table to plan how much material to buy for a new tablecloth; weighing out objects in real life (a pound of potatoes, a letter of 3 ounces).

As to sequencing and the presentation of material, the notes provided in the teacher's edition of each textbook offer detailed guidance for day-to-day instruction. The notes are very helpful in following the lesson plans, helping the student reach the desired objectives, and making whatever adjustments and changes of approach seem advisable for a specific child.

No one needs to feel enslaved by day-to-day instructional plans. On the other hand, there is great value in having an organized plan, in being provided with guidance as to the full scope of what skills a child should master and in what sequence it may be most helpful to present them. Teacher's notes, also, will often give a wealth of ideas as to how to most effectively teach the materials.

It is most important, however, to recognize that the point at which children are ready to be introduced to a new concept varies considerably from child to child. The amount of time it may take for them to thoroughly master a skill and the different approaches that may be needed for them to achieve this mastery can vary as well. A teacher should never hesitate to linger as long as necessary with a specific child on a particular concept, providing extended reinforcement, repetition, a fresh approach; on the other hand, the highly proficient student should be helped to proceed more rapidly. Once a student has truly mastered a concept, he should never simply be given *more* of the same sort of problems to do in order to keep him busy. In a classroom situation, therefore, it is vitally important to make fully adequate provision for the needs of children at both ends of the skills spectrum.

In some cases, adult aides (often parents or grandparents in the school community) can be recruited to come in and work in a one-to-one situation with a child. There are other possibilities; creative solutions which meet the need of each person should always be sought.

Finally, the use of supplementary materials should not be overlooked. These may range from remedial materials on specific problems, to enrichment/special interest books. Some of the latter are listed in *Books Children Love* under Mathematics. In addition, a good public library will have further titles on interesting aspects of mathematics, the sort of thing not usually found in a routine textbook. There are surprising, fascinating things to be learned in every area of study, and mathematics is no exception.

Most teachers who teach mathematics to children are not usually professional mathematicians. In fact, math may be the thing they least enjoy teaching. The subject, however, does not have to be treated as a dreary chore, and the adults responsible for conveying its truths to children should open up to its positive aspects. Students might be asked, for example, to imagine what even one day would be like if all mathematical guidelines were removed (no timepieces, no ability to buy or sell measured quantities, no ability to calculate prices or give change, no way to convey information about distance, number of people in a group)—the possibilities are endless.

Students should also be able to enjoy the fact that unlike other questions with which they must grapple, mathematics (at least at the elementary level) offers tidy, readily learnable, exactly right answers to each problem—something that cannot (or certainly *should* not) be said about many other areas of study, many aspects of life.

Also in this connection, it might be possible for a teacher to share from time to time, some illustration of the fact that only through an advanced application of mathematical principles (principles that are integral to our ordered universe) have all the discoveries in physics, astronomy, broad areas of technology, etc., been made possible.

Note: The subject of pocket calculators and their use by children is a controversial one in many schools. Obviously, they should not be allowed to substitute for the child's own ability to *know*, to *think*, and to *do* in the area of arithmetic problems. Calculators are, however, a fact of contemporary life. A number of schools and parents feel that at some point the skill of operating such calculators in a maximally efficient manner should be a part of the mathematics program. A number of books have been written on the use of pocket calculators, both for practical purposes and for enjoyment. A small representation of such books is included in *Books Children Love*.

9 Mathematics

An understanding of mathematics is vital in the modern world since it includes computer science and operational research. Math should not be viewed as a separate entity but should be integrated into the daily experiences of the students. Children should understand what causes the processes used to work, the meaning of the facts learned, and discover when and how to apply them to problem solving. Conceptual understanding is as important as the basic skills and the rote memory of addition and subtraction facts and the multiplication tables. Each child should feel confident that math basics can be learned and that a special "mathematical mind" is not necessary in order to learn them.

There is a logical progression to the presentation of the skills and concepts. The ability to understand and apply advanced concepts is dependent on the mastery of those learned at a lower level. The development of a mathematical vocabulary should take place within a meaningful context. A balance between basic facts, processes, and application to real situations should be maintained. All experiences need to relate to the emotional, developmental, and academic readiness of the student. Manipulatives (concrete objects used to aid in the learning process) should be used extensively at all levels.

There is often more than one way to solve a problem, and children should be taught alternate methods and allowed to use them. A problem should be counted correct if the answer is right, no matter how it was solved. (Mary had 6 bowls of apples. Each bowl contained 11 apples. How many apples did she have in all? Jack solves the problem by adding $11+11+11+11+11+11=66$. The answer is correct. If multiplication was the intent, Jack could be asked if it would be possible to multiply and get the answer. This would cause Jack to think and discover principles and ideas for himself. He would be more likely to remember them and relate them to other situations. It also makes learning more exciting.)

Narration should be used in teaching mathematics. If a child is not able to verbalize the process, then he or she will not be able to apply the process to problem solving.

A horizontal approach (expanding and enriching the material covered on the grade level) rather than a vertical approach (moving to the next grade level) is advocated. Children need a strong foundation in the skills, concepts, principles, and strategies being presented. Expanding these horizontally allows for practical applications, and math is seen to be relevant to daily living and not simply as information.

Note: These math skills are not necessarily listed in the sequence in which they should be taught, but there should be progression from the easier skills to the more complicated ones. Many of them will be taught simultaneously. The teacher's edition of the math series will suggest a sequence, give suggestions on how to approach teaching the skills, and present ideas for reinforcement and enrichment. Teacher's editions should be viewed as guides. The teacher will need to choose what to use and what to delete and how to adapt the material for the individual needs of the children being taught. Always keep in mind that it is not a textbook which is being taught, but children.

First Grade Math

The first grade math program provides a beginning background in mathematical skills, concepts, and strategies. Students are encouraged to apply what is being learned to classroom experiences as well as to other areas of their daily experience. Math should be correlated with other subject areas as an aid in making skills and concepts relevant. A foundation is begun for the development of independent learning.

Curriculum

1. First grade math vocabulary should be developed in context and not as isolated words.
2. Recognize, read, and write Arabic numerals from 1-100 and understand that each represents a certain number property.
3. Recognize, read, and write number words from zero to twenty.
4. Counting—Develop an understanding of the number property of each numeral before reciting and writing them in sequence.
   a. Count by 1s (1–100).
   b. Count by 10s (10–100).
   c. Count by 5s (5–100).

d. Count by 2s even (2,4,6, etc., to 100).

e. Count by 2s odd (0,1,3, etc., to 99).

5. Sets
   a. Recognize sets.
   b. Group objects into sets.
   c. Recognize how many objects a set contains.
   d. Group objects into like sets—objects that are the same color, same size, same shape, etc.

6. Place value—develop an understanding of ones and tens.
   a. Use concrete objects.
   b. Write ones—1,2,3, etc., to 9.
   c. Write tens—10, 20, 30, etc., to 90.
   d. Write the numeral that stands for the number of objects shown and discuss how many ones and how many tens.
   e. Regroup sets by joining two sets. (Start with a set of 2 bundles of 10 straws and a set of one bundle of 10 straws and 5 single straws. Join sets. Write the numeral that represents the two sets when joined—35.)

7. Ordinals to the tenth
   a. Learn in context of daily activities

      • First row or group of desks

      • Third girl in line

      • Sixth boy to paint at the easel

   b. Learn in other contexts

      • Second week of the month

      • Fifth tree from the corner

      • Third day of rain

8. Geometry
   a. Recognize plane figures (circles, rectangles, squares) and space figures (cylinder, cube, cone, sphere).
   b. Classify by shape or size.
   c. Begin developing an understanding of area and perimeter. (See measurement, number 14.)
   d. Spatial relations—inside, outside, on, beside, above, below

9. Money
   a. Recognize pennies, nickels, dimes, quarters.
   b. Form sets of different coins with the same value—5 pennies are the same as 1 nickel, 5 pennies and 1 nickel are the same as 1 dime, etc.
   c. Use money in addition and subtraction problems.

d. Select which coins would be needed to buy an item by reading its priced value.

e. Begin developing the ability to make change.

10. Addition
    a. Use concrete objects, place them in sets, join the sets.
    b. Recognize the mathematical symbol for addition.
    c. Read, write, and solve addition sentences.

    $1+\square=3, \quad \square+2=3, \quad 1+2=\square$

    d. Read, write, and solve vertical addition problems.
    • one-digit

$$\begin{array}{r} 4 \\ +1 \\ \hline \end{array} \qquad \begin{array}{r} 5 \\ +2 \\ \hline \end{array} \qquad \begin{array}{r} 3 \\ 1 \\ +2 \\ \hline \end{array}$$

    • two-digit

without regrouping			with regrouping	

$$\begin{array}{r} 42 \\ +\ 3 \\ \hline \end{array} \quad \begin{array}{r} 21 \\ +12 \\ \hline \end{array} \quad \begin{array}{r} 5 \\ +\ 2 \\ +21 \\ \hline \end{array} \qquad \begin{array}{r} 56 \\ +\ 5 \\ \hline \end{array} \quad \begin{array}{r} 72 \\ +18 \\ \hline \end{array}$$

    e. Use zero in addition.
    f. Use a number line in addition.
    g. Understand the inverse relationship of addition.

$$\begin{array}{r} 2 \\ +3 \\ \hline \end{array} \qquad \begin{array}{r} 3 \\ +2 \\ \hline \end{array}$$

    h. Speed tests of basic facts through sums of 18 (doubles through 20). The competition should focus on bettering one's own score and not on individuals competing against one another. (A bar graph can be kept.)

11. Subtraction
    a. Using concrete objects, form one set by using 2 different sets of objects (6 pencils and 3 erasers), remove the pencils, and observe how many are left in the set. Use the same procedure with a set of like objects.
    b. Recognize the mathematical symbol for subtraction.
    c. Read, write, and solve subtraction sentences.

    $4-2=2, \quad 4-\square=2, \quad \square-2=2, \quad 4-2=\square$

    d. Read, write, and solve vertical subtraction problems.
    • one-digit

$$\begin{array}{r} 5 \\ -1 \\ \hline \end{array} \qquad \begin{array}{r} 8 \\ -3 \\ \hline \end{array}$$

- two-digit

without regrouping	with regrouping
26 44	51 62
− 2 −11	−24 −38

e. Use zero in subtraction.
f. Use a number line in subtraction.
g. Speed tests of basic facts through minuends of 18 (20 when subtracting 10). The competition should focus on bettering one's own score and not on individuals competing against one another. (Use a bar graph to record results.)
h. Introduce the four addition/subtraction facts or fact "families."

$$
\begin{array}{cccc}
2 & 6 & 8 & 8 \\
+6 & +2 & -2 & -6
\end{array}
$$

$2+6=8$ $6+2=8$ $8-2=6$ $8-6=2$

12. Time
    a. Calendar—divide into a year, a year into months, a month into weeks, a week into days.
    b. Divide a day into hours.
    c. Divide hours into half hours, half hours into quarter hours, and for any indicating readiness, quarter hours into minutes (5 minute intervals, 10 minute intervals, 15 minute intervals, etc., to 60 minutes).
    d. Learn to read time on both a standard and digital clock.
13. Fractions
    a. Recognize equal sized parts of a whole—1/4 through 1/10.
    b. Recognize and write the numeral for the fractional units—1/4 through 1/10.
    c. Understand that the top number (numerator) always stands for how many parts in the whole are being talked about and that the bottom number (denominator) always stands for how many equal parts there are in the whole.
14. Measurement—linear and liquid
    a. Compare things that are the same length and different lengths.
    b. Compare length and height.
    c. Compare things that are long and short.
    d. Classify things by longest and shortest.
    e. Measure classroom items using both inches and centimeters.

f. Measure liquids and solids using both metric and customary standard units.

g. Begin developing an understanding of distance measurement.

h. Introduction to area (inches, square inches, centimeters, square centimeters)

i. Introduction to perimeter (counting inches to find distance)

15. Problem solving
    a. Complete addition and subtraction sentences.
    b. Select the correct method for measuring—ruler, cup, etc.
    c. Word problems—select the correct procedure (addition or subtraction).
    d. Word problems—select the information needed to solve the problem.
    e. Have students write their own problems and solve them.

16. Graphs
    a. Introduction to bar graphs
    b. Introduction to pictographs
    c. Simple outcome graph—such as a science experiment on plant growth
    d. Simple statistical graphs—such as how many plants grew from the seeds planted

17. Greater than (>) and less than (<)
    a. Recognize if a number from 1–100 is greater than another number.
    b. Recognize if a number from 1–100 is less than another number.

Second Grade Math

Beginning skills, concepts, and strategies are continued and expanded in second grade. As new areas are introduced, the students are encouraged to apply the math knowledge to situations they encounter daily. Children are encouraged to become independent learners and are guided to think through processes and draw their own conclusions. Provision is made for the correlation of mathematics with other subject areas.

1. The mathematics vocabulary for second grade should be developed in context and not as isolated words.

2. Recognize, read, and write Arabic numerals from 101 through 999 and understand that each numeral represents a certain number property.

3. Counting
   a. Review the skills studied in first grade.

- Counting by 1s (1–100)

- Counting by 10s (10–100)

- Counting by 5s (5–100)

- Counting by 2s even (2,4,6, etc., to 100)

- Counting by 2s odd (0,1,3, etc., to 99)

b. Count by 1s (101–999).
c. Count by 10s (100–990).
d. Count by 5s (100–995).

1. Develop the ability to write a standard form number from an expanded form (60 + 4 expanded form, 64 standard form). Guide the students in discovering that the tens digit and the ones digit in the expanded form are used to make the standard form (6 tens, 4 ones=64).

5. Sets
   a. Develop an understanding of even numbers by making sets with the same number of objects in each set.
   b. Develop an understanding of odd numbers by making sets with an odd number of items and discovering that one or more will be left over when forming equal sets. (15 balloons=3 sets of 4 with 3 left over.)

6. Place value
   a. Review ones and tens and introduce hundreds.
   b. Add and subtract pennies and dimes to expand understanding of ones and tens.
   c. Add and subtract dollars, dimes, and pennies to expand understanding of hundreds, tens, and ones.

7. Ordinal numbers
   a. Review and expand previous knowledge.

      - Identify 1st–10th in the context of daily activities.

      - Identify 1st–10th in other contexts.

   b. Recognize, read, and write ordinal words (first-tenth).

8. Geometry
   a. Continue developing an understanding of area and perimeter and introduce volume.
   b. Expand the understanding of three-dimensional shapes.
   c. Develop the ability to identify sides, corners, and square corners.
   d. Introduce the concept of a line of symmetry.

9. Money
   a. Review pennies, nickels, dimes, and quarters.

    b. Recognize the half dollar and dollar.

    c. Form sets of different coins with the same value—2 quarters are the same as 1 half dollar, 2 dimes and 1 nickel are the same as 1 quarter.

    d. Add and subtract money.

10. Addition

    a. Review and expand previously learned skills.

- Mathematical symbols

- Reading, writing, and solving number sentences

- Reading, writing, and solving vertical problems—one-digit and two-digit problems with and without regrouping

- Using zero in problems

- Inverse relationships

    b. Expand vertical (column) addition to include 3-digit numbers.

- Without regrouping

$$\begin{array}{r} 214 \\ +142 \\ \hline \end{array}$$

- With regrouping 1s

$$\begin{array}{r} 628 \\ +105 \\ \hline \end{array}$$

- With regrouping 10s

$$\begin{array}{r} 721 \\ +293 \\ \hline \end{array}$$

- With regrouping 1s and 10s

$$\begin{array}{r} 267 \\ +154 \\ \hline \end{array}$$

    c. Addition with three addends

- Without regrouping

$$\begin{array}{r} 21 \\ 6 \\ +\ 2 \\ \hline \end{array} \qquad \begin{array}{r} 32 \\ 5 \\ +21 \\ \hline \end{array} \qquad \begin{array}{r} 10 \\ 35 \\ +44 \\ \hline \end{array}$$

- With one regrouping

$$\begin{array}{r} 4 \\ 5 \\ +\ 7 \\ \hline \end{array} \qquad \begin{array}{r} 8 \\ 21 \\ +36 \\ \hline \end{array} \qquad \begin{array}{r} 22 \\ 15 \\ +33 \\ \hline \end{array}$$

  ↲ With two regroupings

$$234 \qquad 148$$
$$+176 \quad +362$$

  d. Use the number line for adding.
  e. Develop speed and accuracy by using speed tests of the basic addition facts. The competition should focus on bettering one's own score and not on individuals competing against one another. A graph should be used to record the results.

11. Subtraction
  a. Review and expand previously learned skills

  • Mathematical symbols

  • Reading, writing, and solving subtraction sentences

  • Reading, writing, and solving vertical problems—one-digit and two-digit problems with and without regrouping

  • Using zero in problems

  • Addition and subtraction fact families

  b. Subtract three-digit numbers

  • Without regrouping

$$542$$
$$-121$$

  • With regrouping 1s

$$624$$
$$-205$$

  • With regrouping 10s

$$834$$
$$-453$$

  • With regrouping 1s and 10s

$$922$$
$$-546$$

  c. Use the number line for subtracting.
  d. Develop speed and accuracy by using speed tests of the basic subtraction facts. The competition should focus on bettering one's own score and not on individuals competing against one another. A graph should be used to record the results.

12. Time
  a. Review and expand the previously learned skills and concepts.

- Calendar—year, months, week, day.

- Hour, half hour, quarter hour.

b. Read time at 10-minute and 5-minute intervals on both a standard clock and a digital clock. (Introduce 1-minute intervals to students indicating readiness for this concept.)
13. Fractions
   a. Review previously learned skills and concepts.

   - Recognize equal size parts of whole (1/4 -1/10).

   - Recognize and write a numeral for the fractional part of a whole (1/4 -1/10).

   - Understand the meaning of *numerator* and *denominator.*

   b. Identify fractional parts of a whole or of a set (1/4 -9/10).
   c. Identify 1/4 inch and 1/2 inch.
   d. Recognize, read, and write the numeral for fractional units (1/4 - 9/10).
14. Measurement
   a. Review previously learned skills and concepts—linear and liquid.

   - Same and different lengths

   - Length and height

   - Long and short

   - Measuring by inches and centimeters

   - Liquids and solids—metric and customary

   - Inches, square inches, centimeters, and square centimeters

   - Perimeter—counting inches to find distance

   b. Use additional means to measure—metric, customary, standard, and nonstandard.
   c. Measure height, width, and length as an introduction to volume.
15. Problem solving
   a. Continue expanding previously studied skills, concepts, and strategies.

   - Complete addition and subtraction sentences.

   - Select the correct method for measuring—ruler, cup, spoon, etc.

   b. Use graphs and tables to solve problems.

c. Choose the correct procedure (addition, subtraction, or multiplication) and information to use in solving a problem.

d. Write original problems and solve them.

16. Graphs

a. Continue using and developing previously studied skills and concepts.

- Bar graphs

- Simple outcome graphs

- Simple statistical graphs

b. Develop the ability to make, use, and read pictographs.

c. Develop the ability to make, use, and read grids.

17. Greater than (>) and less than (<)

a. Review the concepts studied previously

- Recognizing if a number from 0–100 is greater than another number

- Recognizing if a number from 0–100 is less than another number

b. Develop the ability to distinguish if a number from 1–999 is greater than or less than another number.

c. Discern if an amount of money is greater than or less than another amount.

18. Multiplication

a. Introduce multiplication as a short way to add. (4 sets of 2 buttons—add $2+2+2+2=8$ or $2\times4=8$)

b. Recognize and write the mathematical symbol for multiplication.

c. Learn the basic multiplication facts using 0–5 as factors.

d. Read, write, and solve multiplication sentences involving products through 25 ($5\times5=25$ $5\times\square=25$ $\square\times5=25$ $5\times5=\square$).

e. Develop a beginning understanding of the inverse function ($2\times3=6$ $3\times2=6$).

Third Grade Math

The third grade math program systematically builds upon and reinforces skills, concepts, and strategies begun in the previous grades. An emphasis is placed on multiplication and division skills. The correlation of math with other subject areas is continued, as is the practical application of what is being learned and the development of independent learning skills.

Curriculum

1. The mathematics vocabulary for third grade is developed in context and not as isolated words.
2. Recognize, read, and write numerals from 1000–9999 and understand that each represents a certain number property.
3. Recognize, read, and write number words from one thousand through nine thousand nine hundred ninety-nine.
4. Learn to round numbers to the nearest ten and understand when rounded numbers should be used.
5. Ordinals
   a. Review previously studied skills.

   - Identify 1st through 10th in the context of daily activities and other contexts.

   - Recognize, read, and write ordinal numbers—first through tenth.

   b. Recognize, read, and write ordinal numbers from 1 through 100 (first, second, third, etc., and 1st, 2nd, 3rd, etc.).
   c. Apply ordinal numbers to everyday situations.
6. Place value
   a. Review previously studied skills.

   - Ones, tens, hundreds

   - Add and subtract pennies, nickels, dimes, and dollars.

   b. Develop an understanding of the place value of thousands, ten thousands, hundred thousands, and millions and apply the knowledge in problem solving.
7. Geometry
   a. Review previously studied concepts and skills.

   - Area, perimeter, volume

   - Three-dimensional shapes

   - Sides, corners, square corners

   - Line of symmetry

   b. Recognize additional plane shapes (pentagon, hexagon, octagon) and space shapes (pyramid, prism).
   c. Develop an ability to identify lines, line segments, and rays.
   d. Recognize right angles.
8. Money
   a. Review previously studied skills.

- Pennies, nickels, dimes, quarters, half dollars, dollars

- Form sets of different coins with the same value.

b. Expand the ability to identify coins, make change, and add and subtract money.

c. Develop the ability to multiply money.

9. Addition

a. Review previously studied skills.

- Addition of 1-, 2-, and 3-digit numbers with and without regrouping.

- Addition of three addends without regrouping and with one or two regroupings.

- Speed tests for accuracy and speed.

b. Introduce adding more than three addends.

c. Add four digits with more than one regrouping.

$$\begin{array}{r} 6268 \\ +2454 \end{array} \qquad \begin{array}{r} 7282 \\ +1859 \end{array} \qquad \begin{array}{r} 6456 \\ +1746 \end{array}$$

d. Expand the ability to add money.

e. Begin developing the ability to estimate sums.

f. Use a number line to solve problems.

10. Subtraction

a. Review previously studied skills.
1) Subtracting 1-, 2-, and 3-digit numbers with and without regrouping
2) Addition and subtraction of fact families

b. Subtract 4-digit numbers.

c. Check subtraction answers.

d. Subtract 4-digit numbers with more than one regrouping.

e. Begin developing the ability to estimate the difference.

f. Expand the ability to subtract money.

g. Use a number line in solving problems.

11. Time

a. Continue developing the ability to tell time—stressing to the quarter hour and minute.

b. Develop an understanding of A.M. and P.M.

c. Compare and estimate time.

d. Develop an understanding of elapsed time.

12. Fractions

a. Review previously studied skills, concepts, and strategies.

- Identify fractional parts of a whole (1/4–9/10).

- Identify 1/4 inch and 1/2 inch.

- Recognize, read, and write numerals for fractional units (1/4–9/10).

b. Compare fractions that have the same denominator.
c. Develop an understanding of the relationship of fractions and mixed numbers to decimals.
d. Use a number line to find fractional parts.

13. Measurement
    a. Continue to build on previous skills—liquid and linear.
    b. Develop the ability to measure using the meter, kilometer, liter and milliliter.
    c. Measure temperature using both Fahrenheit and Celsius.
    d. Develop an understanding of the square centimeter.

14. Problem solving
    a. Continue to develop the ability to use graphs, charts, tables, and maps to solve problems.
    b. Use alternate means to solve a problem.
    c. Apply logic to problem solving.
    d. Increase the ability to solve problems by choosing and using only pertinent information.
    e. Develop the ability to discern what missing information is needed in order to be able to solve a problem.
    f. Write and solve original problems.

15. Graphs
    a. Record data on graphs, charts, and tables.
    b. Expand the ability to use graphs, charts and tables.
    c. Collect the necessary data to be recorded on graphs, charts, or tables.

16. Greater than (>) and less than (<)
    a. Review previously studied concepts.

    - Distinguish if a number from 1–999 is greater or less than another number.

    - Discern if an amount of money is greater or less than another amount.

    b. Order numbers from the greatest to the least and from the least to the greatest (one- to three-digit numbers).

17. Multiplication
    a. Learn the basic multiplication facts using 0 through 9 as factors.
    b. Multiply two factors to get the product.
    c. Multiply by 10 and by 100.

d. Multiply two- and three-digit numbers by one digit without regrouping and with regrouping.

Without regrouping		With regrouping	
24	132	54	453
× 2	× 3	× 6	× 6

e. Develop speed and accuracy in the basic multiplication facts through speed tests. The competition should focus on bettering one's own score and not on individuals competing against one another. The results should be recorded on a graph.

18. Roman numerals
   a. Develop the understanding that when writing Roman numerals symbols are used to represent numbers.
   b. Discover that numbers are shown by adding or subtracting the symbols (1=I and 2=II, 5=V and 6=VI, 10=X and 9=IX).
   c. Recognize, read, and write the Roman numerals I through X.

19. Division
   a. Develop an understanding of the division process, why it is used, and when to use it.
   b. Recognize the mathematical symbols for division.
   c. Read, write, and solve division sentences.

$$40 \div 5 = 8 \qquad\qquad 27 \div 3 = 9$$

d. Learn the alternate way to write a division sentence.

$$4 \overline{\smash{)}32} = 8 \qquad\qquad 6 \overline{\smash{)}36} = 6$$

e. Learn the basic facts with a divisor or quotient of 0-9.
   f. Introduce the four multiplication/division facts or fact "families."

$$4 \times 8 = 32 \qquad\qquad 32 \div 4 = 8$$
$$8 \times 4 = 32 \qquad\qquad 32 \div 8 = 4$$

g. Divide with a one- or two-digit quotient without regrouping and with regrouping.

Without regrouping		With regrouping	
$1 \overline{\smash{)}3}$	$25 \div 5 =$	$4 \overline{\smash{)}52}$	$43 \div 7 =$
$6 \overline{\smash{)}66}$	$4 \overline{\smash{)}48}$	$6 \overline{\smash{)}456}$	$4 \overline{\smash{)}352}$

h. Divide with one- and two-digit quotients with and without a remainder.

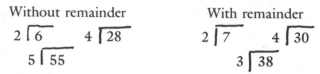

Without remainder

$2 \overline{)6}$ $4 \overline{)28}$

$5 \overline{)55}$

With remainder

$2 \overline{)7}$ $4 \overline{)30}$

$3 \overline{)38}$

i. Develop speed and accuracy in the basic division facts through speed tests. The competition should focus on bettering one's own score and not on individuals competing against one another. The results should be recorded on a graph.

20. Decimals
   a. Develop an understanding of decimals, what they are and how they are used.
   b. Recognize, read, and write decimals that express tenths.
   c. Relate decimals to fractions and mixed numbers.
   d. Add and subtract decimals (tenths).
   e. Write a decimal when measuring by centimeters.
   f. Use a number line to find tenths.
21. Estimating
   a. Understand the difference between estimating and a wild guess.
   b. Use estimating in measuring.
   c. Estimate addition and subtraction answers.
   d. Use estimation in solving problems.
   e. Round to the nearest tenth or hundredth when estimating.
22. Calculators and computers
   Calculators and computer skills and concepts can be introduced if the students have an interest and indicate readiness to comprehend and apply the skills.

Fourth Grade Math

A thorough understanding and mastery of the four basic mathematic operations and the ability to apply them in real-life situations is stressed in the fourth grade mathematics program. New skills, concepts, and strategy areas are introduced. The application of critical thinking skills, including a logical and analytical approach to problem solving, is an integral part of the curriculum. There is an emphasis placed on the correlation of math with other subject areas.

Curriculum

1. The mathematics vocabulary for fourth grade is developed in context and not as isolated words.

2. Recognize, read, and write numerals to 999,999.
3. Recognize, read, and write number words to nine hundred ninety-nine thousand, nine hundred ninety-nine.
4. Round numbers to the nearest 100th or 1000th and increase the understanding of when to round numbers.
5. Greater than (>), less than (<), or equal (=)—expand the ability to distinguish if a number is greater than, less than, or equal to another number.
6. Place value
   a. Review previously studied concepts.

      • Ones, tens, hundreds, thousands, ten thousands, hundred thousands, millions

      • Add and subtract money problems.

   b. Increase the understanding of the place value of a number to billions.
7. Geometry
   a. Review previously studied skills and concepts.

      • Area, perimeter, volume

      • Pentagon, hexagon, octagon, pyramid, prism

      • Line segments, lines, rays

      • Line of symmetry

      • Right angle

   b. Find the area of a triangle.
   c. Introduce the meaning of and be able to identify points, lines, segments, parallel lines, and intersecting lines by using classroom and other familiar items.
   d. Identify right angles in the classroom and on the playground.
   e. Introduce the concept of radius, diameter, and center of a circle.
   f. Review polygons and introduce quadrilaterals, and parallelograms.
   g. Introduce the concept of edge, face, and vertex of space figures.
8. Money
   a. Review previously studied skills and concepts and expand the ability to apply them to daily situations.

      • Coins and paper money

      • Sets of coins with same value

- Making change

- Adding and subtracting money

b. Use multiplication and division to solve problems involving money.

c. Choose the least number of coins or coins and bills that will equal a given amount.

9. Addition

a. Expand previously studied skills and concepts.

- Addition of one-, two-, three-, and four-digit numbers with and without regrouping

- Estimating sums

- Using a number line to solve problems

b. Develop the ability to add five-digit numbers.

10. Subtraction

a. Expand previously studied skills and concepts.

- Subtracting one-, two-, three-, and four-digit numbers with and without regrouping

- Checking answers

- Estimating differences

- Using a number line in solving problems

b. Develop the ability to subtract five-digit numbers.

11. Time

a. Continue developing previously studied skills and concepts.

- Telling time to the minute

- A.M. and P.M.

- Elapsed time

b. Develop an understanding of time zones.

12. Fractions

a. Review and expand previously studied skills and concepts.

- Fractional parts of a whole

- Numeral representing fractional unit—recognize, read, and write

b. Develop an understanding of equal fractions (1/4 and 2/8, 5/10 and 1/2).

c. Use the number line as an aid in finding equal fractions.

    d. Introduce fractions with different denominators and mixed numbers.

    e. Add fractions with common denominators, with different denominators, and mixed numbers.

    f. Subtract fractions with common denominators, with different denominators, and mixed numbers.

    g. Use the number line when adding and subtracting fractions.

    h. Change improper fractions to mixed numbers.

    i. Reduce fractions to the lowest terms.

    j. Develop the ability to distinguish if a fraction is greater than ($>$) or less than ($<$) another fraction.

13. Measurement

    a. Review previously studied skills and concepts—liquid and linear.

    b. Introduce the decimeter.

    c. Develop an understanding of cubic centimeters.

    d. Develop an understanding of the ton as a unit of measure.

    e. Develop the ability to estimate weight and capacity.

14. Problem solving

    a. Review previously studied skills, concepts, and strategies.

      • Choose the correct procedure—add, subtract, multiply, divide.

      • Use graphs, charts, tables, and maps to solve problems.

      • Apply logic to problem solving.

      • Discern what information is missing.

      • Write and solve original problems.

    b. Recognize that the solution to a problem may involve more than just correct computation.

    c. Increase the ability to solve multiple step problems.

    d. Recognize when not enough information is given to be able to solve a problem.

    e. Recognize when too much information is given and select only what is pertinent to solving the problem.

    f. Develop the ability to apply logic to problem solving.

15. Graphs, charts, tables

    a. Review previously studied skills and expand the ability to apply them and to use graphs, charts, and tables.

      • Collect data.

      • Record data.

b. Develop the ability to read, make, and use line, broken-line, and circle graphs.

c. Learn to read, write, and use a tally sheet.

16. Place one- to four-digit numbers in order from the greatest to the least and from the least to the greatest.

17. Multiplication
    a. Review previous skills.

    - Use basic facts 0 through 9 as factors.

    - Multiply two factors to get the product.

    - Multiply by 10 and 100.

    - Multiply two- and three-digit numbers by one digit with and without regrouping.

    - Speed tests—the competition should focus on bettering one's own score and not on individuals competing against one another.

    b. Discover the pattern when multiplying by 10, 100, and 1000.
    c. Develop the ability to estimate products.
    d. Continue to develop the ability to multiply money and to use the skill in daily experiences.
    e. Multiply three- and four-digit numbers by a one- or two-digit factor without regrouping and with regrouping.

Without regrouping			With regrouping		
123	2213	1234	324	1215	2163
× 3	× 2	× 21	× 3	× 4	× 23

18. Roman numerals—expand the understanding of and ability to use Roman numerals.

19. Division
    a. Review previously studied skills.

    - Discern when to use division.

    - Read, write, and solve division sentences.

    - Multiplication/division fact families.

    - Divide with a one- or two-digit number with and without regrouping.

    - Divide with one- and two-digit quotients with and without remainders.

- Speed tests—the competition should focus on bettering one's own score and not on individuals competing against one another.

    b. Develop the ability to divide where the quotient is two or three digits and contains a 0.

    c. Learn to check the quotient—multiply the quotient by the divisor, add the remainder if there is one, and the answer should be the same as the dividend.

    d. Learn to estimate the quotient and to change an overestimate or an underestimate.

    e. Develop the ability to divide money and to apply the skill to daily experiences.

    f. Use division as one process in a two-process problem.

    g. Divide using a two-digit number as the divisor.

20. Decimals

    a. Expand the use of the previously studied skills and concepts.

- Read and write decimals that express tenths.

- Relate decimals to fractions and mixed numbers.

- Add and subtract decimals.

- Write decimals when measuring by centimeters.

- Use a number line to find tenths.

    b. Use decimal values to distinguish if one number is greater or less than another number (234.024 or 234.052).

    c. Learn to round decimals to the nearest whole number.

    d. Add decimals—tenths and hundredths.

    e. Subtract decimals—tenths and hundredths.

    f. Relate decimals to fractions and mixed numbers.

21. Estimation

    a. Continue developing previously studied skills and concepts.

- Difference between estimating and wild guess

- Estimation in measuring

- Estimating addition and subtraction answers

- Estimation in problem solving

- Rounding to nearest tenth or hundredth

    b. Acquire the ability to estimate products and quotients.

22. Calculators and computers

a. Continue developing the ability to use calculators as a tool in solving math problems.
b. Expand the knowledge of computers and use software to reinforce and enrich math skills, concepts, and strategies.

Fifth Grade Math

The fifth grade math program presents new areas and offers a thorough review and expansion of previously studied skills, concepts, and strategies. Proficiency, accuracy, and the practical application of all math areas are increased through practice. Critical thinking skills are stressed as a necessary technique for solving problems. As in other grade levels, math is correlated with other subject areas.

Curriculum

1. The mathematics vocabulary for fifth grade math is developed in context and not as isolated words.
2. Recognize, read, and write numerals through hundred billions.
3. Recognize, read, and write number words through hundred billions.
4. Continue developing the ability to round off numbers.
5. Percent
    a. Develop an understanding of what percent is and how to use it.
    b. Write percent as a decimal and a decimal as percent.
    c. Write percent as ratio and ratio as percent.
    d. Find the percent of a given number.
    e. Use percent in problem solving.
    f. Apply percent to daily experiences.
6. Ratio and proportion
    a. Develop an understanding of the use and function of ratio and proportion.
    b. Read and write ratios—2-30 or 2:30 or $\frac{2}{30}$
    c. Compare two items and write the numeral that represents the ratio of one item to the other. (Given ten boys and eighteen girls, the ratio of boys to girls is 10-18 or 10:18 or $\frac{10}{18}$.)
    d. Use multiplication to find ratios.
    e. Understand that proportion is formed by two equal ratios.
7. Geometry
    a. Review, apply, and expand previously learned skills and concepts.

    • Area, perimeter, volume, distance

- Pentagon, hexagon, octagon, pyramid, prism, polygon, quadrilaterals, parallelograms

- Area of triangles

- Points, line segments, parallel lines, intersecting lines

- Right angles

- Radius, diameter, center of circle

- Edge, face, vertex of space figures

b. Develop the ability to identify rays and perpendicular lines.
c. Develop an understanding of the meaning of congruent segments, figures, and angles.
d. Understand that rays, segments, angles, points, and lines are geometric ideas and are not tangible, but tangible representations can be drawn and used.
e. Understand that squares, rectangles, parallelograms, trapezoids, and rhombuses are quadrilaterals and that the same quadrilateral can have more than one name—the same figure could be called a square, rectangle, parallelogram, or rhombus.
f. Associate an angle with its name (right, acute, straight, obtuse), use letters to name the angle (angle abc), and learn to measure angles.

8. Money
   a. Continue expanding the skills and concepts previously studied.

   - Coins and paper money

   - Sets of differing pieces of money but with the same value

   - Make change.

   - Add and subtract money.

   - Solve problems involving money using multiplication and division.

   - Apply skills and concepts to everyday situations.

9. Addition
   a. Review and expand previously learned skills.

   - Addition of one-, two-, three-, and four-digit numbers with and without regrouping

   - Estimating sums

   - Using a number line to solve problems

   b. Expand the ability to use and apply addition to daily experiences.
   c. Add five- and six-digit figures without regrouping and with regrouping.

Without regrouping		With regrouping	
15,732	384,271	42,537	689,247
+54,164	+412,618	+34,624	+220,865

10. Subtraction
   a. Review and expand previously learned skills.

   • Subtracting one-, two-, three-, and four-digit numbers with and without regrouping

   • Checking answers

   • Estimating differences

   • Using a number line to solve problems

   b. Expand the ability to use and apply subtraction to daily experiences.
   c. Subtract five- and six-digit figures without regrouping and with regrouping.

Without regrouping

67,481	524,679
−24,360	−411,324

With regrouping

704,213	30,245
−365,854	−18,662

11. Time
   a. Review, expand, and apply previously learned skills to daily situations.

   • Telling time—digital and non-digital

   • A.M. and P.M.

   • Elapsed time

   b. Add and subtract time.
12. Fractions
   a. Review, expand, and apply previously learned skills to daily experiences.

   • Fractional parts of a whole

- Equal fractions

- Using a number line to find equal fractions

- Fractions with different denominators and mixed numbers

- Adding and subtracting fractions

- Changing improper fractions to mixed numbers

- Reducing to lowest terms

- Greater than (>) or less than (<) another fraction

b. Change mixed numbers to fractions
c. Multiply and divide fractions.
13. Measurement
   a. Review, expand, and apply previously learned skills to every-day living situations.

   - Liquid and linear

   - Decimeter

   - Cubic centimeters

   - Ton

   - Estimating weight and capacity

   b. Measure angles. (See fifth grade, number 7f.)
   c. Add, subtract, and compare customary units of length, weight and liquid measure.
   d. Measure ingredients for a recipe; cook and eat the finished product. Many areas of math will be applied—purchasing ingredients (money), double or triple the recipe (multiplication), cut the recipe in half (division), measuring, fractions, etc.
14. Problem solving
   a. Review, expand, and apply previously learned skills, concepts, and strategies.

   - Choose the correct procedure—add, subtract, multiply, divide.

   - Use graphs, charts, tables, and maps to solve problems.

   - Apply logic to problem solving.

   - Discern what information is missing.

   - Write and solve original problems.

   - Discern if too much or too little information is given.

      b. Use ratios in problem solving.

      c. Increase the ability to apply problem solving to daily situations.

15. Graphs, charts, tables, statistics, and probability

      a. Review the skills learned previously.

        • Collect and record data.

        • Read, make, and use graphs—line, broken-line, and circle.

        • Read, write, and use a tally sheet.

      b. Conduct probability experiments and graph the results.

      c. Collect statistical data and graph the information.

16. Greater than (>), less than (<) or equal (=)—continue to expand and apply this skill.

17. Multiplication

      a. Review, expand, and apply previously learned skills.

        • Multiply two-, three-, and four-digit numbers by a one- or two-digit factor with and without regrouping.

        • Multiply by 10, 100, and 1000 and note pattern.

        • Estimate products.

        • Multiply money.

      b. Expand the ability to use and apply multiplication to daily experiences.

      c. Multiply five- and six-digit factors.

18. Roman numerals

      a. Review recognizing, reading, and writing numerals I through X.

      b. Read and write Roman numerals to 100.

      c. Discover where Roman numerals are encountered in life experiences.

19. Division

      a. Review, expand, and apply previously learned skills.

        • Discern when to use division.

        • Divide with a quotient of two or three digits that contains a zero.

        • Check quotient.

        • Estimate quotient.

        • Divide money.

        • Use division as one of the processes in a problem of more than one process.

- Divide by a two-digit divisor.

b. Expand the ability to apply and use division in daily experiences.
c. Increase division proficiency through short division.
d. Develop the ability to divide with the quotient being a mixed number.

20. Decimals
    a. Review, expand, and apply previously learned skills.

       - Read, add, and subtract decimals—tenths and hundredths.

       - Relate decimals to fractions and mixed numbers.

       - Use decimals to distinguish if a number is greater or less than another number.

       - Round decimals to the nearest whole number.

    b. Develop an understanding of what a repeating decimal is and how to read and write one ($4.222 = 4.2$, $0.141414 = 0.14$, $2.31111 = 2.31$)
    c. Multiply a decimal by a whole number, by a decimal, or by a power of ten.
    d. Form a generalization regarding multiplying by 10, 100, or 1000.
    e. Divide a decimal by a whole number, by a decimal, or by a power of ten.

21. Estimation
    a. Apply and expand previously learned skills.

       - Estimate measures.

       - Estimate addition, subtraction, multiplication, and division answers.

       - Use estimation in problem solving.

       - Round estimates to nearest tenth or hundredth.

    b. Estimate sums, differences, or products of decimals.

22. Calculators and computers—continue to expand the ability to use calculators and computers to increase math proficiency and for daily experiences.

Sixth Grade Math

The sixth grade math program focuses on enriching and broadening the student's math experience. There is continued emphasis placed on proficiency, accuracy, practical applications, the development of critical thinking and problem-solving skills, and the correlation of math skills, concepts, and strategies with other subject areas. All sixth grade students should have a thorough understanding of the concepts presented in the elementary grades and should have become independent learners.

Curriculum

1. The mathematics vocabulary for sixth grade math is developed in context and not as isolated words.
2. Recognize, read, and write numerals through hundred trillions.
3. Develop the ability to distinguish between a prime number and a composite number and understand that 0 and 1 are neither prime nor composite. Prime numbers are whole numbers that are greater than 1 and have two factors, itself and 1 (2, 3, 5, 7, 11, 13, etc. —1×3=3   3×1=3). Composite numbers are whole numbers greater than 1 that have more than two factors (4, 6, 8, 10, 21, 25, etc.—1×21=21   21×1=21   3×7=21   7×3=21).
4. Integers
   a. Develop an understanding of what integers are and how to use them.
   b. Compare positive and negative integers.
   c. Add positive integers with positive integers, negative integers with negative, and positive integers with negative.

   $$^+4+^+2=^+6 \quad ^-4+^-3=^-7 \quad ^+7+^-3=^+4 \quad ^-5+^+2=^-3$$

   d. Subtract positive integers from positive integers, negative integers from negative, and positive integers from negative.

   $$^+4-^+2=^+2 \quad ^-8-^-3=^-5 \quad ^+10-^-8=^+18 \quad ^-3-^+2=^-5$$

5. Percent
   a. Review previously learned skills

      • Write percent as a decimal and a decimal as percent.

      • Write percent as ratio and ratio as percent.

      • Find the percent of a number.

      • Use percent in problem solving.

   b. Increase the understanding of the relationship of percent to fractions and decimals.
   c. Use fractions and decimals to find the percent of a number.
   d. Use percent to find simple and compound interest.
   e. Use percent to find the amount of discount.
   f. Apply percent to daily experiences.

6. Estimation
   a. Review previously learned skills.

   - Apply estimation in problem solving.

   - Estimate addition, subtraction, multiplication and division answers.

   - Estimate sums, differences, or products of decimals.

   b. Apply estimation to real-life situations
7. Ratio and proportions
   a. Continue developing and expanding previously learned skills.

   - Read and write ratios.

   - Compare two items and write the numeral that represents the ratio of one item to the other.

   - Use multiplication to find ratios.

   b. Discover that the ratio of the sides of similar figures are equal.
8. Geometry
   a. Review, expand, and apply previously learned skills.

   - Area, perimeter, volume, distance

   - Shapes—recognizing and naming

   - Points, line segments, parallel lines, intersecting lines are geometric ideas, but tangible representations can be drawn and used.

   - Angles—right, acute, straight, obtuse

   b. Use points, lines, segments, rays, and planes in solving problems.
   c. Classify triangles by the angle measurement.
   d. Apply geometry concepts to everyday experiences.
9. Continue to expand the ability to use money in everyday situations.
10. Master and expand addition skills and apply them to daily living experiences.
11. Continue expanding and mastering subtraction skills and apply them to real-life situations.
12. Apply the skills involving time to life situations.
13. Fraction skills and concepts should be mastered and applied to daily living situations.

14. Measuring surface areas should be a skill added to those already learned, and all measuring skills should be expanded and applied to real-life situations.
15. Problem solving should utilize all the skills, concepts, and strategies that have been learned in previous grades.
16. The skills for reading, making, and using graphs, charts, and tables, and for gathering and using statistics should be reviewed and applied; experiments implementing probability should also be engaged in. All of these should be applied to real situations.
17. Multiplication
    a. Review all previously learned skills.

    • Multiply one-, two-, three-, four-, five-, and six-digit factors with and without regrouping.

    • Apply to daily experiences.

    • Multiply money.

    • Estimate and round estimates of products.

    b. Develop the ability to find the factors of a number and the greatest common factors of two numbers (1, 2, and 4 are factors of 20 and 32. 4 is the greatest common factor of the two numbers).
    c. Recognize, read, write, and use exponents.
    d. Understand that an exponent is a number that tells how many times the base number is used as a factor—$4^3=64$ (the exponent 4^3 is a shortened way to express the operation $4\times4\times4=64$).
    e. Use prime and composite numbers. (See sixth grade math, number 3.)
18. Continue developing the ability to recognize, read, write, and use Roman numerals.
19. Division
    a. Review and expand skills learned in the previous grades.

    • Discern when to use division to solve a problem.

    • Divide with a mixed number quotient.

    b. Divide numbers that result in a four-digit quotient.
    c. Use divisibility rules for 2, 3, 5, 9, and 10 as an aid in division (add 4, 6, and 8 for those indicating readiness.)

    • A number can be divided by 2 if the last digit of the number is an even number.

    • A number can be divided by 3 if the sum of the digits of a number is a multiple of 3 (3, 6, 9, 12, etc.).

- A number can be divided by 5 if the last digit of the number is 0 or 5.

- A number can be divided by 9 if the sum of the digits of the number is a multiple of 9 (9, 18, 27, etc.).

- A number can be divided by 10 if the last digit of the number is 0.

- A number can be divided by 4 if the sum of the last 2 digits of the number is divisible by 4 (2384—8+4=12 and 12 is divisible by 4).

- A number can be divided by 6 if it is also divisible by both 2 and 3 (384—can by divided by 6 since it can be divided by both 2 and 3).

- A number can be divided by 8 if the last 3 digits of the number are divisible by 8 (267,480 is divisible by 8 since 480 is divisible by 8).

20. Decimals
    a. Review previously learned skills and apply them to daily life situations.

    - Read and write repeating decimals (4.222=4.2, 0.141414=0.14, 2.31111=2.31).

    - Generalization of multiplying by 10, 100, 1000

    - Divide a decimal by a whole number, by a decimal, or by a power of 10.

    - Write percent as a decimal and a decimal as percent.

    b. Recognize, read, and write decimals to millionths.
    c. Develop an understanding of the density of a number (finding decimals between two whole numbers—between 2 and 3 would be 2.1, 2.14, 2.328, etc.).
    d. Divide a decimal by a whole number, by a decimal, and form a generalization about dividing decimals by 10, 100, and 1000.

21. Calculators and computers
    a. Continue using calculators to solve problems and use computer software to reinforce and enrich the math experience.
    b. Use a calculator for finding percent and in calculating integers.

10 Social Studies (Geography and History) Overview

The overview which follows is a brief comment on our approach to the teaching of elementary geography and history. We believe it is in harmony both with the Child Light philosophy of education and with attitudes and methods already being practiced by many dedicated teachers. It is not intended to outline the specific scope and sequence of social studies objectives for the curriculum.

The basic qualities offered by the recommended texts are substantial content, material which is well written in language and style, attention to skills which should be mastered in connection with the subject matter, and a format that is visually appealing. In addition, the notes in the teacher's editions provide a measure of background information and may list ideas for related projects that teachers or parents will want to use. While an appropriate text and the extensive use of supplementary materials are both essential, the way in which the teacher approaches the subject is, by far, of the greatest importance.

When, many years ago, the study of geography and history in most elementary schools was combined into a single subject called social studies, the reasoning behind the change was essentially sound. As children are introduced to the world around them, and to the world of the past, it is necessary to lay a unified foundation. They need to be given from the start an understanding of the ways in which the nature (the geography) of the places where people live affects their lives (their history) and, conversely, the effect of human life on the natural world. All this should be presented in such a way that students are conscious of being very much a part of the whole process.

The study of geography and history should, then, involve for students a sense of place, a view of who and where they and others

□ *137*

are, and an awareness of past and present geographical and cultural relationships. Eventually (and ideally) children's sense of place will embrace both the familiar in the observable world and the different: the reality of what *is* in the present and what man's experience has been in the past for a wide diversity of cultures. There should be a growing awareness of how each place and way of life relates to the other and, equally, of the relationship borne by the present to the past, the past to the present. The viewpoint should be broad, sweeping, panoramic, yet it should come alive through details.

The goal, therefore, should always be to relate details to this panoramic view, giving meaning to each detail as it relates to the whole. Focusing interminably (and sometimes disconnectedly) on clumps of detail has little or no meaning to the student. These details have not been related to his or her own sense of place and of reality. Neither have they been related to any kind of comprehensive view either of the physical world or of the span of human history.

Good textbooks attempt, of course, to take a broad, integrated approach. But unless the teacher also has a comprehensive vision, the subject matter may be presented to students in a way that lacks unity and seems merely to jump about the world arbitrarily. The teacher's own sense of place and of relationships, his or her own ability to implicitly convey such a vision, is of key significance.

Inextricably linked to what has just been said, and also to the use of supplementary materials, is a quality that may be the single, preeminently important element in the successful teaching of geography and history: the existence, for both the teacher and the students, of an inexhaustible sense of wonder and of curiosity. These two immeasurably valuable qualities come from *seeing*, whether in actuality, or with the mind's eye, and from thinking about what has been seen. The natural world, for example, this amazing creation of God, is remarkable, diverse, endlessly supplied with wonder-making realities about which it is natural to think, to be curious—or simply to contemplate with awe. Geography becomes a delight in such a context. And what of human beings who are in some ways the most wonder making of all of God's creation? The story of human life, both as to groups and in relation to specific persons, will, if truly *seen*, provoke lifelong wonder, lifelong curiosity. History, then, is really an endlessly fascinating story.

Weighed down as they are with long lists of objectives to meet, with structures of all kinds imposed on their material, textbooks offer guidelines and structure, but they often fail to look with wonder and curiosity at the natural world and at the human story. It is important, then, to supplement texts. First of all, put children constantly in touch with "the real thing." In geography this would include the nearby rooms and areas to measure and map, the landforms to sketch, the weather to observe, a trip to plan, or the news account of a volcanic eruption to discuss. In addition to that, reading should be supplied in which places and travels are written about with excitement, with obvious wonder and curiosity. *Books Children Love* will be helpful in this regard.

In the study of history, a sense of the past should begin, for children, in such things as a grandparent's stories of things as they were in his or her own childhood, and of the changes that have taken place over a lifetime. Older persons in a community who are longtime residents might be guests in class to tell of the town's past. Locations of historic interest can be visited, putting students in touch with concrete places and objects that relate to the past. In every case, the comprehensive view, the place of events and people in the broad flow of time, should underlie the teaching approach.

As in geography, supplementary reading is important: the stories (either fiction or nonfiction) of significant or representative people of the past, told with a sense of wonder at the overcoming of difficulties, at the greatness of courage or loyalty; or the curiosity of suspense: what is going to happen next? Evaluation: why did Alexander the Great lose some qualities of good judgment and become extremely arrogant and conceited after he became powerful? Well-told stories of the events of the past stay in students' memories, but they generate questions. Questions related to values, the development of character, and cause and effect are vitally important in equipping children to think logically, to recognize truth and to make wise choices and decisions.

Finally, it is necessary to add a note about some valuable, sometimes neglected skills which are of great significance in making children confident and free to learn and grow in their study of geography and history.

In geography, children need to develop ever-growing skills in the use of the subject's primary tool—maps. Some map work is included in the texts, but in most cases not nearly enough to meet the student's need. Students should be able to automatically locate specific places on the map and to have a mental picture of just where that place is, both in relation to its own continental (or national, state, province, county, etc.) identity, and in relation to other geographical units. At first, this skill is practiced in the simplest and most basic forms in which children learn to map a room, a few blocks of their neighborhood, or a local park. It is not long, however, before they are ready to start systematic work (memorization) of their own national map outlines and divisions. The students will learn to recognize, for example, the states of the United States, or the regional divisions of the British

Isles, by shape and by their relationship to the other divisional units and to their nation as a whole. They are also learning (at appropriate levels) about compass directions, the measurement of distance and the use of scale in mapping.

Even before students have reached the point of focusing in detail on the maps of nations other than their own, they should be growing familiar with globes, world maps, the shapes and locations of continents, the concept of the northern and southern hemispheres, and much more. Eventually, children should have been given the opportunity to learn the configurations, identities and relational locations of the world's nations and, in some cases, more detailed divisions of these nations. These memorizations, of course, are always given significance. They are perceived as ways in which each person is able to orient himself or herself to the physical world, and are studied as part of the exciting panorama of the amazing world.

As for history, children should be given, within the broad framework of the thousands of years of which there is some historic record, a timeline sense of when significant events occurred and when key historical figures lived. This kind of organization of history can be started in a simplified form in the early grades. The birth of Christ is the orientation point, and a simple chart can be made by drawing columns vertically on a sheet of paper to the left and right of that orientation point. For the very early periods of history each section might represent several hundred years; later, as civilizations spread and more recorded events occurred, each section might cover 100 or even 50 years.

Throughout the social studies courses, key occurrences may be entered on such a chart. In most cases, knowing the century or half-century in which an important event took place, or a notable person made an impact on history is sufficient for a long-range picture of the march of history. There is a modest number of exact-year dates which it is appropriate—and relatively easy—to memorize, but the chief objective should be to give children a comprehensive idea of major developments: When was Greece at the height of its glory? What were the centuries of a strong Roman Empire, and when was its fall? When was the medieval era, and when did modern civilization begin? etc.

As children study specific details and do supplementary reading with this overall timetable becoming ever more firmly established in their minds, the details once again make sense because they don't stand alone; they are being absorbed as part of a pattern of time and human experience in which each child shares.

Note: Two of the books listed in *Books Children Love* under both "Geography and History," and "Reference," are valuable resources when a teacher or parent is attempting to present a unified view of history. In these books (*The Timetables of History* by Bernard Grun, and *The Timetables of American History* by Laurence Urdang, both published by Simon and Schuster), the reader can look across each double page spread of vertical columns and see what was being done in a variety of categories (History and Politics, The Arts, Science and Technology, etc.) across the civilized world during the same time period.

In addition, Susan Schaeffer Macaulay has developed an alternative social studies curriculum, covering grades three through six. It includes many useful ideas, particularly for those teaching small classes or in the home. The curriculum also has a somewhat international flair, allowing for studies in countries outside the U.S. This curriculum can be found in Appendixes I, II, and III.

11 Social Studies

Social studies is an exciting subject. Children are exposed to the flow of history and see their country and their place in history as part of the whole picture. They begin to see for themselves what happens when certain absolutes are missing and a Christian worldview that gives value to life is absent. The Bible takes on new meaning as they discover that it is the story of people who lived at a point and time in history. How the time in which a person lives affects that person and how he in turn affects history should captivate their minds. A thirst for learning begins to grow as the children are exposed to folktales, myths, and the historical and geographical study of the world in which they live.

Children learn that problems need to be interpreted in light of reliable material and that movies, television, and printed materials can present an inaccurate, biased, or questionable point of view. It is essential that the ability to read and listen critically be developed in order for accurate conclusions to be drawn. The desire to exercise behavior that is consistent with a Christian worldview should be developed. Whether current world problems, the Dark Ages, Asia, or a school playground argument are the focus, the result should be a sense of individual responsibility, which is the essence of Christian behavior.

The curriculum for each grade level provides for a sequential development of knowledge about the world—both past and present. Child Light recommends the use of living books to add richness to the study and other materials to aid in stimulating and motivating learning.

A study of the state in which the child lives should be included in the social studies program. It should be placed at the level specified by the individual state.

Children's interests and abilities vary; therefore, it is important to provide a choice of activities for each area studied. What might appeal to and motivate one child, might not help another. Flexibility is also a key to a good learning situation. When children express curiosity and interest in an area it should be capitalized on and plans for the day laid aside in order to take advantage of the opportunity.

Newspapers and news magazines should be used in all grades. With younger children, just the front page of a local newspaper can be shown, the headline read and the teacher can tell the main facts connected with it. If pictures of local, state, or national leaders are printed, the children can be shown these so that they begin to recognize those in authority in their country. As the children get older articles can be read and discussed in both newspapers and magazines. Pictures of world leaders should also be included. If children are to affect their world they must be informed individuals. Sixth graders should also listen to the words of popular secular musical groups or individuals and note the questions that are being asked and the answers or solutions given. They should discuss what the Biblical answers would be (not superficial, pat answers, but Biblical absolutes and principles).

Note: Books recommended for use at each grade level are found within this curriculum. For additional suggestions see *Books Children Love*.

First Grade Social Studies

The first grade social studies program seeks to broaden a child's view of the world. Understanding that the world is larger than the area, state, and country in which one lives is developed. Maps and globes are introduced, seasonal holidays are emphasized, American folktales and Aesop's fables are read and narrated. The study of Biblical and national heroes develops an understanding of the characteristics of a good role model.

Curriculum

1. Aesop's fables and American folk tales
   a. Suggested books:

   The Caldecott Aesop   Randolph Caldecott

   American Tall-tale Animals   Adrien Stoutenburg

   American Folk Tales

   Heroes in American Folklore   Irwin Shapiro

Yankee Doodle's Cousins   Anne Malcolmson

The Rooster Crows   Maud & Miska Petersham

   b. Read one or two weekly and narrate orally. Oral narration can be followed by the children drawing pictures to illustrate the story, a mural being drawn by the class, etc.

2. Individual state and United States national holidays
   a. Read a story or stories about the holiday, followed by oral narration which can be followed by drawing a mural, making a booklet, etc.
   b. Dramatize a holiday—play, puppets, pantomime, role play, "TV program."
   c. View and narrate movies and filmstrips about holidays.
3. Christian religious holidays
   a. Read the Biblical account and narrate orally, followed by drawing a mural, creating a "TV program," making a booklet.
   b. Dramatize the holiday—play, puppets, pantomime, role play.
   c. View and narrate movies and filmstrips.
   d. Read stories about the holiday, followed by narration.
   e. Note the cultural and the Biblical aspects of the holiday customs.
   f. Include Christmas and Easter.
4. Overview of famous Americans—develop within the child a love for and loyalty to the United States.
   a. Construct a simple time line showing when the people lived.
   b. Use various forms of narration to enhance the study.

     • Presidents of the United States

     • Benjamin Franklin

     • Susan B. Anthony

     • George Washington Carver

     • Martin Luther King

     • American authors

     • John Winthrop

     • Sam Houston

     • John Brown

     • Clara Barton

- Frances Perkins

- Clare Booth Luce

- Others of particular interest to the child, or the city or state in which the child lives

5. Study of the home
   a. Discover that families differ in the way they function.
   b. Learn about families around the world.
   c. Read about Biblical families.
   d. Recognize the responsibility of the individual to the family.
   e. Understand that Biblical principles and absolutes apply to all Christian families, no matter what cultural or individual differences exist.

6. Study of the school
   a. Learn how the school functions.
   b. Develop a sense of the responsibility of the individual to the school.
   c. Draw a simple map of the school.

7. Community workers and other occupations
   a. Read about different community workers and other occupations and narrate—orally and by other forms of narration.
   b. Take field trips to the fire station, post office, bank, a construction site, etc.
   c. Use resource people—invite people with different occupations to speak to the class.
   d. View movies and filmstrips about different occupations and narrate.
   e. Begin an understanding of the difference between vocation (the area in which God has given a person abilities and gifts to use for His glory) and occupation (the activity from which a person gains a livelihood). A person's vocation and occupation may or may not be the same.

8. Transportation
   a. Read books and stories about different modes of transportation and narrate—orally and by other forms of narration.
   b. Take field trips to the airport, train station, bus depot, car dealership, etc.
   c. Use resource people—invite people involved in transportation-related occupations to speak to the class.
   d. View movies and filmstrips about transportation and narrate.

9. Biblical and national heroes—introduction to selecting character traits and values as a pattern for individual goals.

   a. Biblical—Daniel, Shadrach, Meshach, and Abednego, Laza-
      rus, Mary the mother of Jesus, and Mary and Martha. Note
      the character traits that made them godly men and women.
   b. National—select men and women from the study of fa-
      mous people. (See first grade, number 4.) Note the charac-
      ter traits that make them good role models.
10. Geography
   a. Increase the children's knowledge of lakes, ponds, creeks,
      oceans, hills, and mountains.
   b. Take field trips for personal observation.
   c. Gain information from books, films, and filmstrips.
11. Maps and globes
   a. Maps—on a large map of the United States locate the state
      and city in which the child lives, the state where the child
      was born, the state where grandparents live, etc.
   b. Globes—locate the United States and the state in which the
      child lives and notice how land and water are distinguished.
12. Book suggestions:

Who Built the Bridge?   Norman Bate

True Book of Policemen and Firemen   Irene Miner

Big Book of Real Fire Engines   Elizabeth Cameron

If You Grew Up With Abraham Lincoln   Ann McGovern

The Thanksgiving Story

Benjamin Franklin   Ingri and Edgar D'Aulaire

The Columbus Story   Alice Dalgliesh

The Fourth of July Story   Alice Dalgliesh

An American ABC   Maud and Miska Petersham

The Story of the Presidents of the United States of America

Old Liberty Bell   Frances Rogers and Alice Beard

Note: Numbers 1, 2, 3, 4, 9, 10, and 11 will be taught throughout the
whole year. The other areas should be divided into units of six to nine
weeks.

Second Grade Social Studies

   In second grade social studies an individual's conception of the
world continues to be broadened. An understanding of the child's

community and an appreciation for and understanding of the diversity of communities is developed. The ability to use maps and globes is expanded, seasonal holidays are emphasized, a deeper sense of love and loyalty for the United States of America is fostered, a study of wild and domestic animals is introduced, Greek and Roman myths and folktales of the world are read and narrated, and the character traits of Biblical and contemporary heroes are seen as a basis for choosing a role model.

Curriculum

1. An introduction to Greek and Roman myths and folktales of the world
   a. Suggested books:

   The First Book of Mythology   Kathleen Elgin

   Book of Myths   Helen Sewell

   One Hundred Favorite Folktales   Stith Thompson

   b. Read and narrate one or two weekly.
2. National holidays—United States and Canada
   a. Read books and stories about the holidays and narrate orally and by other narration forms; make booklets or murals.
   b. Use dramatization—plays, puppets, "TV programs," pantomime, role play.
   c. View movies and filmstrips and narrate orally.
   d. Include: United States—New Year's Day, Martin Luther King's birthday, Lincoln's birthday, Washington's birthday, Presidents' Day, Mothers' Day, Memorial Day, Father's Day, Flag Day, Independence Day, Columbus Day, Thanksgiving. Canada—Victoria Day (first Monday before May 25), Dominion Day or Canada Day (July 1), Thanksgiving (second Monday in October).
3. Religious holidays—Christian and Jewish
   a. Read about, narrate, discuss, and list the major holidays. Include: Christian—Good Friday, Resurrection Sunday (Easter), Christmas. Jewish—Hanukkah (Feast of Lights) and Passover.
   b. Note how the same holiday may have different customs in different countries.
4. Overview of local and selected world communities
   a. Learn about the local community by observation, by talking to elderly people, by studying the history of the community, by visiting museums, by reading books, and by any other available resources.

b. Compare the local community with other communities and note the diversity that exists among communities and the interdependence of community members. Pay special attention to the necessity that exists for members of a community to work together and for each individual to make a positive contribution to the community if it is to function properly.

c. Compare the way of life and customs of selected communities throughout the world.

5. Flag of the United States of America
   a. Read about the history of the flag and narrate.
   b. Learn the regulations for the care and use of the flag.
   c. Draw or make a flag; make a booklet or mural about the history of the flag; write a story or poem about the flag.

6. National and state historical sites
   a. Recognize pictures of sites such as the White House, the United States Capitol, the Washington Memorial, and the Lincoln Memorial and know why they are significant.
   b. Learn about any local and state historical sites.
   c. Take field trips to historical sites.
   d. Read books and view movies, filmstrips, and slides about historical places.
   e. Resource people—invite people to speak to the class about historical sites.

7. Animals
   a. Domestic—read about, observe, and learn about caring for pets and other domestic animals.
   b. Wild—read about, observe in zoos, and understand the need for conservation of endangered species.

8. Occupations
   a. Read books about different occupations and narrate—orally and by other narration forms.
   b. Have parents and other resource people speak to the class about their occupations.
   c. Take field trips to observe people at work in different occupations.
   d. Increase the understanding of the difference between vocation and occupation. (See first grade, number 7.)

9. Communications
   a. Introduce the various means of communication that exist in the world today.
   b. Apply critical-thinking skills to TV and radio programs, newspaper and magazine articles, and books—distinguishing between fact and opinion.

10. Biblical and contemporary heroes—recognizing character traits that make a good role model
    a. Biblical—Noah, Abraham, John, Elizabeth, the widow of II Kings 4:1-7
    b. Contemporary—people such as Mother Teresa, a missionary known to the class, or a member of the local community.
11. Geography
    a. Continuation of the skills begun in first grade
    b. Learn how geographical features affect communities—by observation locally, and through books, movies, filmstrips, and slides.
12. Maps and globes
    a. Read and narrate *A Map Is a Picture* by Barbara Rinkoff.
    b. Compare photographs with maps.
    c. Locate the North and South Poles on maps and globes.
    d. Begin picture symbol understanding.
    e. Locate individual states on a large map of the United States.
    f. Locate the countries where the myths and folktales that are being read take place.
    g. Draw a simple map of the local community or area.
13. Suggested books:

I Want to Be a Pilot Donna Bake (also the other *I Want to Be . . .* books)

Come to the City

All Around the Train

What Happens When You Mail a Letter? Arthur Shay

People on Long Ago Street

Family Life and Customs Throughout the World

Daniel Boone James H. Dougherty

Columbus Ingri and Edgar D'Aulaire

Abraham Lincoln Ingri and Edgar D'Aulaire

George Washington Ingri and Edgar D'Aulaire

Our Country's Freedom Frances Cavanah

Pilgrim Stories Elvajean Hall

In My Mother's House Ann Nolan Clark

Around the World in Ninety Minutes Rocca Feravob

Third Grade Social Studies

An overview of the western world is presented in third grade social studies. The diversity of past and present communities, the individual's response and responsibility to the community, and climate and its affect on daily living are emphasized. Map and globe study is expanded. Nordic myths and folktales are read and narrated.

Curriculum

1. Nordic myths and folktales
   a. Suggested books:

   Norse Gods and Giants Ingri and Edgar Parin D'Aulaire

   Gods and Heroes from Viking Mythology Brian Branston

   The Wonderful Adventure of Nils Selma Lagerlof

   b. Read and narrate one or two weekly.
2. National holidays—United States, Mexico, Central America, South America
   a. Read books and stories about the holidays and narrate orally and by other narration forms.
   b. Dramatize—play, puppets, pantomime, "TV program," role play
   c. View movies and filmstrips and narrate.
3. Religious holidays—Christian and Jewish
   a. Expand the knowledge begun in the second grade. Include: Christian—Maundy Thursday, Twelfth Night or Epiphany (January 6), Palm Sunday, Advent Sunday (Sunday nearest Nov. 30). Jewish—Rosh Hashanah (New Year).
   b. Review by listing and discussing the major holidays.
   c. Read books and stories for more information about specific holidays and narrate.
   d. Compare and contrast the actual customs with the Biblical account.
4. Overview of the Western world
   a. Read and narrate orally a book such as *Datelines of World History* by Guy Arnold.
   b. Create a mural timeline that highlights the main events of each era.
5. Communities
   a. Compare present-day communities with communities of the past.
   b. Note the diversity and compare and contrast the differences between communities of the past and present.

    c. Note the necessity that exists in communities for individuals to work together for the good of the community.

    d. Begin to perceive what happens when the members of a community do not feel a sense of responsibility toward the community.

    e. Develop an understanding that a sense of compassion should cause each individual member to respond to the needs and problems of the community.

    f. Begin to understand that the value that is placed on life has an enormous effect on the community—Christian worldview versus non-Christian worldview.

6. Biblical and historical heroes—selection based on the character traits that a role model should possess

    a. Biblical—Joseph, Moses, Stephen, Sarah, Dorcas

    b. Historical—selected from the study of the Western world using criteria established for choosing a role model.

7. Career education

    a. Continue the study of vocation and occupation (See first grade, number 7 and second grade, number 8.)

    b. Learn about different career opportunities.

8. Geography

    a. Increase the knowledge of the local climate by learning about and comparing major kinds of climates—polar; ice cap; cold and moist; rainy and warm with rain throughout the year; rainy and warm with dry summer and rainy winters; semiarid; desert; tropical with rain throughout the year; and tropical with a rainy season.

    b. Introduction of the reason why climates differ.

    c. Observe the local climate throughout the year.

    d. Begin to understand how climate affects daily living.

    e. Vocabulary development—hurricane, tornado, blizzard, temperature, thermometer, high pressure, low pressure, precipitation, humidity, wind chill, trade winds, monsoon, tidal wave, barometer

9. Maps and globes

    a. Review of previous skills (See first, grade number 11, second grade, number 12.)

    b. Locate the equator on different maps and globes and discover its significance.

    c. Develop an understanding of scale and apply it when using maps and globes.

    d. Learn the difference between political and physical maps and globes.

   e. Begin developing an understanding of special purpose
      maps.
   f. Construct a relief map of the local area.
10. Suggested books:

   Famous Explorers for Young People   Ramon Peyton Coffman and
   Nathan G. Goodman

   A Day in the Life of President Kennedy   Jim Bishop

   George Washington's Birthday   Wilma P. Hays

   Ike Eisenhower: Statesman and Soldier of Peace   Delos W. Love-
   lace

   With Lincoln in the White House   Earl S. Miers

   First Adventure   Elizabeth Coatsworth

   Fourth of July Story   Alice Dalgliesh

   Adventures of Lewis and Clark   Ormonde DeKay

   Martin and Abraham Lincoln   Catherine Coblentz

   On the Way Home   Laura Ingalls Wilder

   Colonial Farm   June Behrens

   Thanksgiving   Edna Barth

Fourth Grade Social Studies

   An overview of the history of the Eastern world is presented in
fourth grade social studies. The interdependence of people and the
individual's response and responsibility to local, national, and world
needs and problems is stressed. Map and globe skills are increased and
desert, plain, forest, and mountain regions are studied and compared.
Greek mythology is read and narrated.

Curriculum

1. Greek myths
   a. Suggested books:

      Greek Myths   Olivia Coolidge

      Book of Greek Myths   published by Doubleday

      Gods, Men and Monsters from Greek Myths   Michael Gibson

      Greek Gods and Heroes   Robert Graves

   b. Read and narrate one or two weekly.

2. National and religious holidays
   a. National (American) holidays—read about and discuss the significance of each as they occur during the school year.
   b. Religious (Christian) holidays—read about, narrate, and discuss how the celebration of the various Christian holidays is the same and how it varies in different countries. Note which aspects can be cultural and which are absolutes.
   c. Religious (American Indian) holidays—read about, narrate, and discuss religious holidays of different American Indian tribes.

3. Overview of the Eastern world
   a. Read and narrate a book or portion of a book that gives a broad overview of the Eastern world.
   b. Create a pictorial timeline.
   c. Note the presence or absence of Biblical absolutes and the effect this has on the societies.

4. World regions
   a. Compare desert, mountain, plain, and forest regions.
   b. Compare the local region with other regions of the United States.
   c. Develop an understanding of how different regions depend on each other.
   d. Note how daily living differs in different kinds of regions and the similarities that exist in the same kinds of regions.
   e. Apply geographical, map, and globe skills to the study of the different regions of the world.

5. Communication
   a. Develop the realization that there is a need for communication between countries as well as within countries.
   b. Discover which means of communication are used in different areas.
   c. Apply critical-thinking skills to discover how fact, opinion, and propaganda are used in communication between countries and within countries.

6. Biblical and historical heroes—selected on the basis of character traits that a role model should manifest
   a. Biblical—Elijah, Joshua, John the Baptist, Esther, the widow of Mark 12:41-44, Luke 21:1-4
   b. Historical—selected from the study of the Eastern world using criteria established for choosing a role model

7. Career education
   a. Develop a clear understanding of vocation versus occupation. (See first grade, number 7.)

  b. Understand talents, interests, education, and other qualifications needed for different careers.
8. Geography
  a. Correlate with regional studies—desert, mountain, plain, forest. (See fourth grade, number 4.)
  b. Learn what type of climate exists in the four types of regions. (See third grade, number 8.)
  c. Note how latitude, elevation, surface features, oceans (and other bodies of water), and position of the earth affect climate.
  d. Learn how a compass functions and how to use one—correlate with nature walks.
  e. Learn to read graphs and diagrams related to climate and compare geographical features of different regions.
9. Maps and globes
  a. Construct a topographical map of the local area or state.
  b. Recognize the different land and water shapes—coast, lake, gulf, ocean, sea, river, island, isthmus, peninsula, delta, and harbor.
  c. Introduce color and symbols as tools for reading maps and globes.
  d. Introduce longitude and latitude. Locate the child's state and major cities using longitude and latitude.
10. Suggested books:

The First Book of Ancient Bible Lands   Charles Robinson

Thomas Jefferson   Vincent Sheean

The Blacksmiths; The Printers; The Glassmakers; The Cabinetmakers; The Shoemakers   Leonard Fisher

First Book of the Constitution   Richard Morris

Four Days in Philadelphia   Mary Phelan

John Billingham, Friend of Squanto   Clyde Bulla

The Matchlock Gun   Walter Edmonds

Little Navajo Bluebird   Ann Nolan Clark

George Washington Carver   Anne Terry White

Martin Luther   May McNeer

The Apache Indian; The Cherokee and other books about Indians Sonia Bleeker

Desert Life and others in The Living Earth series

Fifth Grade Social Studies

In fifth grade social studies an overview of United States history is presented. There is an emphasis on world events, especially those involving the United States and her neighbors. The development of map and globe skills is continued and the geography of North and South America is compared and contrasted. Roman mythology is read and narrated.

Curriculum

1. Roman myths
   a. Suggested books:

      Heroes, Gods and Emperors from Roman Mythology Kewy Usher

2. National and religious holidays
   a. National (American) holidays—read about and discuss the significance of those that occur during school vacation times.
   b. Religious (Christian, Jewish, and Muslim) holidays—read about, narrate, and discuss the similarities, differences and significance of the holidays. In addition to holidays previously studied include: Jewish—Yom Kippur (Day of Atonement). Muslim—Ramadan (in honor of the Koran being "revealed" to Muhammad), Muhammad's birthday, and the special party in honor of a child and teacher when the child has memorized the Koran.
   c. List the holidays that have a Biblical basis.
   d. Discover why Christians do not celebrate all the holidays that have a Biblical basis.
3. Overview of the history of the United States of America
   a. As a review construct a broad overview timeline of the world history to 1492.
   b. Read and narrate a book or portion of a book that presents a broad overview of United States history.
   c. Construct an in-depth timeline of the United States from 1492 to the present. Include the use of tables, maps, graphs, and diagrams.
   d. Note the presence or absence of Biblical absolutes and the value placed on man during the different historical periods and the effect of these beliefs on the history of the time.
4. Study of the United States
   a. American Indians—Plains, Southwest, Eastern Forest, and Northwest

    b. Founding, growth, and development of the United States
    c. Past and present daily life
    d. Past and present economics
    e. Governmental system—national, local, and state
    f. Neighbors of the United States—Canada, Mexico, Central America, South America, the Caribbean
    g. World events with emphasis on the United States and her neighbors—apply critical-thinking skills in distinguishing fact from bias or an individual's viewpoint.

Note: An interesting approach to the study would be to choose a person from United States history and have that person look back in history to see what happened before his/her time and then look beyond his/her time to see what came after.

    Another approach would be to choose a person and study the time in which that person lived from the perspective of what affected him/her, how he/she affected the time, and what was going on in the world during the time in which that person lived.

5. Heroes—selected on the basis of character traits that a role model should have
    a. Biblical—David, Hezekiah, Stephen, Ruth, Hannah. Note the strengths and weaknesses of each and decide what character traits had to be developed in order for the weaknesses not to have had a negative effect in the individual's life.
    b. Choose heroes from United States history using the criteria of positive character traits and manifested evidence of a desire to grow and mature in areas of weakness.
6. Geography
    a. Note which regions are found in North America, Central America, South America, and the Caribbean.
    b. Identify the types of climate that are found in the different regions.
    c. Construct graphs and diagrams that show crops, products, temperature, and rainfall for the different regions.
7. Continue to develop an understanding of careers with emphasis on the difference between vocation and occupation. (See first grade, number 7.)
8. Maps and globes
    a. Locate the seven continents.
    b. Note that longitude and latitude grids are the same on all maps.

      c. Use longitude and latitude to locate countries, states, islands, and cities.

      d. Increase the ability to use keys and symbols.

9. Suggested books:

Famous Pioneers for Young People

Famous Women of America

Famous American Statesmen   William Oliver Stevens

Martha, Daughter of Virginia   Marguerite Vance

The Story of Martha Washington   Marguerite Vance

Amos Fortune: Freeman   Elizabeth Yates

Ethan Allen   Slater Brown

James Bowie and His Famous Knife   Shannon Garst

Soldier, Statesman . . . Aaron Burr   Jeannette Nolan

Kit Carson: Mountain Man   Margaret Bell

Geronimo   Edgar Wyatt

America's Robert E. Lee   Henry S. Commager

And Then What Happened, Paul Revere?   Jean Fritz

Betsy Ross   Jane Mayer

Colony of Connecticut; Story of the Thirteen Colonies   Clifford Alderman

Colonial Georgia   Clifford Capps

Colonial South Carolina   Eugenia Burney

Colonial New York   Gardell Christensen

Colonial New Jersy   John Cunningham

Colony of Massachusetts   Alice Dickinson

Maryland Colony   F. Van Wyck Mason

Colony of Georgia   Harold Vaughn

The American Indian   Ann White

America's Past   National Geographic publication

The French Explorers in America; The Spanish Conquistadores in North America   Walter Buehr

The Santa Fe Trail Samuel Hopkins Adams

Wild Bill Hickok Tames the West Stewart H. Holbrook

Front-line General, Douglas MacArthur Jules Archer

Dolly Madison Jeanette Nolan

America's Mark Twain May McNeer

Sixth Grade Social Studies

An overview of Western and Eastern history is compared and contrasted in sixth grade social studies. An understanding of current world events is developed, the geography of Europe and Asia is studied, and map and globe skills are explained. Greek, Roman, Nordic, and other myths and legends are read and narrated.

Curriculum

1. Greek, Roman, Nordic, and other myths and legends
   a. Suggested books:

      Mythology Edith Hamilton

      The Myths of Greece and Rome H. A. Guerbver

      Hero Tales from Many Lands Alice I. Haxeltilne

      The Heroes Charles Kingsley

   b. Read and narrate one or two weekly.
2. National and religious holidays
   a. National (American) holidays—write poems, plays, or stories about the holidays as they occur during the school year.
   b. Religious (Christian and Eastern) holidays—read about, narrate, discuss, compare, and contrast the holidays.
   c. Compare the manner in which Western and Eastern Christians celebrate the Christian holidays. Note how culture affects the manner in which the various holidays are celebrated. Compare the manner of celebration with the Biblical account to discover what the absolutes are and where there is freedom for cultural differences.
   d. See *Books Children Love* for book suggestions.
3. Overview of the Western and Eastern world
   a. Create a timeline that indicates what is happening simultaneously in history, art, music, religion, economics, and politics.
   b. Note the result when absolutes are ignored. Construct

graphs, tables, or diagrams to illustrate the difference that exists when Christian absolutes are present and when they are absent.

c. Note the results that exist when a low value is placed on human life.

4. World societies
   a. Develop an understanding of the role and responsibility of individuals.
   b. Note the differentiation between the value systems of different societies.
   c. Compare different political systems and develop an understanding of how they function and how they affect the lives of individuals throughout the world as well as those living under a particular system—monarchy, democracy, republic, communism, fascism, socialism.
   d. Develop an understanding of and compare different economic systems.
   e. Compare a, b, c, and d above with Biblical standards and models and note what elements are missing in the different societies.
   f. By drawing conclusions, formulate a generalization of how and why cultures change.
   g. Develop an understanding that Biblical absolutes do not change, but cultures do; therefore the application of absolutes in contemporary society can reflect the culture without compromising the absolute.
   h. Awareness of current world affairs—apply critical-thinking skills to distinguish between fact and opinion, absolutes being applied or ignored, what the individual's responsibility should be, and what the church's response is or should be.

5. Heroes—chosen for the manifestation of positive character traits
   a. Biblical—Samuel, Nehemiah, Paul, Rebecca, Deborah
   b. Choosing contemporary heroes—use the evidence of positive character traits being manifested and evidence of a desire to develop in areas of weakness as criteria for the selection. Perfection should not be looked for (it will not be found), but evidence that a person is growing in their development of the character traits that will cause him or her to be a positive force in society should be seen. Contrast this approach with the manner in which heroes are usually selected.

6. Career education
   a. Research different careers, noting the qualifications and preparation for each.

    b. Emphasis on vocation versus occupation and the Biblical work ethic versus the American work ethic. (See first grade, number 7.)

7. Geography
   a. Discover what geographical regions are located in Europe, Asia, and Africa.
   b. Note the topography and climate of the different regions.
   c. Construct rainfall, product, and temperature graphs and diagrams for the various regions. Compare the different regions located on the same continent.

8. Maps and globes
   a. Develop the ability to use and make special purpose maps— weather, climate, temperature, time zone, road, historical, products, natural resources, population.
   b. Discover how maps are made—books, movies, filmstrips, field trips, resource people.
   c. Each child should be able to demonstrate an ability to use graphs, keys, legends, symbols, longitude, and latitude.

9. Suggested books:

Famous Generals and Admirals for Young People

Famous Kings and Queens for Young People

Caesar's Gallic War   Olivia Coolidge

Men of Athens   Olivia Coolidge

Whatever Happened to the Human Race?   Francis Schaeffer

How Should We Then Live?   Francis Schaeffer

The Story of Albert Einstein   Mae Freemon

Johann Gutenberg   Brayton Harris

Martin Luther   Harry Fosdick

Jeanne d'Arc   Aileen Fisher

The Magna Charta   James Daugherty

Winston Churchill   Quentin Reynolds

Voyages of Christopher Columbus   Armstrong Perry

Ten Brave Women; Ten Brave Men   Sonia Daugherty

First Book of How to Run a Meeting   David Powers

Christmas Book of Legends and Stories   Edna Smith

From Bush to City: A Look at New Africa   Marc Bernheim

The Roman Republic   Isaac Asimov

Golden Days of Greece   Olivia Coolidge

Dwellers of the Tundra   Aylette Jenness

The United Kingdom, a New Britain   Marian Moore

$\boxed{12}$ Science Overview

T he overview which follows is a brief comment on our approach to the teaching of elementary science. We believe it is in harmony both with the Child Light philosophy of education, and with attitudes and methods already being practiced by many dedicated teachers. It is not intended to outline the specific scope and sequence of science objectives for the curriculum.

Textbooks are recommended that offer a strong foundation in the life, physical, earth and space sciences. Experiments and related activities demonstrate the concepts under consideration and students are encouraged to develop an understanding of the scientific approach. In this they learn that specific facts about the natural world and the way its laws operate are demonstrable. But they also learn that science has its limitations and that the opinions of scientists change as new facts are discovered.

It is unfortunate that even the idea of science has become a disturbing issue for some Christian educators, simply because many non-Christian scientists have gone beyond the facts they possess and have in some cases presented theory as fact. This should not, however, put Christians on the defensive. Neither the original acts of divine, supernatural creation, nor evolution by chance from some minute, inexplicably existent life-form can be *scientifically* proven. Instead, a faith is held and known facts are viewed from the perspective of that faith, whether it is the faith that a pre-existent God created the universe, or a faith that some elements of the universe and a spark of life were pre-existent and eventually developed into the orderly universe now known. For believers of either faith, there are still many unanswered questions about the natural world which can only be placed in a mental file marked "pending."

There is every reason for the Christian to have a positive viewpoint. First of all, Christians *know* the One who revealed Himself to man as the Creator, and it is with confidence and assurance that they accept His word. Second, all known laws of probability make the idea that everything that *is* was formed by chance, utterly untendable even from an entirely mathematical point of view. But the whole idea of a Creator, a supreme all-powerful being who consciously designed the universe, its precise laws and its complexity of detail, is totally unacceptable to many scientists and others who influence contemporary thought. They cling tenaciously to their "all-by-chance" faith, supporting it with their interpretation of scientific facts and, for the most part, choosing not to focus on the unanswered questions in their belief.

From time to time in children's experience, whether in books or classes, on television programs or in conversations, they will encounter the "by chance" belief. It is important to help them to realize that this view is simply one aspect of a total worldview that doesn't acknowledge God. It is not something about which to feel defensive or hostile.

The teaching of science in the Child Light program maintains a broad perspective: that the children live in a universe designed and made by God, on a planet brimming over with beauty, wonder, intricacy, variety and delicately balanced interrelationships. Furthermore, because God made an orderly universe, there are natural laws that govern its ongoing motion and life.

The study of science, then, is simply finding out, in an organized way, as much as possible about the universe, and particularly about the natural laws, qualities and life-forms of the planet earth.

In this exploration of science, the spirit of wonder and curiosity which has already been spoken of in connection with other subject areas should be very much in evidence. Certainly the natural world is an endless source of fascinating, surprising realities. The recommended science texts offer a variety of lively, interest-provoking projects, but in addition, supplementary material from *Books Children Love* should be drawn upon. And wherever possible, experiments illustrating a particular concept should not only be conducted in the classroom, but should also be applied in real-life situations.

Work in the field should be regularly included in the science program. A weekly nature walk, notebooks in which observations made during the walks are recorded, and a variety of nature collections (leaves, pressed flowers, insects, etc.) all bring students into close contact with nature. Such contacts provide both tangible and intangible benefits and in some cases mark the start of a lifelong interest in nature.

$\boxed{13}$ Science

The study of science is approached with the understanding "that science and religion cannot, to the believer in God, by any possibility be antagonistic."[1] New areas of understanding and wonder are explored. Facts are learned, ideas are dealt with, and answers to questions are sought "so that the child can enjoy and understand his relationship with the world and the universe he lives in."[2]

Observation of the natural world is a vital part of the Child Light science program. Charlotte Mason found that by observing nature a child was stimulated to want to know more and to view science as an exciting subject. The wrong approach to the teaching of science can quickly kill any excitement for the subject. Observing and experimenting to discover answers and increase understanding are the most effective ways to acquire scientific knowledge.

All areas will be included at every grade level. However, the emphasis placed on each will vary from grade to grade.

Children will learn to use and understand the scientific method which will involve the use of reading and math skills—developing a scientific vocabulary, noticing likenesses and differences, classifying, sequencing, drawing conclusions, making generalizations, making inferences, noting cause and effect, measuring, and making graphs, charts, and diagrams. In addition, hypothesizing will be introduced.

As with all subject areas the science program should provide for individual interests and abilities. Enrichment, reinforcement, and a variety of activities need to be provided. Teacher's editions will give some suggestions. The teacher will need to select those that are applicable, delete others, and add any additional information, experiments, and activities needed in order to meet individual needs. *Books Children Love* also suggests books relating to science. It should be kept in mind that there is knowledge that is basic for all children to know.

Procedure

1. Nature walks and nature notebooks
   a. It is recommended that the children take a nature walk once a week. In some urban areas there may not be a park or other area that is accessible. In that case field trips to an area beyond the city should be planned during the year. Plants, flowers, and insects brought into the classroom, clouds viewed from the windows or playground, etc., are some ways that will give the children opportunity to observe if nothing else is available.
   b. During the walk the children observe all that they see—this is a time for observation, not instruction. The teacher should give the name of a plant, tree, or flower, and any other information only when asked to do so by the children. The children should be allowed to see things for themselves.
   c. Flowers, twigs, leaves, insects, etc., can be collected.
   d. Each child should have a nature notebook. The date of the walk should be recorded and anything else the child desires to record (what is seen, felt, or heard, drawings of what is seen, etc.). The recording can be done during and/or after the walk. How the notebook is done should be left up to the child. It should not be corrected or graded.
   e. Any specimens that were collected can be displayed or made into collection displays. Flowers or leaves can be pressed and saved, etc.
   f. Many lessons will grow out of the walk—the parts of a flower or plant, how the wings of a bird function, classifications, different types of clouds, weather, seasonal changes, etc.
   g. Textbooks and supplementary books should be used as an adjunct to the nature walk and observation.

2. Use the Scientific Method—teaches children to think for themselves.
   a. Ask a question—identify the problem.
   b. Seek to find the answer—investigate the problem.
   c. Form a hypothesis—a tentative answer to the question.
   d. Collect data.
   e. Observe and experiment to discover if the hypothesis is correct—answer the question.
   f. Continue to explore—gather information, observe, and experiment to test the solution in light of any new conclusions.

Note: A two-year science project for grade school children in any environment/climate is available by mail from England. Called *Starting From A Walk*, this has to be used carefully, or the free child-centered exploration outlined above could be spoiled.

However, it gives a bridge by suggesting projects initiated in the real world, but going on into the scientific discipline using more formal observation, recording and experimentation.

Order: *Starting From a Walk*, Wes, Murray House, Vandon St., London SW1 OAJ, England

First Grade Science

The first grade science program provides for observation of nature and an introduction to basic areas of science. The scientific method is presented and applied. Provision is also made for the correlation of science with other subject areas.

Curriculum

1. Vocabulary development—children should understand and be able to correctly use words and terms connected with the science program.
2. Participate in a weekly nature walk and keep a nature notebook.
3. The five senses—participate in activities that make use of the senses (seeing, hearing, touching, tasting, smelling), understand their importance and the adjustments that must be made when one of them does not function properly.
4. Weather
   a. Observe different types of weather throughout the school year.
   b. Keep a daily weather indicator (class and/or individual).
   c. The effect of weather on type of clothing worn
5. Plant growth
   a. Observe during nature walks.
   b. Observe plants in the classroom, on the school grounds, and at home.
   c. Plant seeds and observe the growth process—include what plants need in order to grow.
   d. View films, filmstrips, slides, TV, videos, and read books.
   e. Field trips—garden centers, nurseries, farms
   f. Have resource people share their expertise with the class.
6. Globes
   a. Locate land and water.

b. Use a flashlight to represent the sun. Shine it on a globe to show the cycle of day and night.

7. Seasons
   a. Observe the different seasons throughout the school year.
   b. Discuss clothing that is needed for the different seasons.
   c. Discuss food that is available in different seasons.
   d. Read books and view films, filmstrips, slides, TV, and videos to learn how seasons are the same or different in different parts of the country.

8. Health
   a. Growing—compare each child's height and weight at the beginning of the school year with those at the end of the year.
   b. Nutrition—learn what foods are necessary for good health.
   c. Sleep—develop an understanding that sleep is necessary for good health.
   d. Cleanliness—understand that clean bodies and teeth contribute to good health.
   e. Exercise—discover that it is an essential ingredient for a healthy body.
   f. Safety—know and use safety guidelines.
   g. Substance abuse prevention

   • Recognize that God made each individual unique and special.

   • Learn to identify feelings.

   • Develop good health habits.

   • Distinguish between safe and unsafe substances.

   • Learn how to handle pressure and stress.

9. Animals
   a. Observe animals—hamster or gerbil in the classroom, visit the zoo.
   b. Wild and domestic—observe the differences between an animal kept in the classroom, those in the petting zoo, the children's pets, and wild animals in the zoo. If there is not a zoo nearby use films to illustrate the differences.
   c. Read books about wild and domestic animals and view films, filmstrips, slides, TV, and videos.

10. Classifying
    a. Describe different objects noting details.

b. Place objects in groups according to size, color, or shape, etc.
11. Solids and liquids
    a. Develop an understanding that some elements can be in a solid or a liquid form.
    b. Observe water as a liquid and as a solid—compare and contrast.
12. Magnets
    Magnets should be introduced by allowing the children to experiment with them using the scientific method.
13. The earth we live on
    a. Created by God
    b. Develop an understanding that people who do not believe in the true God formulate their own ideas of how the earth came to be.
    c. Discover that the earth is made up of air, soil, rocks, and water.
    d. Learn about the effect of the sun and moon on the earth.

Second Grade Science

Second grade science continues to provide for the observation of nature and the development of knowledge in the basic areas of science. The scientific method is continued as is the correlation of science with other subject areas.

Curriculum

1. Vocabulary development—children should understand and be able to correctly use words and terms connected with the science program.
2. Knowledge of food groups
   a. Learn that eating from a variety of food groups is necessary for good health.
   b. Discover that food can be divided into various food groups and that foods from each group are needed for good health.
3. Substance abuse prevention
   a. Recognize that God made each individual special and unique.
   b. Learn to identify one's own feelings and the feelings of others.
   c. Learn how to express feelings.
   d. Learn to make good choices.
   e. Evaluate peer pressures in light of Biblical values.

     f. Identify people who can help with solving problems.
4. Understanding human growth
     a. Develop an understanding of physical growth.
     b. Understand that there are different life cycles—birth, infant, toddler, childhood, preadolescence, adolescence, young adult, middle years, older years, death.
5. Animals
     a. Classify animals into basic groups—mammals, birds, fish, reptiles, amphibians, insects, spiders.
     b. Learn about animals' homes.
     c. Develop an understanding of the eating habits of animals.
6. Sound and light
7. Earth
     a. Created by God
     b. Continue developing an understanding that men form creation ideas of their own if they do not believe in the true and living God.
     c. Observe different types of soil.
     d. Rocks—observe, collect, read about, and view films, filmstrips, slides, and videos.
     e. Introduce minerals with emphasis placed on those found in the local area and state.
     f. Learn about fossils through field trips, books, films, filmstrips, slides, and videos.
8. Introduce space studies.
9. Begin developing an understanding of the importance of ecology.
10. Plants and trees
     a. Observe.
     b. Classify—type, size, shape, etc.
     c. Field trips and nature walks
11. Weather
     a. Develop an understanding of how weather affects the way people live.
     b. Observe different types of weather and record observations.
12. Ocean
     a. Locate on maps and globes.
     b. Introduce oceanic plant and animal life.

Third Grade Science

    Observation of nature, application of the scientific method, and correlation of science with other subject areas are continued in the third grade science program. New areas of knowledge are introduced.

Curriculum

1. Vocabulary development—children should understand and be able to correctly use words and terms connected with the science program.
2. Participate in nature walks and keep a nature notebook.
3. Wild animals
    a. Natural habitats of wild animals
    b. Growth and development
    c. Care of the young
    d. Field trips to zoo and natural history museum
    e. Species classification
4. Health
    a. Food for good health
    b. Other elements necessary for good health
    c. Life cycles with emphasis on childhood
    d. Substance abuse prevention

    • Recognize that God loves each individual and made everyone special and unique.

    • View rules as guideline helpers.

    • Understand the effect of advertising on decision-making.

    • Learn about the dangers of ordinary household substances.

    • Develop an understanding of how medicine can be misused.

    • Recognize some of the harmful effects of cigarettes.

    • Recognize some of the harmful effects from the misuse of alcohol.

    • Learn to apply Biblical absolutes and principles to making decisions.

5. Plants
    a. Observation of plants under different conditions
    b. Planting and observing growth
    c. Experimenting to discover what plants need in order to grow
6. Earth
    a. How the earth began—for those who believe in God and for those who do not believe in the true God
    b. Continue to study rocks and fossils.
    c. Begin developing an understanding of the solar system.

    d. Continue the development of knowledge about space travel.
    e. Ecology and the Christian's responsibility
7. Electricity
    a. What it is
    b. How it is used

Fourth Grade Science

Fourth grade science provides for the application of knowledge to new and different problems. The use of the scientific method is further developed and the children are encouraged to conduct experiments as a means of learning. Observation of nature continues to be emphasized.

Curriculum

1. Vocabulary development—children should understand and be able to correctly use words and terms connected with the science program.
2. Participate in nature walks and keep a nature notebook.
3. Health
    a. Continue to develop the understanding that a variety of foods are necessary for good health.
    b. Biblical principles

      • Laws and habits of the Old Testament

      • New Testament position regarding food and health laws of the Old Testament

      • Application for today
    c. World health needs and the Biblical response
    d. Continue to develop the understanding of the activities that are essential for good health.

      • Care of the teeth

      • Proper amount of sleep

      • Exercise

      • Bathing

      • Immunizations

      • Proper fluid intake

      • Good safety habits

e. Substance abuse prevention

- Accepting one's self
- Understanding that man is made in God's image and therefore is of worth and value
- Developing good problem-solving skills
- Learning the proper use of nonprescription and prescription drugs
- Recognizing the dangers of smoking and alcohol abuse
- Learning how to break bad habits

4. Understanding human growth and development
   a. Increase the understanding of human growth and development
   b. Life cycles—birth, infant, toddler, childhood, preadolescence, adolescence, young adult, middle years, older years, and death. Emphasis should be placed on childhood.
5. Plants
   a. Observe, read about, and view films, filmstrips, slides, and videos.
   b. Ecology and the Biblical response in light of man being given dominion after the fall
   c. Food cycle—from seed to full growth. Include from seed to the wholesaler, to the market, to the retail purchaser.
   d. Classification of various types of plants
6. Machines
   a. Development of machines
   b. Uses of machines
   c. Future development and needs
7. Space exploration
   a. Development of space exploration
   b. Present exploration
   c. Future exploration
8. Earth's surface
   a. Origin—Christian belief and that of those who do not believe in the living and true God
   b. Changes that take place
9. Animals
   a. Observation
   b. Life cycles
   c. Ecology

10. Weather
    a. Observation
    b. Effect on people
    c. Effect on crops
    d. Effect on ecology
11. Oceans
    a. Review oceanic plants and animals.
    b. Tides and their effect on the earth
    c. Currents
    d. Resources and their use and misuse
12. Solar system
    a. The planets, how they function and their relationship to the earth
    b. Meteors, asteroids, and comets

Fifth Grade Science

Fifth grade science continues to provide for observation of nature, the application of knowledge to new areas, the use of the scientific method, and experimenting. Origins are studied more in depth. Science studies are correlated with other subject areas.

Curriculum

1. Vocabulary development—children should understand and be able to correctly use words and terms connected with the science program.
2. Nature walks and nature notebooks
3. Human body
    a. Growth and development including life cycles—birth, infant, toddler, childhood, preadolescence, adolescence, young adult, middle years, older years, death. Emphasis should be on preadolescence.
    b. Nutritional needs

       • Food groups and daily amounts needed from each for good health

       • Abuses of food—overeating and undereating

    c. Health needs

       • Prevention as a means to good health

       • Exercise, rest, and cleanliness

    d. The five senses

     e. Skeletal system
     f. Circulatory system
     g. Excretory system
     h. Safety guidelines
     i. Substance abuse prevention

- Understanding that the Christian's body is the temple of the Holy Spirit

- Learning to accept yourself

- Realizing that people are made in the image of God and therefore are of worth and value

- Developing an understanding of Biblical absolutes and principles and learning how to apply them when dealing with feelings, pressures, stress, and conflicts

- Developing an understanding that advertising can affect choices that are made

- Understanding the dangers of smoking and alcohol and medicine abuse

4. Living organisms
    a. Cells
    b. Plants
    c. Animals—vertebrates and invertebrates
5. The world in which we live
    a. Origin—Biblical and non-Biblical positions
    b. Oceans—Pacific, Atlantic, Indian, Arctic, Antarctic ⊬

- Uses

- Misuses

- Plants and animals of the ocean

    c. Solar system

- Constellations

- Galaxies

- Measuring distances

    d. Ecology and the Christian's responsibility in light of man being given dominion after the fall
6. The atom
    a. What it is
    b. Uses

7. Light and sound ʁ
8. Matter
    a. Physical properties and changes
    b. Mixtures, solutions, and suspensions
    c. Chemical changes
9. Energy
    a. Fuels
    b. Nuclear, solar, geothermal, wind
    c. Electricity ʁ
10. Space travel
    a. People involved
    b. Future of space travel
    c. Effects of space travel

Sixth Grade Science

The sixth grade science program continues to emphasize the observation of nature, use of the scientific method, and application of knowledge to new and different areas. There is a continued in-depth study of orgins. The correlation of science with other subject areas is included.

Curriculum

1. Vocabulary development—children should understand and be able to correctly use words and terms connected with the science program.
2. Nature walks to observe nature—nature notebooks are kept.
3. Emotions—what they are and how to handle them
4. Cells
    a. Parts of a cell
    b. Classification of cells
5. Use and care of scientific equipment and models with emphasis on the individual's responsibility
6. Human body
    a. Prevention of disease
    b. Effect of spiritual condition on physical condition
    c. Effect of physical condition on spiritual condition
    d. Food and nutrition
    e. Body functions
    f. Heredity
    g. Systems of the body

        • Endocrine

        • Nervous

        • Disorders

h. Life cycles—emphasis on preadolescence and adolescence. The tape series *Preparing for Adolescence* by Dr. James Dobson is recommended. It is an excellent help in presenting this stage of the life cycle.

i. Substance abuse prevention

- Recognize that every individual is created in God's image and is of worth and value.

- Apply Biblical absolutes and principles to daily living.

- Identify personal likes and dislikes, the effect of feelings on decision-making, and the consequences of poor choices and good choices.

- Establish individual goals.

- Know what resources are available to aid in solving problems.

- Increase the understanding of the dangers of smoking, alcohol abuse, and abuse of medicines.

7. Matter
   a. What it is
   b. Classification—elements, compounds, mixtures
   c. Atoms
   d. Acids, bases, salts
   e. Chemical changes

8. Energy, motion, force
   a. Identify and understand how they function.
   b. Develop a more thorough understanding through experiments.

9. Earth
   a. Origins—a deeper understanding of creation and evolution
   b. Resources
   c. Changes
   d. Ecology and the individual's responsibility in light of man being given dominion after the fall

10. Electricity
    a. Electrons
    b. Radio, telephone, TV
    c. Sound waves
    d. Computers

11. Light
    a. Nature and behavior of light
    b. Laser light and its uses

      c. Effect on daily life

      d. Sources of light

12. Weather

      a. Observing and recording different types of weather

      b. Reading and constructing weather maps

      c. Understanding how weather predictions are made

      d. Learning the causes of different types of severe weather—thunderstorms, tornadoes, hurricanes

      e. Understanding the effect of weather on daily living

13. Space travel and exploration

      a. Exploring from the earth

      b. Exploring from space

      c. People involved

      d. NASA

      e. Future plans and possibilities

      f. Effect on daily living

14 Bible Overview

Because each group, and even each home, has strongly held views of Biblical truth and how to present it, Child Light is not offering extensive overview comments on the study of the Bible.

Child Light does, however, strongly urge that children read the content of the Bible itself—first in the form of a child's story Bible and then, as early as appropriate for the particular child (or children) in a good translation of the Bible.

The importance of a child's becoming at home in the Scriptures and of having a thorough knowledge and understanding of both the facts and the applications of God's Word in its entirety, cannot be overestimated. Education in both the content and practical application of Biblical truth should be the first priority in a child's learning experience. (The suggestions made in the Reading section of the Language Arts Overview about involving young children in the reading process are fully applicable to the reading of Bible stories to young children in the home.)

The Child Light program includes a class period in which the Bible is read aloud daily. Child Light recommends the use of the New International Version, but obviously the selection of a particular translation is left to the discretion of each school or home. For the early grades, story Bibles on two reading levels are recommended for use when material that is more simply stated than the Biblical text seems appropriate.

The Bible reading is done orally at all levels—by the teacher or parent in the early grades and by students or teacher/parent in more advanced grades.

The narration process is used in these classes. During this time questions as to meaning will arise, opinions will be expressed in relation to values and Biblical teachings, and the teacher/parent and students alike will be involved in the bringing out of truth and the illumination of the passage that has been read.

An important resource in the lively discussions that will often bubble up after a Bible reading relating to the children's lives, their own thinking, and what is important to them is the supervising *adult*(s), whether parent or teacher. The adult must be ready for the questions. Therefore, this important aspect is given full attention in Chapter 23, "Developing a Christian Mind and a Christian Worldview." Some of the books listed there for the adults will also be relevant to discussions with older children, and could be referred to with abler thinkers of ten or eleven years old, especially *What Happened to the Human Race?, How Should We Then Live?, Christianity Is Jewish*, and *How to Be Your Own Selfish Pig*. Short passages that the adult finds interesting and relevant will be appreciated by older children accustomed to discussion. But the *ideas* in the chapter are important for discussions in kindergarten as well.

In addition, *Books Children Love* includes a number of biographies, stories, and other appropriate books with a Christian emphasis.

$\boxed{15}$ Bible

T he application of a Christian worldview in contemporary society is the result of being able to think Christianly. The Bible is God's truth and it is only as all of life is viewed from a Biblical framework of reference that a Christian worldview is possible. Therefore, the natural integration of Scripture into all subject areas is an essential part of the Child Light program. In addition, Child Light emphasizes the importance of developing the habit of reading and studying God's Word because it *is* truth and the basis for all of life.

Charlotte Mason felt that "the knowledge of God is the principal knowledge, and no teaching of the Bible which does not further that knowledge is of religious value."[1]

Reading, studying, and memorizing Scripture; prayer; obedience to God's Word; and living a lifestyle that is consistent with the Bible are best learned in the home. The school does not assume the responsibility of the parent, but is a support system that assists in furthering the child's knowledge of God.

Bible Teaching

The recommended method for teaching Bible is that which Charlotte Mason used. The Scripture is read to the children and is allowed to speak for itself. The children are not told what it says or what to think, but are allowed to see for themselves what God says. An Old Testament passage is read on Monday, Wednesday, and Friday and a New Testament passage on Tuesday and Thursday. The major and minor prophets are read in connection with the books about the kings.

Procedure

1. Review the passage read previously.
2. The teacher presents background material for the new passage—vocabulary, pictures, illustrations, customs, geography, setting, etc., and emphasizes "briefly but reverently any spiritual or moral truth."[2] For younger children an accurate pictorial account is read from a Bible storybook. For older children a pictorial or background account on their level is read.
3. The reading is then briefly discussed.
4. The teacher then reads reverently, carefully, and with expression the "incident or definite teaching"[3] directly from the Bible. The passage should not be too long and should be read only once.
5. Immediately following the reading the children narrate what has been read and "they do this with curious accuracy and yet with some originality, conveying the spiritual teaching which the teacher has indicated. Now this is no parrot-exercise, but is the result of such an assimilation of the passage that it has become a part of the young scholar."[4] Any research which has a bearing on the passage is discussed.

Memorization

Since the Word of God serves as a source of information, a means of communication with God—and as a source to shape and reshape our mentality, our outlook on life and the renewal of our mind which brings us into a closer correspondence with the mind of God[5]—Child Light stresses the importance of passage memorization. Charlotte Mason also emphasized the memorization of Scripture: "It is a delightful thing to have the memory stored with beautiful, comforting, and inspiring passages, and we cannot tell when and how this manner of seed may spring up, grow, and bear fruit."[6] The memorization process should be a relaxed, natural part of the Bible program and never become a burden. By following the recommended procedure the children will learn whole passages without feeling pressured.

Procedure for Memorizing Scripture

1. The first day the teacher reads the entire passage to the children two or three times.
2. The next day the entire passage is read once. The teacher then recites a short section (two or three verses) several times until the children think they know it. The children and the teacher then recite the section together three or four times.
3. On succeeding days the entire passage is read. The teacher and

children recite the portion that has already been learned. The teacher recites the next section several times. Then the children recite the new section with the teacher. This procedure is continued until the whole passage has been learned.

Outreach

Opportunities should be provided for the children to develop a Christian compassion for others on a local, national, and world level. Concern needs to be followed by practical action being taken to meet physical, material, and spiritual needs. The application of a Christian worldview in contemporary society is an essential part in the development of Christian character traits.

Curriculum

The Bible introduces children to people who lived at a specific time in history and to the God who worked in their lives and continues to work in the lives of those living at the present time in history. They learn about the triune God—the Father who is caring, loving, and just; the Son who paid the penalty for their sin; and the Holy Spirit who helps them in all areas of their lives. That there should be no separation in their lives between the secular and the spiritual is emphasized in their study of the Bible and by the natural integration of a Biblical framework of reference in all subject areas.

In order for the entire Bible to be covered during the elementary years, it is suggested that stories and incidents be selected from the books listed for each grade level. As much as possible, stories should be presented in chronological order to give students a sense of the flow of history. Suggestions for passage memorization are also given.

First Grade

Old Testament—Genesis Jonah
New Testament—Luke James
Memorization—Psalms 1, 100, 150 Luke 2:8-14 Luke 24:36-47
Luke 6:46-49

Second Grade

Old Testament—Exodus Leviticus Numbers Deuteronomy
New Testament—Matthew Acts
Memorization—Psalms 23, 117, 121 Matthew 2:1-12 Matthew 6:9-13 Matthew 28:1-10 Exodus 20:1-17 or Deuteronomy 5:6-21 (Ten Commandments)

Third Grade

Old Testament—Joshua Judges Ruth Ezra Nehemiah Esther Job
New Testament—John Philemon I & II Thessalonians I & II Timothy Titus
Memorization—Psalms 119:9-16, 133 John 3:16-21 John 20:11-18 Matthew 5:3-11 II Timothy 6:17-19

Fourth Grade

Old Testament—Haggai Zechariah Malachi I Samuel 1-8 Joel
New Testament—Mark Hebrews I & II Peter
Memorization—Psalms 111, 148 Mark 16:1-7 Luke 10:25-37 Hebrews 11:1-13 Proverbs 3:13-18

Fifth Grade

Old Testament—I Samuel 9-30 II Samuel I Kings 1-11 I Chronicles II Chronicles 1-11 Ecclesiastes Obadiah
New Testament—Galatians Ephesians Philippians Colossians Revelation
Memorization—Psalms 98, 136 Proverbs 3:3-6 Galatians 5:13-26 Ephesians 6:10-18 I Chronicles 29:10-13

Sixth Grade

Old Testament—I Kings 12-21 II Kings Ezekiel Lamentations Jeremiah Isaiah Hosea Amos Micah Nahum Habakkuk Zephaniah Song of Solomon
New Testament—Romans I & II Corinthians I, II, & III John Jude
Memorization—Psalms 24, 92 Proverbs 2:6-15 Romans 11:33-36 I Corinthians 13 Isaiah 53

All Grade Levels

Selected Psalms and Proverbs should be read to or by the children at all grade levels.

Many Bible passages and verses, the books of the Bible, and the names of the disciples, etc., have been set to music. Learning these songs is an easy way for additional memorization to be done.

Hymns, contemporary songs, and children's songs should be included in the Bible program. See the music curriculum guide for suggestions on the correlation of music and Bible.

Prayer, music as a means of praise and worship, and missions should be emphasized. The fact that cults and Eastern religious thought are not based on Biblical truth must be understood by today's child. Jesus is the only way and the truth and the life and no one comes to the Father except through Him (John 14:6).

Note: It is highly recommended that pages 92-104 of *For the Children's Sake*, by Susan Schaeffer Macaulay be read for a more complete understanding of the importance of the Bible in the Child Light program.

SUGGESTED BOOKS
The Child's World series is recommended for use with first graders. There are ten books in the series—*Caring, Honesty, Love, Courage, Obedience, Kindness, Joy, Self-Control, Hugging, Helping Is*.
(Children's Press, 1224 West Van Buren Street, Chicago, IL 60607)
See *Books Children Love* for suggested books on all levels.

16 Art and Music Overview

The development of art and music programs is necessarily a very individualized matter for most schools or home education situations. The interests, tastes, skills, resources and abilities of the people involved will vary widely, but Child Light urges as much participation in, and exploration of, these rewarding and significant arts as possible. *Books Children Love* contains a number of fine entries in both areas.

Three lines of activity are suggested in art: first, the creation of drawings and paintings, collages, molded or carved objects, photographic art and a wealth of other art forms, by the students; second, the study of the paintings of renowned artists on a methodical basis in which students observe reproductions of several works by the same artist during, say, the nine weeks of a school quarter. (Further discussion of this is found in the art subject guide.) The third suggested art activity is field trips to museums, galleries and other locations so that the students may see fine art firsthand.

In addition to the specific focus on art as a subject, Child Light urges the inclusion of graphic representations by students in connection with all the other subjects. For example, children may be asked to sketch a landform or an artifact in social studies, make charts or graphs in mathematics, attempt to depict a character or setting from literature and draw a plant in science.

However broad or limited the scope of the art emphasis may be in a particular school or home, there should be an ongoing awareness and acknowledgement of, and focus upon, the beauty, artistic form and expression seen on every hand, both in the natural world and in man's varied creations.

As in art, three areas of activity are suggested in music. First of all, personal participation in some kind of musical activity is something

□ *187*

no child should be denied, even if it is simply to clap and sing with others. Combinations of motion and music are particularly appealing to children and create a wonderful atmosphere of joy and freedom. A number of entries in *Books Children Love* and sections in the music subject guide offer details on such activities. Also, in some schools, children's musicals, choral singing programs, etc., are done each year and can be a source of valuable learning and great enjoyment.

Ideally, in the second area of activity, instruction will be offered in the academics of music: interpreting and reading a musical score (a valuable and much-neglected skill), learning about the various musical instruments, the components of a symphony orchestra, etc., and studying the lives and works of famous composers.

Finally, frequent experience of listening to tapes or records of a wide range of music should be part of the everyday program and also, if possible, a variety of professional concerts attended. A word of caution here: it is important that the adult who supervises such activities has a true love and appreciation for the music selected, however untrained in music he or she may be. The fact that the adult may also be having a learning experience is not a disadvantage; the only negative situation is one in which music is "taken" like a distasteful medicine—an approach clearly to be avoided.

17 Music

T he music program endeavors to help the children develop an appreciation for various types of music, learn a variety of songs and hymns, understand the elements of music, identify and appreciate various musical instruments, and become familiar with various composers. There should be a specific time during the school week for music instruction as well as the correlation of music with other activities.

Curriculum

1. Development of a music vocabulary: rhythm, tempo, tone, accent, meter, register, staff, whole note, half note, quarter note, key, rest, scale, major, minor, sharp, flat, a cappella, chord, clef, measure, pitch, part singing, round, soprano, alto, contralto, tenor, baritone, bass, baton
2. Suggested materials—rhythm instruments; flutaphones; autoharp; guitar; piano and/or pitch pipe; chalkboard staff liner; records and tapes; phonographs; cassette players; pictures—composers, orchestras, bands, musical instruments
3. Suggested activities
   a. *Grades one to three*
      • Musical games

      • Songs—nursery rhymes, children's songs, hymns, choruses, Bible verses, folk, patriotic, foreign, traditional, etc.

      • Music for movement—ballet, folk dances, square dances, physical fitness exercises, aerobics

      • Developing the ability to sing on pitch with good tone quality

- Rhythmic patterns—rhythm band, games, clapping to develop an understanding of accented and unaccented notes and rests

- Recognizing the shape and sound of individual instruments

- Listen to music and identify the mood, feeling, or emotion that is expressed.

- Recognize high and low sounds.

- Recognize that styles of music vary according to the time in history in which the music was written.

- Develop the ability to recognize simple pitches—middle C, G, A.

- Recognize fast and slow tempos.

- Learn the names of the five lines and four spaces in treble clef.

- Identify whole and half rests.

- Field trips—visit music stores, have small groups from the local symphony come to the school to present a program, have resource people come and sing, play, or dance for the children, attend a concert or children's musical.

b. *Grades four to six*
   - Learn the music symbols.

   - Learn to read the key signatures.

   - Develop the ability to read notes--three octaves, bass C to treble C (fourth grade) and four octaves (fifth grade).

   - Identify note values—whole, half, quarter, eighth, sixteenth.

   - Ability to identify quarter, eighth, and sixteenth rests

   - Develop a beginning understanding of music composition.

   - Learn to play a flutaphone.

   - Learn to play an autoharp.

   - Use proper breathing and enunciation when singing.

   - Recognize key signatures.

- Recognize time signatures.

- Identify sharps and flats.

- Learn the rhythm patterns for sixteenth, eighth, quarter, half, whole, and dotted half notes.

- Know the major scales—including pattern of steps.

- Be able to sight read new songs (sixth grade).

- Take field trips—to music stores, concerts (including orchestra, band, and vocal), have resource people in to play an instrument and tell about it or to sing or dance, attend a musical.

4. Ideas for correlation activities—these suggestions are not intended to be an exhaustive list.
    a. Language arts—listen to music from the period in which the literature being studied was written, learn the alphabet song and songs from movies of various fairy tales, listen to records and tapes that use songs to tell stories being used in literature, write original words for a favorite tune, write music for an original poem or for a favorite poem.
    b. Social studies—learn songs from the countries being studied and listen to music representative of the period being studied.
    c. Math—note value, rest value, number of notes or rests in a measure, number of measures in a song
    d. Science—learn songs about nature and the universe.
    e. Bible—learn hymns, choruses, and Bible verses set to music, and listen to music such as *The Messiah,* Bach fugues, and contemporary Christian music.
    f. Art—listen to a piece of music and draw a picture representing what was felt or seen in the mind while listening.
    g. P.E.—musical games, exercises, dance, aerobics
5. Great composers—one composer should be selected for each nine-week period. Good quality recordings (records or cassettes) which illustrate various aspects of the composer's work should be listened to. These can be played at a specific music time, during a rest period, as the children enter in the morning, or at other times throughout the day.

Procedure For Studying Great Composers
    a. Introduce any new vocabulary.

- Briefly introduce the composer—his/her country (locate on map or globe), his/her life (locate his/her time in history on a historical timeline), people that influenced him/her, and any other pertinent information.

- Introduce a short selection by the composer. After the children listen to it, allow them to react to it—how it made them feel, etc.

- Play a selection several times during the nine-week period so that the children learn to recognize it. Two to four selections should be chosen to be played often and others listened to once or twice to illustrate different types of music that the composer wrote. The children could be allowed to choose their favorites from those which are played and these should be played often. Write the name of the composer and the composition on the chalkboard so that the children become familiar with them. This should be a very low-key, relaxed time.

- Take the children to a concert featuring work of the composer who is being studied.

- Use resource people if they are available.

- Some suggested composers: Henry Purcell, Antonio Vivaldi, Johann Sebastian Bach, George Handel, Joseph Haydn, Wolfgang Amadeus Mozart, Ludwig van Beethoven, Franz Schubert, Felix Mendelssohn, Frederic Chopin, Robert Schumann, Franz Liszt, Richard Wagner, Giuseppe Verdi, Johnnes Brahms, Georges Bizet, Peter I. Tchaikovsky, Antonin Dvorak, Nicholas Rimsky-Korsakov, Giacomo Puccini, Niccolo Paganini, Gustav Mahler, Claude Debussy, Johann Strauss, Sergei Rachmaninoff, Maurice Ravel, Richard Strauss, Igor Stravinsky, Aaron Copland, Leonard Bernstein, George Gershwin, Morton Gould, Fritz Kreisler, Edward MacDowell, Camille Saint-Saens, John Williams, and other present-day composers

Note: Two composers could be introduced each nine-week period in grades four through six, if desired.

8. Suggested books:

Modern Composers for Young People   Gladys Burch

Famous Women Singers   Homer Ulrich

Famous Modern Conductors   David Ewen

Famous Composers   Gladys Burch and John Wolcott

Famous Conductors   David Ewen

The Nutcracker   adapted and illustrated by Warren Chappell

American Indian Music and Musical Instruments   George S. Fichter

Aida   Guiseppe Verdi (Franklin Watts, Inc.)

American Composers   Elsa Z. Posell

Peter and the Wolf   Sergei Prokofiev (Alfred A. Knopf)

First Book of the Opera   Noel Streatfield

Great Performers   Patricia Young

Famous Violinists for Young People   Gladys Burch

Star-Spangled Banner   Peter Spier

Let's Learn About the Orchestra   Carla Green

Haydn   Reba P. Mirsky

See *Books Children Love* for additional suggestions.

Art

The art program provides for the development of artistic and creative abilities, an appreciation for various art forms, and a familiarity with the works of great artists. Art is easily correlated with other subjects, but there should also be a specific time set aside each week for art instruction.

Curriculum

1. Development of an art vocabulary: color words, mosaic, collage, texture (descriptive words), light and dark, shapes, foreground, background, composition, arrangement, organization, design, pen and ink, papier-mâché, shading, shadows, portrait, landscape, still life, perspective, crayon resist, abstract, warp and woof, embroidery stitch names, etching, sketch, oil paint, tempera paint, watercolor, pastels, acrylic paint, sculpture

2. Basic supplies: newspapers; magazines; crayons; scissors; tempera paint; easel brushes; paste or glue; newsprint; manila paper; construction paper (varied colors); wallpaper scraps and sample books; plastic sponges; paper towels; tissue paper; crepe paper; charcoal; pastels; acrylic paint; watercolors; watercolor brushes; clay; masking tape; *X-acto* knives; boxes of scraps—yarn, material, felt, cotton, buttons; glitter, string, egg cartons, small boxes, plastic flowers, etc.; cameras and film; books about artists, paintings, and other art areas; reproductions of paintings; pictures of sculptures

3. The same types of activities are applicable for each grade level but with a different emphasis. The children should be allowed to experiment with various mediums and each child should feel a sense of satisfaction as they express their creativity and enjoy

different art forms. Suggested activities include: self-portrait; sketching (still life, landscape, trees); papier-mâché; tempera painting; crayon, chalk, pastels, charcoal drawings; torn paper pictures (construction paper, pictures from magazines); collage (cloth, yarn, seeds, pictures, leaves, twigs); clay; printing—sponge, potato, cork; carving; models; designs; patterns; visit art museums, art galleries, artists' studios, art supply stores, etc.; have resource people come to the school—artists, museum personnel, etc.

4. Suggested correlation activities—every subject offers many opportunities for art correlation. The following suggestions are not intended to be an exhaustive list.

   a. Language arts—illustrate poems or stories from literature, illustrate an original poem or story, make backgrounds for plays, draw pictures to make a "TV program," make backgrounds for a puppet show.

   b. Math—construct graphs, diagrams.

   c. Social studies—murals, timelines, draw pictures to illustrate a folktale or myth, construct models, draw or make models of different types of architecture.

   d. Science—graphs, charts, diagrams, illustrations

   e. Music—illustrate what a piece of music makes you see or feel.

   f. Bible—backgrounds for plays or puppet shows, pictures for a "TV program," murals, booklets

5. Paintings and artists—one artist should be selected for each nine-week period. Four to six reproductions (4" x 6" or 5" x 7") which represent different aspects of the artist's work should be mounted on cardboard and placed in a folder—one set for each child. If small prints are not available then large ones can be mounted and displayed in the classroom. (Some public libraries have reproductions that can be borrowed.) The class could work together as a group or be divided into small groups and each group work with a different picture. The groups would need to rotate so that each group would study every picture during the nine-week period. It should be kept in mind that "the object of these lessons is that the pupils should learn how to appreciate rather than how to produce."[1]

Procedure for Study of Artists

   • Introduce any new vocabulary and give background information. (If the painting is in a rural setting and the children live in the city, information would need to be given about country living, etc.)

- Briefly introduce the artist—his/her country (locate it on a map or globe), his/her life (locate the time in history on a historical timeline), people that he/she knew, etc.

- The children then study a reproduction. "Children learn, not merely to see a picture but *to look at it,* taking in every detail."[2] After two or three minutes, have the children close their eyes, visualize the picture and then open their eyes and check their visual image.

- After the children have had sufficient time to study the picture it should be turned over and the children should describe it by means of narration—the narration can be done in pairs or as a class.

  . . . a dog driving a flock of sheep along a road but nobody with the dog. Ah, there is a boy lying down by the stream drinking. It is morning as you can see by the light so the sheep are being driven to pasture, and so on; nothing is left out, the discarded plough, the crooked birch, the clouds beautiful in form and threatening rain, there is enough for half an hour's talk and memory in this little reproduction of a great picture and the children will know it wherever they see it, whether a signed proof, a copy in oils, or the original itself in one of our galleries.[3]

- Give each student a piece of paper and let them do a rough sketch of the picture from memory.

Of course, as with the narration, children are offering something of themselves. We must not jump on it critically. "You're wrong, you made the house bigger than it was." We must let them see for themselves. They then turn the picture over and look at it *hard.* Maybe they'll want to try again.[4]

- At the end of the nine-week period let each child choose his/her favorite reproduction and, if possible, give them a small print of it to keep.

- If a museum or gallery has the original of any of the pictures being studied or other pictures by the same artist, take the children on a field trip to view them.

- If there is someone in the area who is an expert on a certain painter, that person might be able to give a brief background talk about the artist.

- Suggested books:

  Famous American Painters   Roland Joseph McKinney

  Famous Old Masters of Painting   Roland Joseph McKinney

  Famous French Painters   Roland Joseph McKinney

  Visiting the Art Museum   Laurene K. Brown and Marc Brown

  Famous Artists of the Past   Alice Chase

  The Great Picture Robbery   Leon Harris

  The Art of Africa and others in The Art of . . . series   Shirley Glubok

  Looking at Art   Alice Chase

  See *Books Children Love* for additional suggestions.

- Suggested artists:

  American: Norman Rockwell, Mary Cassatt, Frederic Remington, Charles Russell, Andrew Wyeth, Grandma Moses, Grant Wood, Winslow Homer, John Audubon
  English: Thomas Gainsborough, John Constable, Joseph N. W. Turner, Sir Joshua Reynolds, Sir Henry Raeburn, William Blake
  Swiss: Paul Klee
  Dutch: Rembrandt, Vincent Van Gogh, Jon Vermeer, Pieter de Hooch
  Italian: Leonardo da Vinci, Raphael, Michelangelo
  French: Claude Monet, Jean Francois Millet, Henri Matisse, Pierre Auguste Renoir, Edouard Manet, Georges Seurat
  Spanish: Francisco Goya, Pablo Picasso, Diego Valazquez, El Greco
  Mexican: Jose Orozco, Diego Rivera

19 Physical Education Overview

The extent and nature of a physical education program varies with the individual situation. It is, however, very important that children participate regularly in supervised bodily exercise appropriate to their stage of physical development. No group is too small to engage in guided motion activities or fitness exercises. It is important that the person supervising these activities be aware of what should be done, of the importance of the warm-up period, the potential for injury in fitness and aerobic exercising, etc.

Excellent books on these topics and also on games for the various grade levels of children are included in *Books Children Love.*

20 Physical Education

P hysical education should be an important and integral part of the total educational process. A good physical education program provides progressive, sequential instruction that includes basic movement and the development of activities for a lifetime of enjoyment and healthy living. The activities must be appropriate for each child's age level and abilities.

Proper competition in physical education provides excellent motivation for activity and for the development of skills. Competition in games provides a means for children to learn to adjust to winning and losing and to develop positive attitudes. Interclass, intramural, and field day competition are ways in which healthy competition can take place. Extramural competition should not be a part of an elementary school physical education program.

Tennis shoes and socks and comfortable, appropriate clothing should be worn for physical education activities. Some activities, such as those promoting motor development, may best be done without shoes. Good judgment on the part of the instructor should always be exercised in regard to dress and safety measures.

Curriculum

First, Second, and Third Grade

1. Basic Skills
   a. Running—Point the toes forward, bend the knees, and lean forward. Swing the arms with elbows bent. Be sure they move beside the body and not across it. Land on the balls of the feet.
   b. Jumping—the knees should be bent and the arms should

□ *201*

swing down and backward. Push off from both feet, swing the arms forward, and lift the body into the air. Land on both feet with the knees bent.

c. Catching—first and second grade children should begin by catching balls thrown below the waist or underhanded throws that are thrown from a short distance. When a child is learning to catch, several things should be emphasized. Children will usually begin catching with their arms. They should not be penalized for this, but the correct method should be taught.

- Always watch the ball.

- Keep the hands spread.

- Fingers should be pointing up, the thumbs toward each other, and the hands slightly spread when catching above the waist.

- Fingers should be pointing down, thumbs pointing out, and the hands slightly spread when catching below the waist.

d. Throwing
   - Tossing a ball (first grade)—stand with the feet apart and the knees slightly bent. Hold the ball in both hands between the knees. Straighten the knees and bring the ball up, releasing it at waist height.

   - Two-arm shoulder throw—the ball is placed in the right hand, above the right shoulder. It is steadied by the left hand. The left foot is forward and the weight is on the right foot. Vigorously straighten the right arm and release the ball at arms' length and transfer the weight to the left foot.

   - Sidearm throw—turn the body slightly to the right, with the left foot forward and the weight on the right foot. The ball is held to the side and back and the elbow is bent. The arm is swung forward parallel to the ground. The ball is released waist high with a snap of the wrist and the weight is transferred to the left foot.

   - Underhand pitch—stand with the feet parallel and hold the ball in both hands in front of the body. Fully extend the right arm and swing it down and back. Then swing it forward, parallel to the body, and step forward on the left foot, releasing the ball at waist height.

Note: A left-handed child would reverse the hand and foot instructions.

- Jumping—develop the ability to jump rope when turning it oneself or when it is turned by others.

2. Developmental skills
   a. By the time students complete the first grade each child should be able to perform the following skills reasonably well.

   - Skipping

   - Running without falling

   - Throwing and catching beanbags and large balls on the first bounce

   - Rolling a ball

   - Bouncing and catching a ball

   - Managing simple jump rope skills and jumping over objects

   - Kicking a stationary ball with reasonable accuracy

   b. At the end of the second grade each child should be able to perform the following skills.

   - Skipping forward and backward

   - Running (stopping, starting, and changing direction)

   - Throwing accurately and catching from a distance of ten feet

   - Bouncing a ball with skill

   - Dribbling while standing in place and while moving

   - Jumping or hurdling objects about knee high and performing simple skills with a rope

   - Kicking a moving ball forward

   - Striking a ball from the hand for a short distance

   c. In the third grade these basic skill patterns should be developed.

- Running and dodging and making changes in direction while running full speed
- Throwing and catching different sizes of balls with a partner
- Dribbling in a straight line without looking at the ball
- Passing and shooting (chest pass and shot)
- Soccer-style kicking with control and accuracy
- Jumping single and double ropes
- Striking a volleyball for a sufficient distance

3. Movement education—movement education is a method or approach to teaching physical education where the teacher directs but does not show the children how to move. It can be adapted to all age levels. The children experiment, explore, imagine, and move.

a. Basic movements

- Locomotor—walking, running, jumping, hopping, leaping, skipping, sliding, galloping (singly or in combinations)

- Non-locomotor—bending, stretching, twisting

Note: These basic movement skills should be taught through movement experiences, fundamental rhythms, drill, simple games, and relays.

b. Variations

- Direction—forward, backward, laterally, diagonally
- Level—high, medium, low
- Force—light, medium, heavy
- Speed—slow, medium, fast, accelerate, decelerate, uneven, even
- Space—large, medium, small, wide, narrow
- Emotion—frightened, happy, sad, characters, animals, machines

c. Equipment—all of these movements can be employed with or without equipment.

• With equipment—equipment used to teach movement can be such things as ropes, hoops, wands, beanbags, balls, etc.

Example: Place hoop on the floor and instruct the children to: sit inside, jump around it with the left and then the right foot, move around it with part of an arm inside, skip in and out, move clockwise around the hoop, reverse the direction, etc.

• Without equipment—the children can act out anything and exercise at the same time. Example: act like a dog, walk like a bird with a broken wing, slither like a snake, wiggle like a worm, act like a cat catching a mouse, walk quietly, loudly, tall, short, etc.

4. Activities
    a. Always begin with vigorous warm-up activities and end with less demanding activities.
    b. Engage in vigorous and varied exercises that use the large muscles.
    c. Provide frequent rest and relaxation periods.
    d. Develop physical endurance.
    e. Engage in group activities.
    f. Develop basic social qualities—courtesy, cooperation, good citizenship, respect of others, honesty.
    g. Provide games with simple rules.
    h. Develop good sportsmanship by learning to win or lose gracefully.
    i. Include health and safety instruction and the development of Christian values.

Fourth, Fifth, and Sixth Grades

1. Begin with vigorous warm-up activities.
2. Provide longer activity periods and gradually place more stress on skill instruction.
3. Emphasize good body mechanics, posture, and movement in sports and daily living.
4. Encourage movement accuracy and good form.
5. Continue to develop good sportsmanship by learning to win or lose gracefully and manifesting team loyalty.
6. Provide for rhythm and balancing development through folk and square dancing and aerobics.
7. Present a varied program which utilizes many types of activities.

8. Provide for the need of belonging through team and squad games and activities.
9. Keep the competition at the children's level.
10. Include health and safety instruction and the development of Christian values.

Elementary Physical Education Skills Checklist

1. Motor development
   a. Space orientation—move from one space to another, continually move body in space.
   b. Place self in group formations—single lines, circle, square, or triangle, double-column lines, and any other formations.
   c. Balance—ability to keep balance when changing positions and while standing
   d. Development of eye/foot coordination and eye/hand coordination
2. Locomotive skills—running, jumping (either foot, height, distance), jumping rope, skipping, galloping, leaping, and hopping (both feet, either foot)
3. Motor skills—ability to start or stop at a given signal whether visual or audible, ability to avoid stationary and moving objects, pivoting, catching and throwing balls, kicking, batting, and dribbling
4. Gymnastic skills—rolling, swinging, landing, and balancing
5. Ability to follow the rules of games
6. Development of aerobic skills
7. Rhythm skill development
8. Jumping or hurdling objects about knee high
9. Performing simple skills with a rope
10. Kicking a moving ball forward
11. Striking the ball from the hand for a short distance

$\boxed{21}$ Textbooks

The Child Light curriculum guides can be used with any textbooks. Supplementary materials and books, which are referred to as "living books," are also an essential part of the program.

Format, content, clarity, a logical and sequential presentation of skills, the use of concrete activities, readability, and the authors are all areas to consider when choosing a textbook. The authors should be qualified to write on the subjects covered in the book and be competent writers. If a book is not pleasing to the eye or seems cluttered and hard to read it will not be effective as a teaching tool. Basal readers need to be interesting and not trite stories (The cat sat. The cat sat on the mat. Pat sat on the mat. The bat is on the mat.) whose main function is simply the application of a certain skill. Stories should also cover a wide range of interest areas. This allows for the expansion of information in areas that are unknown or are not interest areas. The format of a textbook will greatly affect its effectiveness as a teaching tool. The format should not produce a negative reaction when a child looks at the book. The content should allow for flexibility in presentation and include pertinent information. Skills should be introduced or reinforced that will enable the child to deal with the content. The material should be presented in an interesting manner, and in both the student text and teacher's guide it should be clear and easily understood. Readability is also an important factor. Basal readers are prepared on different reading ability levels. However, content area textbooks are written on one level and often the reading level is above the grade level indicated. Textbook material will need to be read to children if their reading level will cause them to work at a frustration level when using the book on their own.

When choosing a textbook it is important to compare books from different publishers. Books should be evaluated using the criteria stated and each book's strengths and weaknesses should be noted. The book that appears to be the best overall and that will assist in accomplishing the desired purposes should be chosen.

Teacher's guides should offer ideas for motivating, give background information and list resources where more information can be obtained, and provide for the presentation of skills in a meaningful and integrated manner (not just teaching them in isolation where they are simply learned for their own sake). They should also provide for individual differences by giving suggestions for enrichment and reinforcement, recognize the need for the teacher's own creativity and personality to be exercised, and allow for flexibility as to how, when, and in what sequence the material can be presented. The use of manipulatives (concrete objects used to aid in the learning process) should be encouraged and suggestions given for their use.

A textbook is a tool to be used in the learning process. It will not provide all the information needed on a subject, but should whet the appetite and be used in conjunction with other books. Used properly, a textbook is a help in introducing content areas and in developing necessary skills. Used improperly it can turn children off to learning. Reading a chapter and then answering the questions at the end may cause a child to dislike a subject because it seems dull and boring. A textbook should be viewed as a springboard and not an end in itself. Reading pages 1-247 does not guarantee that any real learning has taken place. It must always be kept in mind that it is children who are being taught and not textbooks. If a child already has knowledge of a certain area or has mastery of a skill, he or she should not be "taught" what is already known just because it is in a textbook. This is a waste of the child's and the teacher's time.

In *School Education* Charlotte Mason offered some suggestions, in addition to narration, of ways children can use books. She offers preparation hints for the teacher as well.

Student Use of Books

1. Enumerate the statements in a given paragraph or chapter.
2. Analyze a chapter.
3. Divide a chapter into paragraphs under proper headings.
4. Tabulate and classify series.
5. Trace cause to consequence and consequence to cause.
6. Discern character and perceive how character and circumstance interact.
7. Learn lessons relating to life and conduct.
   "Until they have begun to use books for themselves in such ways, they can hardly be said to have begun their education."[1]

Teacher Preparation

1. Look over the lesson for the day in advance and note what mental discipline as well as what vital knowledge the lesson presents.
2. Plan questions and activities that will allow the students to use their full mental abilities.
3. Mark the teacher's book using numbers, letters, underlining, and notes.

Suggested Textbooks

The textbooks listed have been reviewed and are of good quality. They are suggestions and not an exhaustive list of books that can be used when implementing the Child Light curriculum.

Reading

Economy Reading Series
Copyright 1986
McGraw-Hill Book
Company
School Division
1200 Northwest 63rd
Street
P.O. Box 25308
Oklahoma City, OK
73125
(800) 654-8608
In Oklahoma call collect
405-840-1444

H B J Bookmark Reading
Program
Copyright 1983
Harcourt Brace
Jovanovich, Publishers
6277 Sea Harbor Drive
Orlando, FL 32021

The Headway Program
Open Court Publishing
Company
P.O. Box 599
Peru, IL 61354-0599
(800) 892-6831

SUPPLEMENTARY MATERIALS
Be a Better Reader
(Grades 4-6)
Copyright 1984
Prentice-Hall
Educational Book
Division
Englewood Cliffs, NJ
09632
(800) 524-2349

Specific Skills Series
(Grades 1-6)
Barnell Loft, Ltd.
958 Church Street
Baldwin, NY 11510
(800) 645-6505
In New York call collect
(516) 524-2349

Spelling

Keys to Spelling Mastery
Copyright 1984
McGraw-Hill Book
Company
School Division
1200 Northwest 63rd
Street

P.O. Box 25308
Oklahoma City, OK
73125
(800) 654-8608
In Oklahoma call collect
(405) 840-1444
Zaner-Bloser Spelling
Zaner-Bloser
2300 W. Fifth Avenue
P.O. Box 16764
Columbus, OH
43216-6764
(614) 486-0221

Handwriting

Zaner-Bloser Handwriting:
Basic Skills and Application
Copyright 1984
Zaner-Bloser
2300 W. Fifth Avenue
P.O. Box 16764
Columbus, OH
43216-6764
(614) 486-0221

Building Handwriting Skills
McDougal, Littell &
Company
P.O. Box 1667
Evanston, IL 60204
(800) 323-5435
In Illinois call collect
(312) 967-0900

English

Language: Skills and Use
Copyright 1986
Scott, Foresman and
Company
1900 East Lake Avenue
Glenview, IL 60025
(312) 729-3000

Your English
Copyright 1984
Coronado Publishers,
Inc.

1250 Sixth Avenue
San Diego, CA 92101
(800) 782-9016
In California
(800) 321-1964

SUPPLEMENTARY MATERIALS
In Other Words,
A Beginning Thesaurus
(Grades 3-4)
Scott, Foresman and
Company
In Other Words,
A Junior Thesaurus
(Grades 5-6)
Scott, Foresman and
Company
1900 East Lake
Avenue
Glenview, IL 60025
(312) 729-3000

Math

Silver Burdett Mathematics
Copyright 1987
Silver Burdett and Ginn
Company
Customer Service Center
4343 Equity Drive
P.O. Box 2649
Columbus, OH 43216
(800) 848-9500
In Ohio (614) 876-0371

Invitation to Mathematics
Copyright 1985
Scott, Foresman and
Company
1900 East Lake Avenue
Glenview, IL 60025
(312) 729-3000

Mathematics Their Way
(K-2)
Math a Way of Thinking
(3-6)
Center for Innovation
in Education

19225 Vineyard Lane
Saratoga, CA 95070
(Activity-centered
mathematics pro-
gram)

SUPPLEMENTARY MATERIALS
*Developing Key Concepts in
Math*
*Developing Key Concepts for
Solving Word Problems*
Darnell Loft, Ltd.
958 Church Street
Baldwin, NY 11510
(800) 645-6505
In New York call collect
(516) 868-6064

Social Studies

The World and Its People
Copyright 1984
Silver Burdett Company
250 James Street
CN-1918
Morristown, NJ
07960-1918
(800)-631-8081
In New Jersey
(201)-285-7700
The Story of the Old World
(Grades 5-6)
Christian Schools
International
3350 E. Paris Ave., SE
Grand Rapids, MI
49510
*Concepts and Inquiry:
The Human Adventure*
(Copyright 1971, 1975,
now out of print)
(Grades 5-6)
Allyn and Bacon, Inc.
Text consists of quality
paperback books.
Since they are each 150-
200 pages long, three to
four books can be cov-

ered in a year. They are
available through used
textbook companies
such as Wilcox & Follett.
Wilcox & Follett Book
Co.
1000 W. Washington
Blvd.
Chicago, IL 60607
(800) 621-4272
In Illinois
(000) 621-1171
Titles include:
Ancient Civilization
Four World Views
*Greek and Roman
Civilization*
Medieval Civilization
Age of Western Expansion
*New World and Eurasian
Cultures*
The Challenge of Change

SUPPLEMENTARY MATERIALS
Map and Globe Skills
(Grades 4-6)
Coronado Publishers, Inc.

*Nystrom's Where and Why
Map & Globe Skills Pro-
gram*
*Nystrom Hands-on
Geography*
Nystrom
3333 Elston Avenue
Chicago, IL 60618
(800) 621-8086
In Alaska, Hawaii and
Illinois call
(312) 463-1144

Research Skills
Applied use of charts,
graphs, numbers and
time lines
(Grades 4-6)
Coronado Publishers,
Inc.

Ancient Greece and Rome
Gabriel Reuben, Sheila
Schwartz
(Grades 4-6)
Coronado Publishers,
Inc.
The Middle Ages
Fred King, Herbert
Epperly
(Grades 4-6)
Coronado Publishers,
Inc.
World History:
A Basic Approach
Jerome R. Reich,
Mark M. Krug,
Edward L. Biller
(Grade 6 and up)
Coronado Publishers,
Inc.
1250 Sixth Avenue
San Diego, CA 92101
(800) 782-9016
In California
(800) 321-1964

Science

Silver Burdett Science
Copyright 1985
Silver Burdett Company
250 James Street
CN-1918
Morristown, NJ
07960-1918
(800) 631-8081
In New Jersey call
(201) 285-7700

Scott, Foresman Science
Copyright 1984
Scott, Foresman and
Company
1900 East Lake Avenue
Glenview, IL 60025
(312) 729-3000

Bible

Basic books needed
Bible concordance
Bible dictionary
Bible atlas
Bible lands customs and
manners
Bible story book
Bible

Music

Silver Burdett Music
Copyright 1985
Silver Burdett Company
250 James Street
CN1918
Morristown, NJ
07960-1918
(800) 631-8081
In New Jersey
(201) 285-7700

Music Is for Children Primary
Level 1
(Grades 1-3)
Music Is for Children
Level 2: Rhythm
(Grades 4-6)
Music Is for Children
Level 2: Harmony
(Grades 4-6)
David C. Cook Publishing
Company
850 North Grove Avenue
Elgin, IL 60120

Physical Education

*Dynamic Physical Education for
Elementary School Children*
8th Edition
Victor P. Dauer,
Robert P. Pangrazi
Burgess Publishing
7110 Ohms Lane
Edina, MN 55435

*Complete Elementary Physical
Education Guide*
Copyright 1974
Parker Publishing
Company, Inc.
West Nyack, NY 10994

Ideas and Activities Periodicals

The Good Apple Newspaper
(Grades 3-6)
Shining Star
(Especially for Christian
educators and parents)
Good Apple, Inc.
Box 299
Carthage, IL
62321-0299

22 Kindergarten

Overview

A kindergarten program should establish a basis for the development of critical-thinking and problem-solving skills. The environment should stimulate each child to begin to learn to think Christianly and to exercise a Christian worldview.

The uniqueness of each student should be recognized and each should be helped to enjoy the total kindergarten experience. The child's developmental readiness and individual needs are important considerations. Skills need to be taught progressively throughout the year as the child is developmentally ready.

A foundation that strives to promote love and excitement for lifelong learning is provided through a readiness program. Areas presented are prereading and beginning reading skills; oral language development; listening skill development; an introduction to science and social studies; and Bible stories and memorization.

Emphasis is placed on vocabulary development; listening and comprehending; and exploring, observing, questioning, and making new discoveries about God's world. A flexible, stimulating environment and a warm, loving atmosphere allow the child to develop physically, emotionally, socially, intellectually, and spiritually.

Christian Kindergarten Objectives

1. To lead the child to trust in the true and living God.
2. To lead the child to appreciate the wonders of God's creation and His great love in sending Jesus Christ as the Savior.

The Christian Kindergarten objectives are quoted from *The Christian Kindergarten* by Morella Mensing, © 1953, 1981 and is reprinted and adapted by permission of Concordia Publishing House.

3. To guide the child in understanding that he/she needs to believe in Jesus as his/her personal Lord and Savior.
4. To teach the child to speak to God in prayer and to put his faith into action.
5. To help make the child's adjustment to school happy and wholesome.
6. To help the child become aware of and have an interest in the world around him/her.
7. To give each child many opportunities to work and play cooperatively in a group.
8. To teach the child to act and think for himself/herself and to make good evaluations and judgments about situations, information, and ideas.
9. To help the child feel at ease when talking to a group.
10. To help each child develop desirable speech habits—to speak correctly and distinctly and to grow in vocabulary.
11. To teach good sportsmanship—to be willing to lose at times.
12. To give the child all kinds of experiences in a stimulating, challenging environment.
13. To foster creative expression by providing opportunities to work with many kinds of materials.
14. To follow the child's progress in all phases of growth through teacher observation and conferences with parents.
15. To help the child feel a real sense of belonging and full acceptance with adults and with his/her peers.
16. To help the child grow in the courtesies commensurate with his/her age.
17. To teach the child how to live happily with and show concern for others.
18. To teach the child to develop simple health and safety rules.
19. To help the child develop love and tolerance for all people.
20. To develop in the child a desire to share the story of Jesus and His love with others.
21. To help the child manifest some degree of self-discipline and self-control.
22. To develop in the child a sense of pride in his/her school, church, home, and community.

Kindergarten Curriculum Guide

A kindergarten program should offer a stimulating educational environment which allows for the conceptual, perceptual, language, social, emotional, and spiritual development of each child. A strong foundation on which the elementary continuum of learning is based needs to be provided. Materials provided should aid in the implementation of the program. How every teacher ought to use his/her own creativity and select what to use, delete, change, or add so that the needs of the children will be met. Teacher's editions are guides and materials are tools. It should always be kept in mind that it is children—not programs, not books, not curriculum guides—that are being taught.

The skills, concepts, content, and strategies for each area are not necessarily listed in the sequence in which they will be taught, but there should be progression from the easier skills to the more complicated ones. Many of them will be taught simultaneously.

Readiness Development Progress Guide

1. Provide for individual and group activities.
2. Provide for the development of visual and auditory development.
3. Provide experiences that prepare for formal reading.
    a. Distinguish between likenesses and differences.
    b. Look at the picture and tell a story about it.
    c. Develop the ability to distinguish rhyming words.
    d. Recognize when words begin or end with the same sound.
    e. Recognize the vowel sound in a word.
    f. Recognize, name, and write upper- and lowercase letters.
    g. Associate a letter with the sound it stands for.
    h. Develop a sense of left to right progression.
    i. Develop an understanding of top to bottom progression.
    j. Expand the ability to express ideas clearly.
    k. Develop an attention span of no less than ten minutes.
    l. Increase visual and auditory discrimination development.

4. Provide for vocabulary development.
5. Provide for retention development.
    a. Retell a story.
    b. Correctly sequence a story or an event.
    c. Develop the ability to follow oral directions with three or more steps.
    d. Recall a story, experience, or event—immediately after, the day after, a week after, etc.
    e. Memorize Bible passages, poems, and nursery rhymes.
6. Provide opportunities for developing beginning comprehension skills.
    a. Identify the main idea of a story.

    b. Identify important details in a story.

    c. Increase the ability to follow directions.

    d. Answer questions about a story—literal comprehension.

    e. Acquire and use information.

    f. Predict the outcome.

    g. Develop the ability to recall the proper sequence of a story, event, experience, or directions.

    h. Begin developing a foundation for critical reading.

7. Provide for oral communication development.

    a. Learn to speak clearly.

    b. Learn to enunciate distinctly.

    c. Develop the ability to use good eye contact.

    d. Share experiences and ideas.

    e. Role play.

    f. Dramatize events, experiences, and stories.

8. Provide real and vicarious experiences.

    a. Visit a zoo, museum, airport, historical site, library, post office, fire station, park, factory, farm, bakery, etc.

    b. Observe streams, rivers, creeks, ponds, lakes, and other bodies of water.

    c. Take walks or hikes and observe plant life, wild animals, insects, birds, clouds, etc.

    d. Participate in household activities—cooking, setting the table, picking up toys, dusting, pulling weeds, etc.

    e. Engage in creative play and other creative activities.

    f. Care for a pet.

    g. Listen often to stories being read aloud—a wide variety of themes should be included.

    h. Listen to the radio and records and view movies, videos, and educational television.

    i. Participate in Sunday school and other group activities.

    j. Participate in games of many types.

    k. Learn to swim.

9. Provide activities that will stimulate the desire to read.

    a. Read a wide variety of stories to the children.

    b. Have the children participate in writing experience chart stories. (See first grade, number 1.)

    c. Provide a comfortable, stimulating library or book corner.

    d. Label items in the classroom.

    e. Display Bible passages, poems, class stories, etc.

    f. Help the children discover that answers to questions can be found in books, encyclopedias, and magazines.

    g. Provide for experiences that will illustrate the need for reading.

Language Arts Curriculum Guide

English

1. Recognize, read, and write first and last names, address, and phone number.
2. Recite the days of the week and the months of the year.
3. Expand vocabulary by using and understanding new words.
4. Oral communication
    a. Develop the ability to share ideas and experiences.
    b. Describe objects, animals, events, feelings, and people.
    c. Develop the ability to express a personal opinion.
    d. Enunciate clearly when speaking.
    e. Develop good voice modulation.
    f. Use volume appropriate for the situation.
    g. Speak in complete sentences.
    h. Stand properly when speaking.
    i. Use good eye contact.
    j. Develop the ability to use appropriate gestures.
    k. Dramatic play—role playing, puppets, acting out stories, etc.
    l. Recite poems and nursery rhymes.
    m. Recite Bible passages.
5. Listening
    a. Listen to and follow directions.
    b. Use listening as a means of learning.
    c. Learn to be a good listener when interacting in a group situation.
6. Writing
    a. Write upper- and lowercase manuscript letters.
    b. Write chart stories as a group.
    c. Write the letter that stands for a given sound.
    d. Write words that illustrate the rules for two vowels together (boat), final *e* (cake), and one vowel followed by a consonant (pet).
7. Grammar
    a. Develop an understanding that the names of people and places start with capital letters.
    b. Develop an understanding that a sentence ends with a certain punctuation mark.
8. Poetry—listening to and memorizing
    a. Gain a feeling for language usage in expressing ideas, feelings, and emotions.
    b. Use nursery rhymes and other poetry as a means of increasing a child's vocabulary.

    c. Develop the ability to identify visual and auditory images.

    d. Develop a positive attitude toward and an enjoyment of poetry.

    e. Examples of appropriate poems to memorize:

"After a Bath" by Aileen Fisher

"Mrs. Peck-Pigeon" by Eleanor Farjeon

"Mice" by Rose Fyleman

"One, Two, Buckle My Shoe"

"A Bird" by Emily Dickinson

A variety of nursery rhymes

Note: Memorizing poetry should be a positive, delightful experience. The teacher should read the poem while the children listen. The poem can be read two or three times when introduced and then at odd times throughout the day. The following day the teacher should read the poem again. The children can say any words or parts they recall with the teacher as the poem is read. By following this procedure, the children will soon have the poem memorized without feeling pressure. It will be a happy experience.

  9. Literature—to be read aloud to the children

    a. Develop an appreciation for literature.

    b. Provide a feeling for language usage and richness.

    c. Expand vocabulary.

    d. Increase knowledge.

    e. Develop a beginning understanding of nonfiction and fiction.

Reading

1. Alphabet

    a. Recognize the symbol and the sound each consonant letter stands for.

      • Look at the symbol and name it.

      • Look at the symbol and give the sound it stands for.

2. Develop left to right and top to bottom orientation.
3. Develop eye/hand coordination.
4. Look at a picture and tell a story about the picture.
5. Recognize the eight basic color words.
6. Identify items, shapes, figures, letters, words, etc., that are alike and that are different.

7. Identify and use words that rhyme, start with the same sound, end with the same sound, or have the same middle sound.
8. Use a variety of descriptive words when describing objects, events, people, animals, feelings, experiences, or nature.
9. Write experience chart stories. (See first grade, number 1.)
    a. Read the story.
    b. Match sentence strips with the correct sentence in the story.
    c. Match word cards with the correct word in the story.
10. Classifying
    a. By size
    b. By shape
    c. By color
    d. By function
    e. By similarities
    f. By differences
11. Develop comprehension skills.
    a. Use literal comprehension.
    b. Use inferential comprehension.
    c. Recall details.
    d. Recall the proper sequence.
    e. Use contextual clues for word meaning.
    f. Develop the ability to recognize the main idea of a story.
    g. Develop the ability to draw conclusions.
    h. Develop the ability to predict the outcome of a story.
12. Create an ending for a story.
13. Develop the ability to identify cause and effect relationships.
14. Demonstrate an understanding of the meaning of position words.
    a. above
    b. below
    c. beside
    d. between
    e. bottom
    f. in
    g. inside
    h. top
    i. middle
    j. next to
    k. on
    l. outside
    m. right
    n. left
    o. under
15. Identify the vowel and consonant sounds in a one-syllable word.

Use the rules for two vowels together, final *e*, and one vowel followed by a consonant to identify the sound the vowel stands for (for those indicating readiness).
16. Begin reading words, sentences, and simple stories when the child demonstrates developmental readiness.

Handwriting
  1. Use correct posture.
     a. Sit up straight.
     b. Place feet flat on the floor.
  2. Use kindergarten-ruled paper—one inch from top to bottom with a broken line running in the center.

  3. Place the paper correctly according to which hand is used for writing.
     a. Right-handed—slant paper to the left.
     b. Left-handed—slant paper to the right.
  4. Hold the writing tool correctly and loosely enough that it can easily be pulled from between the fingers.
  5. Start at the correct point and move in the proper direction—top to bottom and left to right.
  6. Form letters carefully and leave the correct space between letters and words.
  7. Move the lower arm and hand across the paper and not just the hand.
  8. Learn to form upper- and lowercase letters and numbers correctly.

Mathematics Curriculum Guide

A multisensory approach is used in teaching kindergarten mathematics. Provision is made for progression from the use of concrete examples to the use of the abstract form. The kindergarten math vocabulary is developed in context and not as isolated words.
  1. Recognize and write numerals 1 - 31.
  2. Recognize and read numerals 1 - 31.
  3. Develop an understanding that numerals stand for the number

being dealt with. (Numerals can be read, written, and even erased. Numbers are abstract forms that we use to add, subtract, multiply, or divide.)

4. Associate the numerals 0 - 20 with the abstract concept.
5. Geometry
   a. Develop the ability to recognize and name the basic plane and space shapes—circle, triangle, rectangle, square, ball, can, box.
   b. Develop the ability to discern if shapes are the same, different, or have the same patterns.
   c. Develop an understanding of words that indicate spatial and other relationships

left to right	on	far
over	above	alike
under	behind	different
in	in front of	between
inside	next to the last	heavier
outside	little	lighter
top	big	next to
bottom	large	below
middle	small	first
beside	near	last

6. Classification
   a. By color
   b. By shape
   c. By size
   d. By function
   e. By likenesses and differences
   f. By additional categories
7. Money
   a. Identify pennies, nickels, dimes, and quarters.
   b. Develop an understanding of the value of coins to ten cents.
8. Comparing sets
   a. Identify sets with the same number.
   b. Identify a set that has more than another set.
   c. Identify a set that has less than another set.
9. Ordering numbers
   a. Count, read, and write in order 0-31.
   b. Identify a number than comes after a given number.
   c. Identify a number than comes before a given number.
10. Ordinal numbers
    a. Develop the ability to understand and use ordinal numbers, 1st-5th.
    b. Apply ordinals to daily experiences.

11. Problem solving
   a. Classify and sort by size, color, likenesses, differences, and shape.
   b. Identify an object that is not related to the other objects in a set.
   c. Use pictures to gain necessary information to solve a problem.
   d. Develop the ability to complete and copy patterns.
   e. Develop the ability to use drawings to solve problems.
   f. Make and use simple picture graphs, charts, and tables.
   g. Apply simple logic to solve problems.

12. Measuring
   a. Develop a sense of time relationships.

   • Calendar

   • Clock—to the hour

   • Sequencing of events

   b. Use nonstandard units to measure length, height, and distance.
   c. Compare weight and capacity.

13. Addition
   a. Join sets and note that the new set is more than any of the original sets.
   b. Add horizontally to 6.
   c. Add vertically to 6.
   d. Use addition to solve problems.

14. Subtraction
   a. Remove a set from a given set and note that the number left is less than the original set.
   b. Subtract facts to 6 horizontally.
   c. Subtract facts to 6 vertically.
   d. Use subtraction to solve problems.

15. Fractions
   a. Recognize one half of a given whole.
   b. Recognize equal parts of a whole.

16. Statistics and probability
   a. Use simple picture graphs, bar graphs, tables, and charts to solve problems and record information.
   b. Make an inference, and experiment to test the inference.

17. Estimation
   a. Develop an understanding that one task may take more or less time to accomplish than another task. Make an estimate and experiment to test the estimate.

b. Develop an understanding that one item may weigh more or less than another item. Make an estimate and experiment to test the estimate.

c. Develop an understanding that one item may hold more or less than another item. Make an estimate and experiment to test the estimate.

18. Calculators
    a. Demonstrate how a calculator works.
    b. Use a simple calculator to add sets.

Note: Manipulatives (concrete objects used to aid in the learning process) should be used extensively in the math program.

Social Studies and Science Curriculum Guide

Social studies allows children to learn about themselves and the world in which they live. They learn to observe nature and to appreciate the world God created. A foundation is laid for the development of a Christian worldview.

1. Me
   a. I know my name, address, and phone number.
   b. God made me unique.
   c. God loves me.
   d. Understand the importance of good health habits.
2. School
   a. My teacher and teacher's assistant
   b. The administration
   c. The faculty and staff
   d. The office
   e. The media center
   f. The facilities
3. Family
   a. Develop an understanding that families are God's plan.
   b. Guide the child in developing positive attitudes toward parents and siblings.
   c. Compare contemporary families with early families in the United States.
   d. Compare contemporary families with Biblical families and note the principles that have not changed.
   e. Understand the importance of the Bible and the local church in the life of the family.
4. Pets
   a. How to select a pet
   b. How to care for a pet

5. The five senses
   a. Taste
   b. Hear
   c. Feel
   d. See
   e. Smell
6. Community helpers
   a. Develop an understanding of the individual's responsibility to the community.
   b. Learn about specific services performed by community helpers.
7. Transportation
   a. Learn about different types of transportation in the community.
   b. Develop an understanding of early transportation in the United States.
8. Farm
   a. Farm animals
   b. Farm products
   c. Farm work
   d. How plants and trees grow
   e. The parts of plants and trees
9. Zoo Animals
   a. Learn how zoo animals differ from pets.
   b. Develop a beginning understanding of how an animal's natural habitat differs from their zoo habitat.
10. The world
    a. Understand that the world was created by God.
    b. Learning about God's world

    • Air

    • Water

    • Light

    c. Taking care of God's world

    • Different forms of energy

    • Ways to conserve energy

    d. Learning about people in God's world
11. Weather and climate
    a. Observe different types of weather.
    b. Develop an understanding of how the basic climate affects the weather.

c. Understand that weather affects the type of clothing worn.
12. Birds, insects, and freshwater and sea life
    a. Observe and recognize the characteristics and habits of birds, spiders, and insects.
    b. Learn about sea plants and animal life.
    c. Learn about freshwater plants and animal life.
13. Feelings
    a. People are made in God's image and are of worth and value.
    b. God gave us feelings
    c. How to respond to positive feelings
    d. How to respond to negative feelings.
    e. Learn to respect the rights and feelings of others.
14. Holidays
    a. Biblically based holidays

      • Christmas

      • Easter

    b. Cultural holidays

      • Thanksgiving

      • New Year's Day

      • Martin Luther King's birthday

      • Valentine's Day

      • Presidents' Day

      • Mother's Day

      • Memorial Day

      • Father's Day

      • July 4

15. Seasons
    a. The four seasons

      • Fall

      • Winter

      • Spring

      • Summer

    b. Changing seasons affect people, plants, and animals.
16. Geography
    a. Locate one's state on a map and globe.

b. Locate the United States on a map and globe.
c. Locate the state where the child's parents were born.
d. Locate the state where the child's grandparents live or were born.

Bible Curriculum Guide

A basis for developing a love for and respect of the Bible is established. Narrative portions of the Old and New Testament are read and discussed. Selected portions are memorized throughout the year. Emphasis is placed on character trait development. Biblical principles are naturally integrated into all content areas.

1. Character trait development
   a. Attentiveness
   b. Faithfulness
   c. Creativity
   d. Diligence
   e. Patience
   f. Contentment
   g. Obedience
   h. Wisdom
   i. Tenderheartedness
   j. Thankfulness
   k. Honesty
   l. Joyfulness
   m. Love
   n. Forgiveness
   o. Responsibility
   p. Self-control
2. God the Creator
   a. The world
   b. Man
3. The first family
   a. Adam and Eve
   b. The fall
   c. Cain and Abel
4. God made me special.
5. God loves me and takes care of me.
6. Christmas—the birth of Jesus
7. Jesus on earth
8. Easter—death, burial, and resurrection of Jesus
9. Special people
   a. Noah
   b. Abraham
   c. Jacob
   d. Joseph
   e. Moses
   f. Joshua
   g. Gideon
   h. Samson
   i. Hannah
   j. Ruth
   k. Samuel
   l. David
   m. Esther
   n. Jonah
   o. Mary
   p. Peter
   q. Paul

Music Curriculum Guide

An appreciation for different types of music is established. A wide variety of songs appropriate for kindergarten are learned and a basis for understanding musical elements is begun.

1. Development of a beginning music vocabulary.
2. Rhythmic patterns
    a. Clapping patterns
    b. Even and uneven patterns
    c. Rhythm band
3. Listening to different types of music and learning to understand and enjoy them
4. Listening to different instruments and looking at pictures of them or at actual instruments
5. Distinguishing loud and soft sounds and fast and slow tempos
6. Understanding what a rest is
7. Singing
    a. Game songs
    b. Action songs
    c. Nursery rhymes
    d. Children's songs
    e. National songs
    f. Holiday songs
    g. Christian songs
    h. Part songs
    i. Folk songs

Art Curriculum Guide

The kindergarten child is encouraged to develop his/her artistic and creative abilities. An appreciation for various art forms and for great art is begun. Art is correlated with subject areas and specific instruction is also given.

1. Development of a beginning art vocabulary
2. Drawing
    a. Paint
    b. Crayon
    c. Chalk
3. Constructing
    a. Masks
    b. Mobiles
    c. Costumes
    d. Puppets

4. Using various mediums
   a. Clay
   b. Finger paint
   c. Papier-mâché
   d. Torn paper
   e. Salt and flour dough or play dough
5. Using various techniques
   a. Crayon resist
   b. Crayon etching
   c. Crayon rubbing
   d. Using geometric shapes to form a picture
   e. Collage
   f. Mosaics
   g. String design
   h. Toothpick design
   i. Leaf design
   j. Drinking straw design
6. Printing
   a. Sponge
   b. Potato
   c. Cork
   d. Vegetables
7. Original designs
8. Looking at, understanding, and appreciating great works of art

Physical Development Curriculum Guide

The children are guided in developing an understanding of the importance of cooperating with one another when playing games and the importance of a proper attitude toward competition. Provision is made for the development of gross motor skills, and fine motor skills, and activities that foster eye-hand coordination are also included. In addition, there is an emphasis on good health and safety habits.

1. Fine motor
   a. Using scissors
   b. Using a pencil
   c. Using crayons
2. Gross motor
   a. Hopping
   b. Galloping
   c. Skipping
   d. Walking a balance beam
   e. Throwing a ball
   f. Catching a ball

  g. Rolling a ball

  h. Kicking a ball

  i. Exercises

  j. Tumbling

  k. Playing games

3. Eye-hand coordination
   a. Copying patterns
   b. Pasting
   c. Tying shoes
4. Health
   a. Importance of sleep
   b. Proper exercise
   c. Correct eating
   d. Bathing
   e. Care of teeth
   f. Care of fingernails
   g. Importance of clean hair
   h. Importance of clean hands
5. Safety
   a. Careful use of playground facilities
   b. Correct use of scissors and pencils
   c. Keeping the floor free of objects
   d. How to enter and leave doors
   e. Crossing streets

    • Looking both ways

    • Using crosswalks

    • Obeying signs and signals

    • Importance of walking and not running

   f. Correct way to leave and enter cars

Social and Personal Development

  The children are provided with many opportunities for social and personal development. The goal is to enable each child to become a self-disciplined individual who manifests positive attitudes and self-confidence.

1. Develop the ability to follow classroom, playground, and school guidelines.
2. Increase the ability to follow directions.
3. Recognize the importance of cooperating with the teacher, a teacher's assistant or aide, classmates, other children, and adults.
4. Respect the rights of others.

5. Learn to accept new situations.
6. Show respect for authority.
7. Respect the property of classmates, school, and others.
8. Care for and put away materials.
9. Increase the ability to work independently.
10. Learn to complete a task.
11. Learn to use time wisely.
12. Recognize the importance of always doing your best.

23 Developing a Christian Mind and a Christian Worldview

J esus Himself gave us the key instructions for developing a Christian mind. "Be hearers of the Word, and doers also." We hear something. We do something! In another place, Luke 10:27, 28, He tells us how we can go beyond mere physical existence to enjoy being vitally, abundantly, excitingly alive. In fact He says, "Do this and you will live." Do what? "Love the Lord your God with all your heart and with all your soul and with all your strength and with all your mind and your neighbor as yourself."

We have a fatal tendency to park the words of Scripture in a special compartment, separate from our everyday life. Separate from anything real in life. And then when we do this, we make pretense of saying that we believe Christianity is true.

Why doesn't the church change society? Why aren't Christians' lives much different than other people's? Why do our kids get bored, apathetic, cynical, even about Christianity? One important reason is that Christianity isn't actually lived. This is true in other relationships in life. For instance, if I say to my new foster child, neighbor, or pupil, "I care about you," and then never look up to say "Hi!" and acknowledge them when they come into the room, if I carry on with my absorbing activity and never have time to listen, if I never plan for regular meals, visits, enjoyable activities, the words, "I like/love you" become worse than meaningless; they become hurtful lies. My life, my action shows whether I actually mean what I say.

My late father, F. A. Schaeffer, spent a lifetime telling me the content of Christianity, relating it to the reality around me, and in many other ways communicating that the Bible is true. God is there. But one of the most powerful messages to me as an ordinary person prone to fears, doubts and questions was his actual response to facing his own death. He *knew* that God's promises were true, and I could see him acting on them. Trusting. Believing. I must add that any "preacher's kid" like me often hears things in the pulpit or in Bible class that they know their old pa hasn't yet mastered! It is the attitude here that counts to the child. For instance, I can teach the child that "love your neighbor" means taking turns on the swing, but still admit that I'm finding it hard to cut short time spent watching some favorite TV program to visit a tiring but lonely "neighbor." In other words, I'm honest—"I'm really finding it hard to share my time" (or not lose patience, temper, finish a job, whatever). The child respects the reality of our position: we don't just talk about God's words, we try to *live* them.

Next, note that Jesus—who says we're not to just let our ears be tickled with His words but are meant to put them into our lives—also spells out actual areas that should be touched by our choices, our priority of loving God with all our heart (emotions), soul, strength, and with *minds*.

Now, lots of Christians act as if Christianity were merely wishful thinking. They don't act as if it were *truth* . You know, truth can stand on its own two feet. If you are facing the truth you don't need blinkers, props. You can face reality. And it's OK, because Christianity is *really* true and it does have answers to the questions that bother us all.

In societies that brainwash their members, there are many banned books, ideas, and people. So in Russia we have dissidents literally locked up for writing a poem that puts out a different point of view than the official one; many books and newspapers are banned. Why? Because the leaders are afraid to let people think for themselves! "If they get hold of the Bible they might think that there is a God," or whatever. They fear any point of view different from their own. In some school systems, any history series that doesn't interpret history into a political tract is banned. Why? It is not desired that the person should hear both sides of a question. This approach is a weak one (as well as wrong). The person who is the product of such planned learning is feeble. As soon as they hear an opposite argument or position it seems interesting, exciting even. Without having understood, recognized or evaluated ideas themselves, such a person is especially vulnerable. It is as if the baby was kept in a baby walker, and never used his own muscles to walk. Everything is supported, thought out, decided. Well, such a weak child could never climb a mountain or surmount obstacles. He is not prepared to think capably, not prepared for reality.

If we ourselves enjoy a Christian worldview, we want more than anything that our children should grow into a living relationship with the Christ of the Bible. We want them not to serve their own selfish selves, but to actually place the whole of their lives under the Lordship of Christ. He is not meant to be Lord of Sunday, or, even more narrowly, the Lord of my church life. His truth is part of *everything*, including my mind, my understanding of all reality and knowledge. This means the ideas of Christianity relate to every single aspect of life.

Loving the Lord My God with All My Mind

In applying this principle to educational practice, we first of all identify the mind as part of the whole person created by God. He has made us so that our minds need nourishing with ideas and knowledge, just as our bodies need food.

The small child talks about the world about him or her. I was bringing my two and one-half-year-old grandson home through the twilight. It was my conscious grandmotherly choice to start talking about all we saw. "*God* made the moon," I pointed out as he was awed by the moonlight. "*God* made the tall, tall trees." So far so good! And then his little voice pierced into my rather smug grandmotherly lesson, "Did God make all the trees blow down?" I was startled. Recently a gale had devastated the countryside where he lived. This baby was asking me if God was also the creator of destruction, danger, chaos!

In my experience, children ask all the big hard questions several years before their tenth birthday. If you want to obey Jesus' command in relationship to your children, you have to change your way of life and use *your* mind! For the adult is the resource turned to, and woe betide you if the home or classroom is so busy or pressured that the friendly, natural, warm questioning and discussion never takes place!

So, we're going to make an atmosphere, a setting and a schedule that allows for talk. The child's talk is his response to reality. And my answer is the resource. But here's the rub! *What am I going to answer?*

"Hear, O Israel: The LORD our God, the LORD is one. Love the LORD your God with all your heart and with all your soul and with all your strength. These commandments that I give you today are to be upon your hearts. Impress them upon your children. Talk about them when you sit at home and when you walk along the road, when you lie down and when you get up" (Deut. 6:4-7, NIV).

We are never to forget God's revealed Word. That is *our* first resource, the basis of all this talking (apparently in my bedroom upon waking up, at meals, and in my leisure time). I have a responsibility to use my mind as best I can to grow in the wisdom and knowledge of God's revealed Word.

I can't, simply can't talk about it when I don't give God's Word serious study myself. A Christian mind and Christian worldview means that I so surround myself with God's words that I see things His way, and understand what He is actually saying.

As this godly viewpoint and understanding gets stronger, I'll pray for and start to see and understand reality all around me *the way He sees it*. We must remember here that the Bible isn't only for Sunday or church. God's revealed truth relates to everything: what all my peers say and do; what is right, what is wrong. What would Jesus say to their questions, their fears? What is His view of the laws my government is proposing this year? . . . the values I see on my TV screen? What does He think to be the most important aim in life? When I read history, what does it mean in relationship to the way God sees human life? As male and female roles change, what from God's viewpoint is important to remember? When people starve, what should my attitude and response be? The list of realities that are touched by God's viewpoint is as broad as all of life itself. It touches *everything*.

Christianity as the Bible describes it from Genesis to Revelation is a revolutionary view of reality and life. No part of life isn't touched by it, if it's true. God's truth shines like a bright light, illuminating the chaos, bringing order out of confusion. Truth is under my feet like a strong rock, and I'm not swayed by every current that swirls around me. For, I can say, "I *know* . . ."

In the curriculum guides, we've outlined the practice of bringing children in a planned, regular way to the reading of God's Word. But if the adults don't also pursue this on a lifelong basis, seriously, and in depth, we weaken our integrity. How does God speak to *me* if I don't listen, understand, use my mind, grow? And how can I start to be equipped to answer from God's viewpoint the literally thousands of questions the children ask, if I don't make His words the influence in my life, rather than magazines, other media productions, etc.? I must always aim to find out what God actually means in the text, in His Word. I mustn't go at it to prove a point, but to understand what it says for itself.

I want, now, to return to the point that Christian education should not brainwash. Of course, as responsible Christian adults, we must limit all sorts of materials that could misinform or mislead our children. For instance, over seventy percent of sexual relationships portrayed on TV are not between married persons. That is obviously not the standard we wish to have a child assimilate! Just as we keep them from an all-day diet of potato chips and soft drinks, so we must keep them from junk mind-food and worse, poison itself. For there are actual evils in many media productions; evil books, programs, people, places. *Yes,* we do choose and put limits on our children, if we care about their welfare.

More than that, the whole purpose of Child Light is to so design the entire life of the child that he or she is put in touch with the *best*, including nature, physical experiences, the arts, culture, etc. Now the question of using ordinary books arises, as opposed to using only books in all fields that are produced by Christians.

We try to use a book because it is valuable, well-written, useful. We don't expect that a child must only see the same Christian point of view in print, any more than he or she only meets Christian people, only hears news read by a Christian newscaster, etc. Any such child would be mentally exactly like the baby never allowed to walk but kept in a baby walker.

I'll give an example from a wonderful book, *A Child's History of the World*. When I was teaching my nine-year-old, not only did *he* get in touch with the flow of history, not only was *his* structural understanding of our culture established, so was mine! In fact, it can make an excellent quick history review for persons of any age. But typically, this book starts with three chapters "before written history." The "primitive" people are living in caves, and grunt instead of talking! Many Christians would then be scared off and not dare ever read the book. *Wait a minute!* What you are about to read with the child *will* promote questions, comments, ideas. Please don't follow Moscow and ban this good book! Don't you think your precious child or pupil is going to encounter people outside school who naturally assume this was history's beginning? Don't you want to read it together, discuss it, and *let the child see what he thinks*? If you haven't taught the story of creation *only* in a Sunday school setting, but refer to it casually as different beliefs and faiths about creation are brought up in newspaper items, books, people's stray comments, etc., then this won't pull the rug out from anybody's feet!

What is the panic all about? The panic is that parents and teachers who believe in Christianity don't think they have the answers to the questions and doubts that will be raised. And so, at the end of this chapter, I am proposing a short course for the *adult* in a few basic aspects of Christian thought and truth. It would be a terrible thing if we kept the child in a glass house where only Christian words, ideas, and books existed. It is not the real world.

More than that, if we are to develop a Christian mind, we must set out to understand life around us, not merely tolerate it. It is then that we will be able to discuss and answer questions without resorting to slogans.

> It is not only Christians who can appreciate beauty and
> create it, have keen insights, solve problems both physical
> and spiritual, care for the destitute, uphold justice, do

deeds of heroism. The non-Christian can do these too, for he is made in the image of God.

Therefore, the Christian mind will expect to find the true, the whole, the right, the pure, the lovely, the admirable within all human experiences—even though seriously diminished and hampered by sin maybe. This calls for discernment for the sifting of good and bad. There are no easy solutions, neatly packaged. It is a matter of sifting and weighing, of trying to find out what is pleasing to the Lord, of taking time and trouble, of discerning and listening.

How, for example are movements in art measured? How are priorities in political action decided upon?. . . [1]

Through books we seek to bring to children people who have literary gifts, or understanding of anything from biological structure to architectural history. Just as in everyday living, they will encounter those who have many viewpoints. Through conversation, questions, discussion, the child can relate the Christian viewpoint being developed to all these other thoughts.

"Oh, I don't think I'm up to that! I can't sift out what is important from the Christian perspective myself; I can't judge everything from the theory of evolution to rock music. I think I'll play it safe and stick to all Christian textbooks."

Well, that *might* sound safe, but it really doesn't work! You're just going to have to do some mental "jogging and exercise" work and get into better shape than that! This child who has only seen a Christian biology book is out waiting at the airport and hears the lyrics of a current rock song,

> Love, you're an animal
> Give it what you feel now,
> Fight like an animal
> 'Cause you're all alone tonight . . .

And what *then*? The Christian mind is to judge all things (I Cor. 2:15)."Paul explains in the second half of I Cor. 2 that the Christian has something which no one else has, namely, information from God Himself. This is the wisdom from God we referred to earlier, 'No eye has seen, nor ear has heard, no mind has conceived . . . God has revealed it to us by His Spirit.' (I Cor. 2:9, 10). Therefore the spiritual man (i.e., the one who is properly related to the Holy Spirit through faith in Christ) is able to 'make judgments about all things . . .' (I Cor. 2:15). In other words, is able to really understand what is going on in the world . . . (including science, psychology, etc . . .)."[2]

All of this is vital, for going back to the biology book issue, the question of origins and of the nature of the human being (made in the image of God? animal? machine?) will crop up frequently in rock music, TV, laws passed in government, magazine articles on artificial insemination, etc.

My dad, F. A. Schaeffer, used to say that if you went to China as a missionary and never learned the language, you might as well not go; but, he said, many Christians never "learn the language" or even *try* to understand what is being said and believed today in our own culture. It isn't just a luxury; if we don't learn to understand the people around us, their lives, our culture, if we don't find out where we've come from historically and where the thinking of our age is heading, then we're like a traveler walking blindfolded. We have a duty to understand, and to then talk it all over with our growing children and young adults.

What if we don't? Young people will conclude Christianity isn't for the real world, the world where Bruce Springsteen sings,

> Outside the street's on fire
> In a real death waltz
> Between what's flesh and what's fantasy
> And the poets down here
> Don't write nothing at all
> They just stand back and let it all be
> And in the quick of a knife
> They reach for their moment
> And try to make an honest stand
> But they wind up wounded
> Not even dead
> Tonight in Jungleland[3]

The quivering, feeling human being has always sung his pain, fear, questions. Do we listen, care, understand? The "real death waltz," it turns out, is not knowing what is real and unreal, "flesh and fantasy" . . . the singer turns to the poets, and meets silence. What a powerful lyric for discussion! Understanding! Compassion!

The Essential Grown-ups' Homework List for Christian Mind-Building

You're convinced! Spending disciplined effort on your own mind and developing an understanding of all aspects of life about us, you're ready to start working yourself. You hope to be ready with a background of understanding when questions start and discussions ensue.

First, realize that what I share with you here isn't meant to be a definitive list. It is a core of book reading and tape listening that started hundreds of seekers on their way in this area. It covers enough of the basic areas to give a reasonably sound infrastructure of thought. Who are these hundreds of people?

For the last thirty-four years, I have been involved in the beginning and continuing of L'Abri Fellowship—first in Switzerland where my parents, Dr. and Mrs. Francis A. Schaeffer began this work. Later on my husband, Ranald Macaulay, and I were asked to start a British branch. We lived there for twenty years, but for the last few years have been back in the Swiss branch again!

L'Abri has been a place where we have struggled (failed sometimes, tried, continued) to live according to the teaching of God's Word. Part of this has been the opportunity for people to ask their questions, and for us to discuss together the way various aspects of life relate to God's teaching. In fact, for many, L'Abri was the place where bridges were built from Christian teaching into the real world. Early on, we began recording some of the discussions and lectures. Through the years, a huge catalog of such cassette tapes has been built up. And from some of the early lectures, my father wrote books which had an electrifying effect on certain sections of the reading public (especially the Christian portion).

Coming for a time to L'Abri (there are now residential study branches in Switzerland, England, Holland, Massachusetts, and Sweden) people set aside a period of up to three months to consider the claims of Christianity and the Bible, to consider why and how it could be actually true (apologetics), to share in the challenge to *live* it together, and to study the bridges of thought into the world around us (developing the Christian mind).

Although it is obvious that the experience of such a stay cannot be duplicated from afar, you can most certainly follow a similar study plan yourself anywhere, using the sort of curriculum you'd receive if you came to L'Abri. Missing will be living discussions, personal relationships, and sharing in prayer, worship and Bible study together.

Bible

First, remember the resource of the Bible! This study list assumes you make this study a priority.

What *is* the Bible? Does it contain the Word of God to me, or *is* it God's Word?

Books:

• *The Great Evangelical Disaster,* by F. A. Schaeffer, published by Crossway. In this book Schaeffer says, "Evangelicals today are facing a watershed concerning the nature of Biblical inspiration and authority. Within evangelicalism there is a growing number who are modifying their views on the inerrancy of the Bible so that the full authority of Scripture is completely undercut . . . ."[4]

Our view of Scripture, its authority, its truth, will either give us a firm base or not, depending on whether we accept its claims for itself. A careful study of this book will show the relevance of our choices. Don't let yourself slide into a weak position and find yourself slipping down the wrong slope of the watershed. When we do, a lot of land slides with us! In the preface to *The Great Evangelical Disaster,* Schaeffer gives what could be our aim in this study commitment: "I would want to emphasize from beginning to end throughout my work the importance of evangelism (helping men and women come to know Christ as Savior), the need to walk daily with the Lord, to study God's Word, to live a life of prayer, and to show forth the love, compassion and holiness of the Lord. But we must emphasize equally and at the same time the need to live this out in every area of culture and society."[5]

• *Christianity Is Jewish,* by Edith Schaeffer, published by Tyndale, Coverdale. If the Bible seems like a series of disconnected stories to you, if you've never followed the unifying thread of God's plan for the human race from the Genesis account onwards, this book will change your understanding of what the Bible is all about. How does the Old Testament relate to the New? Did God have a plan to help the human race? The individual? When one talks about the Judeo-Christian tradition, what does that mean?

• *Lifelines:* The Ten Commandments for Today, by Edith Schaeffer, published by Crossway Books. Many of the questions you'll be asked have to do with guidelines for behavior, moral choices, actual living. This book builds important bridges from the Word of God (the Ten Commandments) into our contemporary lives.

Cassette Tapes:

The following are a few of the many L'Abri cassettes on the Bible. These are chosen as essential areas of study: one must consider inspiration (Is the Bible of man, containing the Word of God, or is it the inspired Word of God?), Genesis, the Bible's view of itself, etc. Further Biblical studies, doctrinal teachings, etc. should be followed later.

• *Inspiration of Scripture* by F. A. Schaeffer. (Number 13.1) The validity of the Bible depends upon this concept.

• *Freedom and Limitations in Biblical Cosmogony: Historicity and Interpretations of Genesis* by F. A. Schaeffer. (Number 8.3) Perhaps no other section of the Bible comes under greater skepticism. Everyone will face questions involving Genesis. This book is central in the understanding of Biblical teaching.

The next four are a series by Jerram Barrs:

• *Authority, Revelation and the Bible's View of Itself* (Number 92.1)

• *Authority and Canonicity of the New Testament Books* (Number 92.2)

• *Presuppositions of Critical Biblical Studies* (Number 92.3)

• *The Debate Among Evangelicals on the Scripture* (Number 92.4)

Note: Cassettes referred to are L'Abri cassettes. These can all be ordered from the following addresses. Available also, by request, is a catalog giving a wider selection of L'Abri tapes on many subjects. The catalog is updated from time to time. U.S.A.–L'Abri Cassettes, P.O. Box 2035, Michigan City, IN 46360 (219) 879-7753; England– L'Abri Cassettes, The Manor House, Greatham, Liss, Hants GU 33 6HF (The English address will send tapes by mail order to countries other than the U.S.A., Australia and New Zealand); Australia and New Zealand–L'Abri Cassettes, Square Level, St. Andrews House, Sydney Square, Sydney, Australia

Apologetics

But is the Bible actually true? How do you know? Is it a blind leap of faith? This is the domain of *apologetics*.

Books:

• *How to Be Your Own Selfish Pig,* by Susan Schaeffer Macaulay, published by David C. Cook. This book makes a deceptively easy start! Its stories and cartoons make it seem easy reading. But the questions asked are the deep ones most commonly met. The answers show how one can actually see reality around us explained only if the Bible *is* true. Children have read it to themselves from the age of eleven up. Recently two consultant physicians in different countries became Christians themselves after reading this book! It helped answer *their* questions, helped Christianity make sense to *them*. It is also a great discussion-starter!

• *Common Sense Christian Living,* by Edith Schaeffer, published by Thomas Nelson. Chapters 1 and 2 are part of this study list. Read it in relationship to finding out and explaining whether or not Christianity is true. It contains special reference to creation—chance or by design? (Read the other relevant sections in relationship to areas of practical Christian living like prayer, answering actual questions, what's important in life.)

- *The God Who Is There,* by F. A. Schaeffer, published by IVP, Hodder, and in *The Complete Works of F. A. Schaeffer,* Crossway.[6] This is essential reading, a good basic study you *must* have in apologetics. Many have had a lifetime's understanding opened through this book.

- *He Is There and He Is Not Silent,* by F. A. Schaeffer, published by Tyndale House and in *The Complete Works of F. A. Schaeffer,* Crossway. In this book, Schaeffer goes into the philosophical background of the apologetics given in the *The God Who Is There.* "This book deals with one of the most fundamental of all questions: how we know, and how we know we know. Unless our epistemology [the theory of knowledge] is right, everything is going to be wrong. That is why I say this book goes with *The God Who Is There*—a link emphasized by its title. The infinite-personal God is there, but also He is not silent; that changes the whole world. . . . He is there and is not a silent, nor far-off God."[7]

- *Whatever Happened to the Human Race?* by F. A. Schaeffer and C. Everett Koop, published by Marshall, Morgan and Scott and by Crossway Books in paperback. Chapters 4 and 5 of this book on life issues give an excellent apologetic survey of the answer to the "Why or how is Christianity true?" questions. It is a compact structured approach to the defense of the Bible. You can't afford to miss this book. Although listed under this section because of its apologetic value, it builds vital bridges between the claims of the Bible about the human being and important questions shaking up society this very minute. It is essential reading if you're going to answer the hundreds of important questions asked every day in our generation. In fact, you won't be able to read publications like *Time* or your newspaper from a Christian viewpoint if you haven't grasped the truths in this book.

Tapes:
Once again, L'Abri cassettes can form a short or extensive basis for study in this area.

- *The Christian Mind,* by Ranald Macaulay (two lectures). (Numbers 156.3, 156.4)
Many of the students coming to L'Abri use this to guide their studies, using the Biblical basis for the use of the mind and the development of a Christian mind.

- *Intellectual Proof and Faith,* by F. A. Schaeffer. (Number 8.1)

- *Why I Believe,* by Jerram Barrs. (Number X550) Jerram communicates deeply and yet in an understandable way for us all. Having worked in L'Abri for seventeen years, he is aware of most of our questions and problems!

- *Possible Answers to the Basic Philosophical Questions,* by F. A. Schaeffer (two tapes). (Numbers 1.1a and 1.1b) These two tapes are classics. Schaeffer himself came to believe at seventeen years of age as he read the Bible and found it actually answered the philosophical questions of life. This was an important aspect of Schaeffer's excitement all his life that Christianity is *true.* Don't forget that children ask the philosophical questions very early on. So teachers from kindergarten to the university level need to understand this material.

- *Criteria for Truth: The Relation Between Proof in Science, History, and Faith,* by Ranald Macaulay (two-tape series). (Numbers 116.3 and 116.4) A short survey run at one of the L'Abri branches showed that most people coming to study at L'Abri had found these two tapes essential . . . more essential than any other tape.

- *Christian Evidences: Reasons for Faith,* by Barry Seagren. (Number 8.4) Barry is always very clear and well organized. This tape should be included!

Where Have We Come From? Why Are We Here? What's Here Anyway? Where Are We Going?
     This is a huge section, understanding society, history, people . . .

Books:
- *Being Human:* The Nature of Spiritual Experience, by R. Macaulay and J. Barrs, published by InterVarsity Press. In educational seminars this is listed as a key study book for the Charlotte Mason or Child Light understanding of the basis of Christian education. Sometimes poor educational practices have arisen out of an ascetic view of the person (separating out the spiritual as more important than the ordinary aspects of our lives). This has caused confusion and unhappiness. And then, what about the Fall? We advise anyone thinking through the Biblical infrastructure hoping to then build sound families, churches and schools to include this book in their study plan. It is essential and explains what Charlotte Mason meant when she said "there is no division between the secular and the religious" or when Schaeffer pointed out, "The Lord is Lord of *all* of Life."

- *How Should We Then Live?,* by F. A. Schaeffer, published by Revell and Crossway. Subtitled, "The Rise and Decline of Western Thought and Culture," this is another absolute *must.* Before one can teach history, literature, government/social studies, science, from any textbook, book or program, one has to understand the *flow* of history. "In no way," Schaeffer writes in the Author's Note that begins this book, "does this book make a pretense of being a complete chronological history of Western culture. It is questionable if such a book could be written. This book is, however, an analysis of the key moments in history which have formed our present culture, and the thinking of the people who brought those moments to pass. This study is made in the hope that light may be shed upon the major characteristics of our age and that solutions may be found to the myriad of problems which face us as we look toward the end of the twentieth century."

I believe this is another book that everyone should study and discuss before finishing high school or college.

• Please notice that the book already referred to, *Whatever Happened to the Human Race?* also fits into this category. The ethical issues facing us in our generation, and the choices made, will determine future history.

• Those wishing a greater in-depth study of the history shaping our present lives should make a study of *A History of the Modern World,* by Paul Johnson, published by Weidenfield and Nicolson, London. Although working through this book is a commitment requiring serious reading, anyone wishing to come to grips with our own culture will be well repaid the effort.

Cassettes

L'Abri cassettes cover many cultural areas including society, historical perspectives, psychology, science, law and politics. A very small choice follows, but anyone wishing to do so may draw up a personal study program from the extended lists available from the L'Abri cassettes distributors.

• *A Christian Mind in Today's World,* by Jerram Barrs (Numbers X629 to X633). This series of five lectures covers the subjects: An Uncertain Mind, A Humanist Mind, An Existential Mind, A Marxist Mind, A Christian Mind.

• *Images of Man in Psychology,* by Richard Winter (Number X512). Dr. Winter is a psychiatrist, and he relates the Biblical view of man to the psychological descriptions currently used.

• *Eastern Philosophy and the New Age Movement,* by Ellis Potter (Number X611). Many attitudes in vogue today have originated in eastern religions and philosophies. Everyone working with children and young people should begin to try to understand these ideas, and to be able to identify them when we meet them in conversation, the media, etc.

• *Naturalistic Science Is Poor Science,* by F. A. Schaeffer (Numbers 199A and 199B). Many people assume that scientific theories are based on fact and Christian belief on faith. It is a subject that demands our objective thought.

• *Chance and Evolution,* by F. A. Schaeffer (four cassettes, No. 12.1A, 12.1B, 12.2A, 12.2B). This short series goes into greater depth and refers to Charles Darwin, Arthur Koestler, Michael Polanyi and the DNA template.

• *Some Art Norms and Thoughts for Christian Artists,* by F. A. Schaeffer (Numbers 11.1a and 11.1b). Art is the window for society, people, culture. For the Christian it has value for its own sake, and also puts us in touch with the people who produce it. These two lectures give us twelve criteria for the evaluation of art.

• *Art Forms and Loss of the Human,* by F. A. Schaeffer (Numbers 10.1a and 10.1b). A child looking at a contemporary canvas exclaimed, "Oh, what a mess!" These two tapes explore the effect of the contemporary philosophies upon art development.

• *The Place and Purpose of Literature,* by Donald Drew (Number X204). An Englishman who spent his career in teaching school has concentrated on the place of literature. This art form is one of the most important as it includes philosophical considerations, attitudes, relationships . . . in fact, every aspect of life.

• *The Christian Philosophy of Literature,* by Donald Drew (Number X557). The title is clear, and so is its importance!

• Finally I will include two tapes by Jerram Barrs on *The Christian and the State* (Numbers 77.4 and 67.1).

Although the recommended studies cannot be accomplished in five minutes, it obviously is only a beginning, and introduction. Also, I have limited my choices to those which have come out of L'Abri Fellowship itself. This isn't because there aren't other resources! However, it is a sample of the sort of study program you'd have outlined for you if you *could* come and study in L'Abri. These are the sorts of areas this curriculum guide expects those in charge of the children to have explored and understand in some depth. Of course, when a question is asked and we don't have the answer in our minds, it is always good to say, "Oh what a good question. I haven't thought about that enough, and I'll have to look it up before I can answer it."

In fact, if you did come to L'Abri there would be lots of other areas you'd study that this guide hasn't covered at all. The practical Christian life, Bible study, prayer, a living relationship with God, guidance. Other areas are relationships with people, the church, social problems, ecology. If you write out the word *education,* remember it touches all of life![8]

" 'As a man thinketh, so is he,' is really most profound. An individual is not just the product of the forces around him. He has a mind, an inner world. Then, having thought, a person can bring forth actions into the external world and thus influence it. People are apt to look at the outer theater of action, forgetting the actor who 'lives in the mind' and who is therefore the true actor in the external world."[9]

This study guide is based on the premise that the children we educate will turn to the adults surrounding them for life-giving answers. Their minds are hungry, wondering, exploring. Can the blind lead the blind? Any Christian school board, for instance, should be very careful about choosing *teachers,* as well as concerned about the curriculum! None of us are exempt; we must give time and effort if we are to understand, if we are going to keep a Christian mind.

Susan Schaeffer Macaulay

$\boxed{24}$ Flexibility: Making It Work!

T he curriculum guides are offered to you for use in many situations. To use them, you'll need the three Child Light books, *For the Children's Sake, Books Children Love,* and this one.

Schools today face a big problem. Many children come to them with basic needs unmet. For instance, there may not be time at home for good relationships as both parents are under the stress of draining careers. School may be the only place for conversation, free time to initiate imaginative and creative play, the enthusiasm of books shared, and even a place to rest and eat. This creates problems, as our traditional schools with their rigid classrooms aren't really designed for living in.

You'll realize that without a reasonably balanced life, a child cannot make use of a school curriculum. Each school, even each class must creatively respond to these needs if they are to serve children. There must be an atmosphere where each child is accepted, appreciated, cared about. There must be a *balance* between structured learning time and unstructured time when the child responds to a rich environment, including human relationships.

When you read about Charlotte Mason's ideas, you must be aware that many children never enjoy much of the life she describes. For instance, the freedom and sheer joy of responding to a meadow with a stream to play in, a beach, the woods . . . what can you do for the children if they come to school in bus or car and return to a room, a TV set, and exhausted parents? Christians who believe in the importance of all of life *must* be creative.

The sort of thing a school could try is teachers working in twos. A group of children has an enriched classroom "home" where many activities are available to them. In this "home" they are free to choose where to become involved. A teacher is there to guide and assist. The activities depend on age of children and facilities available. There is possibly an art area, a library center with comfortable cushions, wood-working facilities, kitchen, play areas with dress-up clothes, construction toys. Out of doors there is free play space with trees to climb, grass to run on, etc. Utopia? What price a healthy, satisfied, interested child? This "home" space is available for creative play, interests, projects. However, there is a timetable. A small group of children leaves the "home" area for short but carefully structured schoolwork times. They go with the second teacher to an absolutely quiet, separate classroom area where they may learn to concentrate, and work at an appropriate level.

Such a combination of structured and free time could somewhat imitate the advantages children used to have in pasture, yard, home and neighborhood. The "home" room could furthermore be used as a base for a small home-like community. Meals could be taken as a group there, with the two teachers and any volunteer assistants who are part of the "family." After the meal, all the children in the family could listen with rapt attention while a book is read aloud to them as a group. Work projects (cooking a meal together, clearing a yard) would also be part of life together.

As the family and neighborhoods flounder, if we are to offer what children actually need, we *must* respond to the unmet needs in their lives. Don't be put off thinking of ways to supply some of the children's needs because you can't do everything! A Christian teacher in a public school (grades 2 and 3) revolutionized the lives of the children in her room by putting into practice what she could of C. Mason's ideas. She cut out or down on busywork. She arranged the day so that there was more free playtime. The children became less tense, less naughty. She started reading entire books aloud, such as C. S. Lewis' Narnia tales. They loved it! They sat in rapt attention! Concentration improved dramatically. Children's reading improved; they developed a love of books. She instituted a rest time and played classical music. The children became friendly users of the great composers.

In order to have the right atmosphere at school and at home, we must foster good relationships. In the twentieth century we've been notoriously poor at that! It is a complicated subject, but the following two books are worth careful attention:

• *The Kink and I: A Psychiatrist's Guide to Untwisted Living,* by James D. Mallory, D.D., published by Victor Books. This book is full of sound advice given from a Biblically based view of life and relationships. It's the sort of thing that makes good annual reading, as we never get past the stages and problems discussed!

• *How to Really Love Your Child,* by Ross Campbell, M.D., published by Signet Books and by Victor Books. Again, this book will alert you to the difference between just caring for a child (your own or somebody else's) and letting them *feel,* experience, *know love.*

If you feel you've come up with a really good idea, please do share it with others. The children of today: in urban centers, day-care situations, hyperactive, underachieving, with "low self-image" . . . all desperately need *good ideas.* We're going to try to keep up a Child Light newsletter three times a year. Please send in ideas, plus how they worked out! We'll print up a selection of these for others working with children

I think a secret of good sense in education and child care is what I call the cookbook approach! Many people today look for a blueprint to solve their human problems. But *each* situation, *each* child is different. After you have a basic understanding about the principles of life, *do adopt a selective approach.* There is no one answer right for everyone. Take the little model I outlined of a home classroom with two teachers providing a more living atmosphere for children who don't have much of a life at home. Well, that might work in one situation, and not in another. But one might adapt it partially, and tack on yet another idea.

In fact, in trying to use these curriculum guides, to make them work you'll need to be selective. All of the suggestions aren't usable in their entirety in any case.

Be a collector of ideas for the children's sake! And try to plan a menu from the "cookbooks" that nourish their minds, tell them the truth, show them love, and provide for as satisfying and wholesome a life as possible.

Susan Schaeffer Macaulay

Appendix I:
Alternate Social
Studies Overview

T he description that the words *social studies* gives is a combination of the study of history, geography and people. The relationships of each part to each other is immensely significant. For instance, what were the people thinking, believing when they allowed Hitler to "take over" Germany? What did he do? What were the historical consequences? In order to clearly understand the implications of this history, one also needs the basic information of geography, the stage upon which people's lives are acted out. What countries are Germany's neighbors? How did the physical structure alter the unrolling of the happenings? In all of this there is considerable overlap of various separate studies. But to integrate the different strands, one must clearly see each strand!

In fact, one needs to relate other strands into the total understanding of the situation. Going back to 1938 in Germany, what had happened in the people's thinking? What were they writing? What was the church's theology like? The arts are another expression coming out of the thinking of a people. What do we see in the arts that relates to the whole picture?

The Child Light educational perspective aims to relate all of this picture to a Christian viewpoint. What was right, what was wrong, according to the unchangeable structure of God's righteousness and truth? The grid of the Bible's perspective must be related to such a complex tapestry of various strands often through discussion. Someone has to have a firm understanding both of the grid and also a clear grasp of the strands—this someone may be a teacher, parent or friend.

Seeing this mixture of strands, it is understandable why educational practices in the last years have tried to blur the threads into ready-made felt. That's how I view the common definition of social studies; a felt with all the threads mashed up, cooked, pushed into indistinguishable felt! Although I can see how this happened, it just doesn't work.

If you want competent weavers (the interrelating understanding of different branches of knowledge), you have to first supply the knowledge of the separate threads! A distinct bobbin of, say, blue yarn for history. A fascinating thread of true tales, history, people's lives, their choices, the consequences. This blue thread has a beginning, a middle and an end as it is woven into the whole. But we don't get the whole pattern first! We start with a firm, definite thread of historical understanding.

Other threads interweave with the blue of history. Next to it, say, is a green thread of the ordinary people's lives. This thread relates directly to the main historical flow. How do people live? They marry, have children, either have slaves or don't, write laws, invent things. Now another thread gives the emerging pattern its shape. Geography! All this is going on in a *place*. This stage, or background of threads affects the whole. Is it dry? Too wet? Steep? Flat? The pattern emerges.

Social studies? Maybe, if you like! But you can get no clear pattern, understanding, knowledge, unless the separate threads are clearly taught so they become part of the educational heritage of each person. Of course, something very like this used to be the aim in education.

"Progressive" educators revolted (rightly) against dull, dry lists of facts being taught in textbooks under the titles history, geography, etc. They merged these into seemingly fun projects. "Let's be a tribe of red Indians," or "We'll read about the Vikings, make a Viking mural, and visit a Viking museum." It sounded good, but the clear threads, that flow of sequential history, just never happened for lots of children. These children have, many of them, graduated from high schools and colleges, and they still have trouble looking intelligent if the Punic wars were cited, or if how the ideas of the Renaissance affect us now is discussed, etc. Worse, this muddle hasn't given many of them a passion for knowing *more*.

This curriculum suggests a clearly structured approach to the threads of history, geography, and other "social studies." This will include a growth of understanding in what Christians are doing (missions), and also focus on understanding our own current culture.

Unusual? It most certainly is! Why? Our curriculum development and textbook writers got mixed up and "made felt," that's why (poor quality felt at that)!

According to a 1985 Foundations of Literacy study,
two-thirds of the seventeen-year-old students tested could

not place the Civil War in the correct half-century; a third did not know the Declaration of Independence was signed between 1750 and 1800; a third did not know that Columbus sailed for the New World before 1750 . . . and one-half of our high school seniors did not recognize the names of Winston Churchill or Joseph Stalin.

Several reading specialists have observed that "world knowledge" is essential to the development of reading and writing skills. I call this knowledge *cultural literacy,* the networks of information that all competent readers possess. It is background information that enables them to read a book or an article with an adequate level of comprehension, getting the point, grasping the implications.

Clearly our schools have failed to fulfill their fundamental responsibility to provide students with this world knowledge. . . .

It is the American public school's cafeteria-style curriculum, combined with our unwillingness to place demands on students, that has resulted in a steady diminishment of commonly shared information between generations and between young people themselves. Some have objected that teaching the traditional literate culture means teaching elitist material. That is an illusion. Literate culture is the most democratic culture in our land: it excludes nobody; it cuts across generations and social groups and classes. . . .

Children also need to understand elements of our literary and mythic heritage that are often alluded to without explanation. For example: Adam and Eve, Cain and Abel, Noah and the Flood, David and Goliath, the Twenty-third Psalm, Humpty Dumpty, Jack and Jill, Cinderella, Jack and the Bean-stalk, Peter Pan and Pinocchio. Also: Achilles, Adonis, Aeneas, Agamemnon, Antigone and Apollo, as well as Robin Hood, Paul Bunyan, Satan, Sodom and Gomorrah, the Ten Commandments.

A curriculum reform designed to teach young children the basics of cultural literacy will require radical changes in textbooks. . . .

Of course, we must present material to children in an interesting way. Dry incompetence is not the necessary alternative to lively ignorance. . . . Children don't have to be forced to memorize facts; they do it anyway. The great oversight of a watered-down curriculum for early grades is that while children are busily remembering what they experience in school, their school materials are often not worth remembering. . . .[1]

The Child Light approach to the study of history/people/their world has a clear perspective on why we want children and young people educated in a way that includes a very real sense of the flow of history, the cultural background of our countries, and a relating of this to current thought. It is a Christian reason. The Judeo-Christian tradition teaches that God has revealed His word to us in the Bible. This is truth. This tells us that the human being was given *choice*. And we believe that history and historical consequences flow out of these *choices*.

We believe that what people choose matters. We believe people matter. We believe that it is for a deeper reason than merely being "literate" that our children should be educated. They have the right to have an accurate historical base upon which to build their own choices. Making Christian choices is not an easy or popular thing at the end of the twentieth century. To make strong choices, right ones, followed by commitment, people need to consider questions like, What is right? What are most people saying and why? What are they giving up by this choice? What happened in history when people made choices like this?

> To understand where we are in today's world—in our intellectual ideas and in our cultural and political lives— we must trace three lines in history, namely, the philosophic, the scientific, and the religious. The philosophic seeks intellectual answers to the basic questions of life. The scientific has two parts: first, the makeup of the physical universe and then the practical application of what it discovers in technology. The direction in which science will move is set by the philosophic world view of the scientists. People's religious views also determine the direction of their individual lives and of their society.[2]

If those of us who work with college students, graduates, and professional people often feel that even they have no such historical background, cultural understanding, and philosophic knowledge, aren't we rather overambitious to be referring to such understanding in a curriculum overview and guide for children in the sixth grade and *under*?

That is like saying, what comes first, the cart or the horse? The *reason* we have a generation of cultural illiterates is *because* of the loss of the strong common curriculum our children used to share. Take

Hirsch's comments, quoted above from his book *Cultural Literacy*. Notice, it used to be taken for granted that children had a comprehensive knowledge of the Bible, the literary traditions of the English language such as nursery rhymes, and also the classical tales from Greece and Rome. We expected them to know European history (and classical history behind that). We could refer to great statesmen, kings, constitutions, queens, and the aspirations of citizens who spoke out, who acted, etc. and expect a reasonable knowledge structure.

The recent book by Allan Bloom, *The Closing of the American Mind,* also refers to the educational heritage rooted in the Bible, the family, and the "remarkably unified and explicit" American political tradition centered on the Declaration of Independence.

> The Bible was the common culture, one that united the simple and the sophisticated, rich and poor, young and old. . . .
>
> My grandparents were ignorant people by our standards. But their home was spiritually rich because all things done in it found their origin in the Bible's commandments. Their simple faith and practices linked them to the great thinkers who dealt with the same material. There was a respect for real learning.[3]

Convinced? That true education includes a strong chronological teaching of history, plus many other threads woven in?

If you've also remembered what Charlotte Mason put forward, as I covered her educational views in *For the Children's Sake,* you'll remember that we're looking for good strong history books, with a story-like narrative flow. *If* we can find books such as these, then it isn't at all too ambitious to give children this definite historical heritage. In fact, if you locate the right books, a class can easily have two history "courses" at different times during the week. Children are hungry for stories, and they often plead, "Oh, please go on, what happened next?"

Here is our next problem. And it's a tough one! Books telling a clear story of Western history simply aren't that easy to come by. As Hirsch said in the previous quotation, "A curriculum reform designed to teach young children the basics of cultural literacy *will require radical changes in textbooks* . . . (italics mine).

Where can we find these books ready for our use when we're advising an old-but-new-now approach and content? Listed at the end of the different grade guides are the few we've located so far in this difficult hunt for something that has gone out of style. Some are out of print but are still available in secondhand bookshops, from clearing houses and public schools who've phased them out, etc. It really is worth tracking down lively, accurately clear history books. If you unearth treasures as you search, *please* send in the information to Child Light so we can pass the details on to other interested people!

It is astounding how much children in the sixth grade and under can take in. If a timeline is drawn for them (described later), and stories read entered in their place on the timeline, they can develop a real understanding of unfolding history. Here is an important note that should be attended to! This historical unfolding should be precisely that. It is natural to start a story at the beginning, and follow the sequence in order. Hopping around causes confusion. In other words, Western civilization (ours and so directly relevant to our children) unfolds in a clear order: the Greeks, the Romans, the Middle Ages, the Renaissance, the Reformation, the Enlightenment, etc. If you can find a copy of one of the good narrative histories, it is good to read one chapter after another right through the book.

An age can be explored in greater depth around the chapter read at that time. Say you are reading through the history of the Roman Empire. Go to the local library and bring back an armload of the many excellent pictorial factual books that show what Roman buildings looked like, isolated incidents retold in story form from the Roman age, etc. Prop these up in a welcoming array along a shelf. Leave them for pupils to pick up and explore on their own during "choosing" or free activity times.

If, say, you read the main history story on the Monday, on Tuesday the children may enter the event on the timeline. Two children (or more) may narrate the historical episode back to the class. Depending on the children's ages they might draw a picture to illustrate the episode or write it up from memory in their notebook. Discussion emerging from this feedback should be encouraged. On Wednesday another history episode may be read, etc.

The episode is related to map work. Creativity should be used. For instance, while studying ancient history (the Greeks, the Romans), the children might construct a very large relief wall map starting with the Tigris and Euphrates Valley, right up to Northern Europe. In the middle sits a very blue Mediterranean. The children will naturally refer to the maps to follow Alexander the Great, the Punic Wars, etc.

The more one can "pad out" the historical period, the better. Older children can be assigned individual research projects on aspects relating to the Romans, say, or life in a medieval castle. Children sometimes enjoy looking up extra facts in children's encyclopedias. An appropriate documentary video could be watched.

In literature, myths, tales or poetry from that historical period should be read and enjoyed. Another excellent idea is to read a historical novel set in the historical time being studied.

Older children at the top end of the grade school will be able to relate the history they are studying to some of the books listed at the end of this curriculum guide in the chapter, "Developing a Christian Mind." For instance, a teacher of a combined fifth and sixth grade class in an American city progresses over the history of Western civilization in a two-year cycle. Using the Concepts and Inquiry Series[4] she finds that students grasp the historical flow from the ancient civilizations, through the Greeks and Romans, the Middle Ages, up to the Industrial Revolution, and the "Age of Revolution," etc. This line or thread covers the material commented upon from a Christian worldview standpoint in the book by F. A. Schaeffer, *How Should We Then Live?* As the students progress through the historical chronology, their lively discussions are guided by the teacher's understanding of the sort of insights Schaeffer draws out in that historical commentary. She finds that the film series with the same name as the book, *How Should We Then Live?*[5] is excellent when viewed by these children. Each episode relates to a period in history and bridges the gap between the historical events and the Christian implications. Students of ten and eleven are well able to grasp the questions, problems, and the right and wrong choices history exemplifies.

This is an example of the way it might go. The teacher we're using as an example (an actual person, this isn't theoretical!) has been reading with the children chapters dealing with the Renaissance from the Concepts and Inquiry Series. Of course, even as they read, the children find things to comment on, ask about. Sometimes discussions arise. Now, while all this is happening, our teacher has in the back of *her* mind the sort of Biblical perspective written about in Chapter 3 of the book *How Should We Then Live?* In fact, not only does she keep those ideas in mind as she guides the discussions along (she rereads it the night before even though she knows it well), she sometimes brings out the book and reads relevant paragraphs. The children look at the pictures in it, too, and relate these to other art reproductions brought into the classroom from the library.

Another day, the children watch the episode from the film series *How Should We Then Live?* They understand what they are seeing. They really do understand the ideas talked about, and show this in the discussion afterwards. Of course, they won't remember *everything!* But the thread *is* there, the weaving *is* there.

Without going into the subject of geography as deeply as history here, it should be noted! I could hardly believe the following item in *The Times Educational Supplement* (published in London, England the 5th of February, 1988):

> If America sometimes seems doubtful of her place in the
> world, officials of the National Geographic Society do

not find it surprising. Recent surveys have shown that nearly half of its high school seniors cannot locate the United States on a map or globe.

"Our youngsters today are geographically illiterate," complains Mr. Gilbert Grosvenor, the society's president. "Since World War II, geography has practically disappeared from the school system. If you don't know where you are in the world, you are nowhere. And today, unfortunately, we do not."

The Geographic Society has announced a gift of $20 million to set up an educational foundation that will concentrate on teacher training and the development of geography curricula.

The need educationally is painfully apparent. And Americans, don't shrink with embarrassment! A British survey not long ago found that many teenage British pupils fared little better. Living opposite the French coast, many didn't know where France was, or how big it was, etc.

Yes, use maps, globes and any clear geographical curricula you can find! There is the casual literacy: locating on the map where something happened in 1790 . . . or today, from the newspaper headlines. But there is the science of geography. The mapping out of the world's surface.

Charlotte Mason was in favor of the earlier grades becoming acquainted with their *local* world first. Climb a local hill. Follow a local stream; she meant, wade in it, walk along from gurgling rapids to where it spreads out in a meadow and meanders. Chart it. Learn to make maps from things seen. This is an excellent and important stage in geography. You move from observing (experiencing) the real land to the charting of it on paper. The more variety at this stage, the better. *Climb* a hill, *drive up* a mountain, and *hike* the last bit. *Paddle* in the waves as they roll up a beach, *walk* around a cove and *notice* how the wave patterns change. *Go in boat* to an island, down a river, across a lake. The variety is as broad as the earth itself. Make use of what you have! City children will chart roads, freeways, etc. But they, too, should be taken to land and allowed to run, climb, observe. Sometime during all this activity the children naturally move from simple charts to actual maps.

Older children should learn to enjoy mapping a hike on a large scale map. They can plan whether to climb over the hill, or meander up the valley along a river. Many children travel today. Following the map as you go is fun in cars, airplanes, boats or by foot in the Himalayas for missionary children. Geography! It has to do with the feet on our ground, the water, the oceans. It is also the stuff of dreams, following in the imagination trips you can't take yourself! A stack of old *National Geographics* makes excellent browsing material, armchair travel. Don't make a big lesson of it! Let the child enjoy browsing, talk over the things you see together as interested friends. Merely point out on a handy globe where in the world you are!

In the last grades of grade school the actual study of geography is started. It sounds as if we can look to the National Geographic Society for some good curricula here. We need them.

To sum it up, the goal should be to relate details (or the separate threads of history, geography, etc.) to this panoramic view, to give meaning to each detail as it relates to the whole. This avoids the fragments of mere details of knowledge which float about disconnectedly in a person's mind. These fragments have little or no meaning to the student because these details haven't been related to his or her own sense of place and of reality. Such details also fail to relate to any kind of comprehensive view (such as the Judeo-Christian worldview) either of the physical world or of the span of human history. In fact, today few schools have any such unifying view of reality that makes interrelationships possible. Most students are condemned to a vague fog of muddled thinking made up of unrelated ideas and facts.

As books and textbooks rarely include a real interrelating element, the teacher is the key person here. This teacher must have his or her own sense of place, relationships, etc. There must first be the weaving together of the threads in his or her mind, so that in discussion this all comes out. That is why an integral part of this important curriculum covering so much of life is the teacher's *own* preparation. The chapter on the teacher developing a Christian worldview fits in right here. It is impossible to skim over this element and still reap the product desired! *It takes time and effort for the adults to be prepared. It simply can't work otherwise.*

Susan Schaeffer Macaulay

Appendix II: Alternate Social Studies Curriculum, Grades Three and Four

Third Grade Social Studies

This year a more formal plan is adopted. The main aim is to use the immediate environment as the resource for understanding geography and a sense of history. However, continued national and international awareness is also developed through biographies read (other people's lives), some use of current news, "adopting" a missionary family, and the deliberate use of a globe and atlases.

In some classes, children will find out about their state. Other teachers may relate the local story to the country's overall history.

For abler children, you may wish to include a bit of European background. Next year the focus will be on your country's history. If you feel you can include it, you might choose some books that give a picture of the "old world" out of which your country sprang.

Curriculum

1. Nordic myths and folktales
    a. Suggested books:

       Norse Gods and Giants   Ingri and Edgar Parin D'Aulaire

       Gods and Heroes from Viking Mythology   Brian Branston

       The Wonderful Adventures of Nils   Selma Lagerlof

       See *Books Children Love* for additional suggestions.

    b. Read and narrate an episode once or twice weekly.
2. Biography—Use these suggestions to draw up your own list of

biographies and autobiographies. Before taking in the broad sweep of history, a child relates best to "getting introduced" to people he or she can't meet in person.

The Columbus Story by Alice Dalgliesh

Benjamin Franklin by Ingri and Edgar d'Aulaire

George Washington by Ingri and Edgar d'Aulaire

Lincoln's Birthday by Clyde Bulla

Pocahontas and the Strangers by Clyde Bulla

Little House in the Big Woods by Laura Ingalls Wilder, and others in the series

Whatever you've chosen for your set of biographies, try to include the following autobiographical story which opens a window on missionary work in North Africa. Through it children come to share in the needs of children's lives in very different circumstances, and what it means to one English woman living with them. It is an absorbing and beautiful story. Relate this insight to the mission project listed later.

Star of Light by Patricia St. John (Moody Press)
All God's Children by Pauline C. Webb (Revell)

Although not biographical, these tell stories of children in other lands and foster understanding and interest in other children. Relate this to the missionary project and to geographical locations.

3. Main Study Theme: The World Around Me—Integrated studies of local history and geography.

An in-depth, exploratory program based on your local area. The geographical scene should be literally explored, something as described in the overview of this section. If your area has been built up, use that too. However, you should also arrange several field trips to nearby landforms as well and note topography. Remember, the geographical aspects should be experienced and then charted. Going out once a week would not be too much.

A historical picture of the area should also be built up. Try to relate this to real people. One of the best resources is a senior citizen who can make an interesting story of what the hometown was like seventy or eighty years ago. What was school like? Chores? The Fourth of July? Try to locate the oldest building. Make a local timeline mural chart.

If there is a local museum with a program for children, make full use of its facilities.

After you've taken exploratory walks, charted them, made maps, etc., look up books describing the same sort of topography as you've seen. Extend that something like this, "We climbed a small hill. Look at these pictures of mountains." In other words, use whatever experiences the children have had to help them imagine landforms they haven't seen in other places.

As you're building up a picture of the area, go back a second time covering the same routes again. This time, relate science observations to the whole picture. How many different kinds of trees, grasses, flowers, etc., can you locate growing naturally? What evidence is there of insect life? Notice different kinds of soil, water supply, etc. How does this affect plant growth?

Notice shadows at different times of the day. Notice seasonal changes. The list relates geography to earth sciences.

Now go a bit further. If you've explored and charted a river, for instance, get out a map of a wider area, a map of the whole country, too. Where did this river come from? Where does it go? How about the roads? Where do they lead? Get a road map and trace destinations. Try to relate this to trips individual children have gone on.

Although we've mentioned asking individual older people about the past history of the area, now study in greater depth the *groups* of people who make up the community. Who are they? Where did they come from? What do they believe? What are their customs? If, for instance, there is a group with a different ethnic background, make creative use of that. Can you go shopping with the children and buy the sorts of foods these people use in cooking? Could a member of this group come to a home and cook a typical meal with the children? Can the children actually get to know people from different groups? Could you celebrate a festival as another group does? What are the problems people face in this area? Third graders aren't too young to think about problems. Housing? Employment? Age? Crime? Poverty?

The children might be able to visit a synagogue or in some other way begin to understand the diversity around them. Farm children need a couple of field trips to built-up areas. City children could visit a farm, have a camping weekend in the countryside, have a day's hike in a nearby outdoor area once a month, etc.

Don't forget ecological observation. Is erosion a problem? Notice it. Call the public park service. Is there a reclamation project the children could visit?

Try to record all of the explorations in a meaningful way. Scrapbooks with pictures and stories the children have written, local maps, etc., should be made and left on display. Maybe some of the people who told their stories, explained different ways of life or beliefs, etc., could be invited in for an afternoon tea at the end of the year! Children could bring sandwiches, snacks and cakes, and drinks could be served to the guests who could view the information finally amassed.

By the way, if during your explorations, children notice problems, this is an ideal time to communicate the idea that we're to *do* something about problems. Have a cleanup party for a littered park or beach. Plant trees. Visit a lonely old person. Make friends, and keep going back.

Last of all, do be on the lookout for any books relating to all these topics. Ask at your library. Keep them on display. If there were Chinese people and you met them, found out about them, then get out books on China. (A few!) If you're in the middle of an urban sprawl, look for books that tell about similar land that is *unbuilt.* Also look for books about cities. The list is endless!

This *The World Around Me* theme has more than enough to keep you busy in third grade!

4. Adopt a Missionary Family or Project—A wall space or bulletin board and perhaps a scrapbook should be the focus for a practical awareness of the wider world. In the Christian home or school, it's never too early to find out about, and feel responsible for a particular missionary family, or possibly a specific project like an orphanage or village. This means finding out, caring, and then responding. The first appropriate response is to really pray for one or more of the missionaries. That person will have a prayer list. Make up a class list from it. Children need to find out that prayer is *"really* doing something." Answers to prayer should be thankfully talked about as good news. Many missions have materials suitable for children: books or stories to read about the work, the country, etc. Children needn't be protected from all the problems. The picture they get should be as real as possible.

Obviously, this inside picture means you'll locate your missionary on a world map (with the time-honored pin?) and also trace how they travel to and from the country with your fingers on the globe. You'll read a short library book on the country and continent "your" missionary is in.

Maybe the missionary has children, and letters could be written to them. Would these children enjoy a package of books? Art supplies? Contact? American children studying at home may be able to locate missionary children who even use the same study courses as they do. Pen pals are fun, too.

Read the two suggested missionary books sometime during the year. (Listed under number 2, Biographies in this chapter.)

If you live in a suburb, consider the importance of recognizing the missionary needs much nearer at hand. Have a second bulletin board for a more local home missions project. If you feel like shielding such young children from the grimmer side of their city, remember they've seen worse on TV. And this is something to care about, pray for, act for. It is their real world. In some American cities, instead of providing pregnancy counseling centers, Christians unite to provide residential care for young unmarried mothers. Children of this age could also pray for such a project, care about the people in trouble in their world. They might make a practical caring contribution. Is there anything the children can *do?*

5. News—as you're studying the locality, get a local newspaper regularly. Appropriate news stories can be read, noticed. Events can be located on a local map. A bulletin board could display clippings of happenings interesting to children. Local events (a country fair, an art exhibit, etc.) could be visited. Important national and international news should also be noted.

6. Maps—the class should have a good globe, atlas, map of the locality, relief map and political maps of the entire country and world. These should be referred to. For instance, if a child talks about a grandparent in another country, locate it. When there is a news story, find out where it happened on the map. Keep referring to where things were or are located. If you discover that the black people in your community came from Africa originally, find *Africa,* name it. See if the children can find it alone!

Also see that the children can locate the equator on the globe. What is it? Notice and develop an understanding of scales used in maps. Notice the difference between political and physical maps.

7. Exploring the Wider World—another way of approaching the wider world in an interesting way is through reading the book, *Famous Explorers for Young People* by Ramon Peyton Coffman. This opens up world geography through the topic of its exploration. Be sure to talk about climates in areas explored. Notice continents and oceans.

Fourth Grade Social Studies

Fourth grade will be the year when students will be introduced to the story of their own country. For most schools following this curriculum, this will be the history of the United States.

Students of this age are well able to follow a consecutive history where events unfold one after the other. A text which holds their interest and stirs the imagination should be sought. Beware of lists of facts and treaties! If you cannot locate a lively, story-telling tale of your nation in a single book, you may have to use textbooks only as the teacher's linking infrastructure and for reference. In this case, build up the national history from a biographical standpoint—"real books" and story books written to be read with children.

Students will make their own notebook record of the story of their country.

In geography, a basic geographical knowledge of the child's country is the aim. The development of map and globe skills is continued. Using an atlas for reference is practiced.

Roman mythology is read and narrated.

The missionary project is continued. Awareness of missionary needs and work in the student's own country is developed.

Curriculum

1. Roman myths

   Suggested books: *Heroes, Gods, and Emperors from Roman Mythology* by Kewy Usher. See *Books Children Love* for additional suggestions. Include some appropriate tales from the child's national heritage.

2. National and Religious Holidays

   a. National (American or other) holidays—read about and discuss the significance of them throughout the year. Include those that fall during vacation time.

   b. Religious (Christian, Jewish, and other appropriate faiths present in the nation)—read about and discuss the similarities, differences and significance of the holidays. From the Christian worldview, it is important to establish that although we believe other faiths are not true, not right, yet we respect other people. Being truly tolerant doesn't mean thinking everybody is right, or even has a reasonable point of view. But we believe in freedom of personal choice. Also foster respect for other people's lives, respecting what is important to them. Note which aspects are cultural, and which aspects involve absolutes.

3. History—"The Story of My Country." For most, this will mean a survey of the main events and ideas that shaped the United States of America. Those from other countries can easily adapt this.

   a. Introduction. Find a few short pictoral accounts of Europe in the fifteenth century, so that children have some understanding of the "Old World." Locate Europe on the map. Suitable picture books can be borrowed from a public library.

   b. There are two options for the study of history in the fourth grade.

      • Based on a single book—locate a lively, interesting and accurate narrative history of the United States of America. Read a section (a chapter, if possible). The next day, children narrate that story as remembered. They may draw a picture of some event in the episode. They locate the event and record it on a mural timeline. Other stories of the same period may be read in conjunction with the main history book: historical novels, biographies, etc. Library picture books of the same period are borrowed and are propped up inviting perusal.

Later in the week, the next chapter is read. In this way, the story of the nation is unfolded.

- A year's story told through separate books read in historical sequence—these are linked by charts.

  You may not find a lively narrative history book to read, chapter by chapter. In this case, devise a history through linking up individual books: historical stories, and biographies are chosen—"real books," not textbooks.

  The danger here is that a sense of flow will not be developed. Construct the timeline and enter main events and people as you progress. Make a separate wall chart for each century, and hang them in order. At the top are dates clearly printed: 1600-1700. The teacher reads the chapter on the time span being studied in the children's textbook in preparation for the class. He or she chooses books that will tell something of the story of the century. But there are gaps! Draw an outline of major events and people in the century. Now, you're ready! Say, for example, you've read some preparatory books with the class and now you start with a story of Columbus. You note "Discovery of America—Columbus" both on the chart and the timeline (with the children). There is a gap! The next good readable narrative book you locate is one on people who lived in Jamestown. That leaves you with Spanish exploration untouched. At the local library you find three picture books about Spanish explorers and the routes they took. Fine! After the Columbus story, you have an "easier" lesson, reading the picture books right through together, talking about their clothes, etc. Each child gets a photocopied map of the continent, and traces different explorers' routes in different colors on them. On the chart goes a title, Spanish Explorers in America. The chart and timeline will provide the connecting element.

  Keep the sense of *flow* strong. You may find and refer to two or three clear textbook outlines with maps and pictures so that the children can refer to them and visualize how it all hangs together.

  Be sure to provide the backdrop to the flow, e.g. something about the effect of world history on this story—the country itself, how the geography helps to tell the story. Also don't forget important facts *in* the flow for which you might not find story books—the Declaration of Independence, the Constitution.

The Main Books You'll Read. Find selections from *Books Children Love* and other lists. Look for biographies, historical novels, and autobiographical material. Libraries have lovely picture books of all sorts on historical topics. Make full use of these. The pictoral information will make the child's imagination more accurate when you read the narrative stories.

A few "real book" examples are listed at random, not in order. Check with your public librarian for more titles. Use some of the suggestions from third grade that are appropriate if they weren't used.

Caddie Woodlawn by Carol Ryrie (pioneer Wisconsin—1860s)

Daniel Boone by James Daugherty (living with the Indians, traveling through new territory)

Freedom Train by Dorothy Sterling (the story of Harriet Tubman who knew slavery and escaped, helping others)

America's Paul Revere by Esther Forbes (another biography, also tells the story of a historical period)

The Matchlock Gun by Walter D. Edmonds (New York State and the Hudson Valley, a true story of courage)

George Washington Carver: An American Biography by Rackham Holt (inspiring history of the progression from slavery to scientist)

The Mayo Brothers by Jane Goodsell (short book to include as people changed rural America in various ways. In this case, the founding of the world-famous medical care)

One advantage of the "storybook method" is that children love being read to! Therefore lessons in history like this can be daily ones, and last a lot longer than textbook teaching.

Don't neglect keeping up the outline of historical incidents that shaped the national picture. *Keep the timeline and history charts filled in.*

    c. Whichever option you select for teaching history, remember to fully use other material. Museums, exhibits, visiting buildings and historical sites, some video documentary materials, etc. can be used to enrich the year's study. As in all other subjects, encourage discussion of the *ideas* that lay behind the choices people made and how the consequences shaped history.

d. Use this checklist for areas to be included in the study of the United States.

- American Indians—Plains, Southwest, Eastern Forest, and Northwest

- Founding, growth, and development of the United States

- Past and present daily life

- Past and present economics

- Governmental system—national, local, and state

- Neighbors of the United States—Canada, Mexico, Central America, South America, Caribbean

- World events with emphasis on the United States and her neighbors—apply critical thinking skills in distinguishing fact from bias or an individual's viewpoint

4. Heroes—selected on the basis of character traits that a role model should manifest

a. Biblical—Elijah, Joshua, John the Baptist, Esther, the widow of Mark 12:41-44, Luke 21:1-4

b. Choose heroes from United States history using the criteria of positive character traits and manifested evidence of a desire to grow and mature in areas of weakness. If you've chosen the biographical approach to history, this area may well be covered in daily studies.

5. Geography

a. Construct a relief map of America (North), or the nation the child is a citizen of.

b. Note regions in both North and South America, Central America and the Caribbean.

c. Note climates and weather patterns in the various areas. Develop vocabulary—hurricane, tornado, blizzard, temperature, thermometer, high pressure, low pressure, precipitation, humidity, wind chill, trade winds, monsoon, tidal wave, barometer.

d. Construct graphs and diagrams that show crops, products, temperature and rainfall for the different regions.

e. Spend at least some time on traditional geography study of the child's own country. This will be repeated in the sixth grade, but two overviews in grade school aren't too many! A simple geography book (of the U.S.A.) could be mastered.

   f. Practical local studies should still continue from the third grade. Nature walks should still be part of the curriculum. Learn to use a compass, how does it function? How did pioneers find their way with no roads? Could the children walk West? Where is North, South, East?

6. Maps and globes

   a. Each class should have a copy of *The Children's World Atlas* editor, Brian Dicks (Celestial Arts). This relates to all map work for grades 4-6. Children should have time to look at this alone as well as for work, projects, and reference. Note land and water shapes—coast, lake, gulf, ocean, sea, river, island, isthmus, peninsula, delta, and harbor.

7. Missionary Project

   a. Continue the missionary project by building up a relationship with a real family or work. Suggestions are in third grade, number 4.

   b. Read a missionary book.

   c. Make a class scrapbook about the different *kinds* of missionary/caring work. Orphans; the hungry/agricultural development; inner city projects, street people; hospices; Bible translation, etc. Note the different *skills* people need to serve: medical—doctors, nurses, laboratory technicians, dieticians; agricultural; linguists; secretaries; pilots; communication technicians; teachers; ministers; missionary mothers to keep the family going, etc.

   d. Note some of the realities connected with projects listed above, and the people who serve, leaving home, nice houses, safe hospitals (for some), receiving a lower or poor salary, living in a country where you don't know the language and having to learn it. Living in the inner city isn't nice; what will these families do about their own children? The stress of say, serving in a hospital where you can't get enough medicine, it's hard to clean, not enough staff. How hard is it to tell other people that there is "Good News" that they don't know yet? Will people believe them? How can you make them *want* to know if the Bible and Jesus is real?

   e. Include the serving that Jesus asks every one of us to do. Communicate that everybody is meant to work full-time serving others for Jesus' sake. We're all to be missionaries! What does it mean to love my neighbor as myself in *my* city, *my* town, *my* family, *my* street? Does salary matter as much as obeying this command?

f. For news this year, note news of people-serving projects. Some missionary societies produce colorful periodicals or even children's news. Get other adults to look out for Christian magazines that include features on such projects. Also note secular projects in local and national papers. A hospice for children? A new housing plan for disabled elderly? Food for refugees? Discuss this good news during the year. Don't forget individual acts of caring: a news item about a person's life saved because of someone's courage, etc.

g. Suggested books:

- *Dangerous Journey* by John Bunyan, edited by Oliver Hunkin (Marshall Morgan and Scott/Eerdmans). Using Bunyan's own words, an illustrated *Pilgrim's Progress*

- *Pilgrim's Progress* by John Bunyan (Lippincott, 1939), retold and abridged by Mary Godolphin, or another edition of *Pilgrim's Progress*. See *Books Children Love* for additional suggestions.

Susan Schaeffer Macaulay

Appendix III: Alternate Social Studies Curriculum, Grades Five and Six

T he Child Light overview of history and geography has provided that the child has studied his own local environment, moving on to his national history. Two years will be given to a study of world history, starting with the source of our own civilizations in ancient history. There may be cases where, because a child is only following this course for a year, you need to alter this plan. However, if you consider the scope of this topic, two years will not seem too much! This curriculum guide does not give a timetable for this study. A lot will depend on the books you choose, areas you emphasize, etc. Special importance is attached to a wall chart with a time line so that the sequence of happenings, cultures, eras can be noted. It is assumed that the emphasis on discussion and ideas as brought out in the overview of this subject will be remembered and implemented. It is also assumed that you'll study the material in an ordered sequence that follows history. In other words, Babylonian history comes before the Greeks, etc.

The nature of a two-year course means careful planning is necessary. Also, as such historical studies are fairly unusual in today's schools, special attention needs to be given to appropriate books. The students are now old enough to learn to work right through a book, relating extra material to the basic study. Our main textbook suggestions are listed in Chapter 21.

The recommended Concepts and Inquiry Series is still around in great quantities in back rooms at public schools, available at clearing houses, secondhand textbook suppliers, etc. It is this series that has been found to relate usefully to the *How Should We Then Live?* flow of historical teaching. There is plenty of material for two years.

The Concepts and Inquiry Series published by Allyn and Bacon separates major topics into individual trade paperbacks. Titles include,

Ancient Civilization, Greece and Rome, Middle Ages right up to the *Industrial Revolution* and *Revolution.* There is also a book titled *Four World Views* which gives the background for discussing Christianity in relationship to other worldviews.

Previously mentioned, *A Child's History of the World* by V. M. Hillyer (copyright 1961) is only presently available in print for children enrolled in Calvert School. This excellent book gives one year's worth of history stories. Unique. Especially useful to foster a love of history, it works with children who aren't ready for mature study. Although out of print, teachers and parents have located it in second-hand stores and libraries from California to Boston!

Remember, these books give a good base for the history studied. But the teacher/parent needs to be up on relating ideas to Christian concepts.

However, a Christian publisher has brought out a useful history book that will take the student up to the age of exploration. It is *The Story of the Old World,* published by Christian Schools International, Grand Rapids, Michigan.

Turn to Chapter 21, and note books listed there. Also find further historical suggestions in *Books Children Love.*

Fifth Grade Social Studies

In history the course of world history will be followed. Choose a break-off point where this study will be resumed next year. Be sure to enrich this study with art, travel books with beautiful photographs of unknown places (such as Greece, etc.), related literature, and historical novels. Discussion is an important part of this study.

In geography try to establish that basic geographical knowledge is now understood. Latitude, longitude, the continents and oceans, etc.—basic geography—should be mastered. The development of map and globe skills is continued. The geography of Europe and Asia should be studied as a background to the history. Climate and its effect on daily living should be noted. Large areas of world regions should be noted: desert, plain, forest and mountain regions should be studied and compared.

In discussion (both arising from past history and current news items) the interdependence of people and the individual's response is stressed. Responsibility for individual and group choices is emphasized in relationship to local, national and world need.

Curriculum

1. Roman myths
   Suggested books:

Heroes, Gods and Emperors from Roman Mythology by Kewy Usher.

See *Books Children Love* for additional suggestions.

2. History
   a. Read, narrate and/or discuss the basic historical text you have chosen. As historical understanding is considered essential in the Child Light view of education, quality *and* quantity time should be given to this area. Two or three separate history reading and discussion times should be provided for each week. A twenty-minute history reading is quite long. With discussion or other activities, this may be extended. Some classes have a history reading four times a week.
   b. A history notebook is kept by each student. After the history reading, each student records in list form the main events and people's names in chronological order. Dates are noted—not every small date, but key ones. If desired, students may also keep a separate part of the notebook for other historical work. Drawn maps with relevant places or information marked can be kept together with notes. Some children are ready for narration in written form. (See 6th grade history notes). Another section of the notebook could contain this writing.
   c. Create a mural timeline that highlights main events in the history studied. A few key names of people can also be inserted. Students can each make their own timeline on a long scroll of paper.
   d. Occasionally use a video episode of *How Should We Then Live?* as it relates to the period studied. Use other supporting video material.
   e. If possible, visit any museum or exhibit that has items relating to the period being studied.
3. Discussion/highlights
   a. Compare present-day communities with those of the past. Note the diversity, and contrast the values, economic base, family-life patterns, and philosophical presuppositions.
   b. Note the necessity that exists in all communities for individuals to work together for the good of the whole.
   c. Perceive what happens when members of a community do not feel a sense of responsibility to the whole, or fail to respect the intrinsic value of all other human beings.
   d. Begin to understand the contrast between the Christian view of the person, and that of other cultures. Note the

effect on the laws and social patterns when a community fails to believe in the worth of each separate person. Note that pagan cultures had a low view of the woman compared to the Judeo-Christian traditions.

   e. Note how the two characteristics of God—righteousness and love—need to be reflected in all human communities. Note the effect of un-right laws (unrighteousness) and lack of human compassion, mercy, love, care, affection, gentleness, etc.

4. Heroes—selected on the basis of character traits that a role model should have

   a. Biblical—David, Hezekiah, Stephen, Ruth, Hannah. Note the strengths and weaknesses of each. Notice their belief or trust in God, forgiveness, and choices which required strength.

   b. Choose heroes from the historical period being studied. Find short lively biographies that are enjoyable to read.

5. Maps and globes

   a. Locate the seven continents.

   b. Note that longitude and latitude grids are the same on all maps.

   c. Use longitude and latitude to locate countries, states, islands, and cities.

   d. Increase the ability to use keys and symbols.

6. Geography

   a. Note how the climates are related to desert, plain, forest and mountain regions on the globe or world map. Identify and understand the effects of major kinds of climates—polar, ice cap, cold and moist, rainy and warm with dry summer and rainy winters, semiarid, desert, tropical with rain throughout the year, and tropical with a rainy season.

   b. Choose a geography book that gives a clear overview of Asia and Europe. Note major features: mountain ranges, plains, rivers, etc. Learn to identify countries and their boundaries as they are in the present. Note trade and communication routes: ports, rail systems, cities. Identify the groups of people who live in different areas.

   c. Obtain and view occasional good geographical video material. Leave out *National Geographic* magazines for children to browse through. Be prepared to use their own interest for comment and discussion. Always locate the place on a map!

   d. The student should do at least one geographical project. He or she should look up information in reference books and record it. Maps should be hand copied. Information such as climate, rainfall, etc. should be obtained from special maps in atlases. An essay of "An Imaginary Trip to . . ." could be written or narrated so that he or she tries to imagine the place. A fiction book written on the chosen area could be read.

7. Missionary project

Continue (as first described in third grade) with class mission project/information/involvement *or* begin the world survey of Christian work described in 6th grade, and make it a two-year project.

Suggested book: *Wilfred Grenfell* by Joyce Blackburn

8. News/contemporary thought

Subscribe to a class copy of *Time Magazine, Newsweek,* or some weekly news publication. Leave it out so that children browse through it. Be prepared to answer their questions about articles and pictures. Find out where items are located on the globe. Relate this to the *sort* of country it's in—a democracy? Communist? Some items will be of current events in countries being studied in history. Note this relationship. Many children will have only casually watched news programs on TV. This develops an entertainment attitude toward what is happening in the world. In fact, they should learn to try to assess *factual information* and also note the *ideas* being put across in the article. In discussion, differences of opinions should be welcomed. The adult should ask, "What do *you* think?" "Why?" "If you want to know more, where can you look it up? "Why do you think the article draws that conclusion?"

When appropriate, choose and read an entire item. Discuss it. Note the changing climate of our culture: in the arts, film, rock music, media, behavior of people, medical ethics, etc.

Eternity magazine would be very useful to subscribe to as well in fifth and sixth grade. Note the Christian analysis of these areas. Of course, the teacher must read through the periodicals personally to be ready for the questions! If you haven't, that can be good, too. "Oh, I'm interested that you've asked that. I don't know much about it. What have you found out? I'll read it, but I may have to think this over a bit before answering."

(Some classes will begin further specific discussion as described under *News* in 6th grade.)

a. Suggested books:

Famous Pioneers for Young People

Famous Women of America

Famous American Statesmen

Martha, Daughter of Virginia

The Story of Martha Washington by Marguerite Vance

See *Books Children Love* for additional suggestions.

Sixth Grade Social Studies

The story of world history will be continued from the fifth grade. Refer to the fifth grade subject notes and the subject overview for details of this world history course. When deciding how far to go into modern history, it would help to know what the student will be studying later in junior high school. He may be doing a course then that covers the twentieth century. (A good school will devote a year to the world's history in the twentieth century, and a separate year to more mature study of the student's own national history.) In that case you may decide to leave off the study of this century. However, if you think that the student will not go on and get a chance to study our century soon, you may decide to at least cover the world wars, and discuss the changes in religious belief, technology, social patterns, political realities, etc. As current events are discussed, you may well decide that you wish to come right up to date in the scope of this historical flow.

As students mature, they are able to develop more interest in news and cultural aspects of our society. Ideas such as justice, freedom, and humanism gain more significance.

Geography is studied as a separate subject. The world as a whole is still considered. However, at least part of the year is spent on acquiring accurate geographical knowledge of the student's own country. The old-fashioned ability to sketch a reasonable map of the country should be practiced. Map and globe skills are expanded. Geographical research using a good atlas and other research books is encouraged. Graphs and diagrams should be read and understood.

Myths are read and narrated. Other projects still find a place in sixth grade, such as missionary friends, etc.

Curriculum

1. Greek, Roman, Nordic, and other myths and legends
   a. Suggested books:

   Mythology by Edith Hamilton

   The Myths of Greece and Rome by H. A. Guerbver

   Hero Tales from Many Lands by Alice I. Haxeltilne

   The Heroes by Charles Kingsley

   Read and narrate one or two weekly.

2. History
   a. Read, narrate and discuss the basic historical text you have chosen. This is the continuation of the world history survey course commenced in fifth grade. See that grade's notes for specific suggestions which should be continued.
   b. Personal history study. In addition to the two or three group history lessons each week, it is good to add an extra period for personal historical study.

   Students should keep up the notebook started in fifth grade. Each student records main events and dates in chronological order as the topic is read. Important characters' names are also listed.

   Students should now be capable of writing historical essays. There are two kinds. One is a narration. (See Chapter 2.) In this, the students write from memory on an open-ended question. For instance, "Write all that you can remember about the French Revolution."

   The second essay should involve research. By now students should be familiar with using reference books. Show them how to look in the index for topics or people they are to write about. Essays should support the main historical reading being followed by the class. Students read their essays aloud to each other.

   Some schools may wish to expand personal study to include a more elaborate project of historical research. This could center around something like Life in Early America. It could include drawings, poetry, etc.

   At this age, personal study should not take the place of class reading and discussion. It should be kept fairly simple in scope, and not be a burden. If the skills are developed and an interest maintained in the class readings, children will be more ready than most for true higher learning in later years.
   c. Continue the timeline wall mural. It can indicate what is happening simultaneously in history, art, music, religion, economics, and politics.
   d. Note how beliefs or ideas have actual results in history. Always note the results that exist when a low value is placed on human life.
3. World societies—discussion points to cover
   a. Develop an understanding of the responsibility of individuals in society.
   b. Note the differentiation between the value systems of different societies.
   c. Compare different political systems and develop an under-

standing of how they function and how they affect the lives of individuals throughout the world as well as those living under a particular system—monarchy, democracy, republic, communism, fascism, socialism.

  d. Develop an understanding of and compare different economic systems.

  e. Compare societies studied with Biblical standards and models, and note what elements are missing in the different societies.

  f. By drawing conclusions formulate a generalization of how and why cultures change.

  g. Develop an understanding that absolutes do not change but cultures do and, therefore, the application of absolutes in contemporary society can reflect the culture without compromising the absolute.

4. Heroes—chosen for the manifestation of positive character traits

  a. Biblical—Samuel, Nehemiah, Paul, Rebecca, Deborah

  b. Choose heroes from the historical period being studied. Concentrate on those whose choices affected society: the world was better because of what he or she did. People like Elizabeth Fry, John Newton, Wilberforce, Shaftesbury, and Amy Carmichael are possibilities.

5. Geography

  a. Continue suggestions given in the fifth grade. Students still need a good geography book and need further study in world geography.

  b. Part of the year's geography periods should be set aside to concentrate on the student's own country. What are the main physical areas? How is climate distributed? Rainfall? Temperatures? Where is agriculture best? The communication network. Urban growth: a map of 1890, and a map of today. What are the changes in cities, roads, other developments? The student should become familiar enough with the country to be able to sketch a fairly good map and indicate main physical features and main cities. A geography textbook and an atlas should be used for such studies.

  c. Use graphs and diagrams to consider global geography. Note geographical regions of Europe, Asia and Africa. Note the topography and climate of regions. Construct rainfall, product and temperature graphs for the different regions. Compare different regions located on the same continent.

6. Maps and globes

  a. Develop the ability to use and make special purpose maps—weather, climate, temperature, time zone, road, historical, products, natural resources, population.

    b. Discover how maps are made—books, movies, filmstrips, field trips, resource people.

    c. Each child should be able to demonstrate an ability to use graphs, keys, legends, symbols, longitude, and latitude.

7. Missionary project. In sixth grade give weekly time to a survey of Christian work in all the world. This is good, as world geography and history plus current events give a picture of the world and its problems. What are Christians doing about it? The basis of this survey will be a book which is essential: *Operation World* by Patrick Johnstone. Published by STL books and WEC Publications. This unique book lists all world countries in alphabetical order. Whenever you study a country in geography, or read about it in a news story, you can look in this book for information about that country's religion, physical needs and situation, which Christians are working there, what they do, and what is happening in the Christian church.

    At some point you should also find out about Christian evangelistic and caring work in your own community. Remember, good habits for life are formed in childhood. When you are informed, the appropriate response is prayer responsibility, and then possibly some other form of support.

8. News/contemporary thought

    The same program as fifth grade should be followed.

    Note an additional focus point. Discuss with the class how the media, rock music, television and videos have affected them. Contrast Biblical views of what is right with current accepted behavior. Avoid a list of "shalt nots," but bring out *clearly* Biblical morality. Sixth graders, if they've not already discussed this previously, should especially contrast Biblical sexual morality and its care of each life (abortion and euthanasia) with the common attitudes and practices of today. These are an abomination in the sight of God.

    Bring in a few examples of magazines, and use these as evidence of the attitudes the children may have unthinkingly absorbed. The books that have been read throughout the Child Light curriculum will have given these children an absorbed sense of family life, moral choice, and the value of each human being. But at this stage, the differences must be verbalized, noted, and understood.

    Note the relevance of material available in Chapter 23, "Developing a Christian Mind." Some classes will be ready for the book *Whatever Happened to the Human Race?* listed there, or the video episodes that cover the material in it. For such a class, you can center group discussion around: the value of human life, and why; the unborn; the handicapped; the aged; and problems in genetic engineering, future technology involving human life.

All sixth graders should understand about AIDS and that the Christian method of prevention is that sexual relationships belong *within* marriage to *one person* until death. Compassionate attitudes must also be developed as these children will witness a plague situation, where they as Christians will be called upon to act with compassion and wisdom, bringing comfort to the dying. It is advised that teachers and parents obtain the book: *The Twentieth Century Plague* by Dr. Caroline Collier—a Lion Paperback (copyright 1987, Christian Medical Fellowship. Published by Lion Publishing, Ickneild Way, Tring, Herts, England).

The adult will not read the book to the children. But the information should be passed on verbally. These are the children who must be prepared to cope with the coming epidemic. "The AIDS epidemic of the late 1990s has already happened," according to Dr. Robert Redfield of Walter Reed.[1]

This article states the grim news that "one out of every 61 infants born in New York City harbors . . . HIV" and that health officials know already where the epidemic first wave will strike, in our inner cities.

As all news and contemporary thought is discussed, it must always contain the positive structure of Biblical truth in relationship to the real world which we're meant to understand.

9. Suggested books:

Famous Generals and Admirals for Young People

Famous Kings and Queens for Young People

Caesar's Gallic War   by Olivia Coolidge

Men of Athens   by Olivia Coolidge

See *Books Children Love* for additional suggestions. Note Appendix 6 on Family (Sex) Education.

Susan Schaeffer Macaulay

Appendix IV:
Home Schools

You'll have noticed that the curriculum guides are drawn up in the school mode. Throughout we have references to the class and the teacher. In fact, in home education, all of the twenty-four hours is integrated. However, when you sit down with the youngest child for her hour of "the three R's" plus her looked-for story and narration, this is school! *Her* school . . . and one of the best of all! Mother, Father, big sister, *someone* is the teacher. And so, there is no problem in using the guides as such. In fact, the Child Light curriculum follows ideas initiated by Charlotte Mason, and *she* intended home schools to be catered to as well as the more institutional ones. The methods work especially well on that one-to-one basis. Narration, for instance, is a natural response in the home school. And teacher only has *one* pupil in the class. It really is fantastic! If a question is asked, you don't have ten others who aren't interested. A narration can be enjoyed, and then the whole class has been listened to! Sometimes you *do* give in to the plea, "Just one more chapter, *please.*" And on another day, when your class is restless because something exciting is happening outside, you can at instant notice close school for the day and enrich the child's life.

If the class is having trouble with a mathematical concept, no matter. You either drop it for a while, or spend more time on it. And each child in the class always gets to read, verbalize, explain, and do.

So, *yes,* yes, yes, these guides are for the home school as much as for the institutionalized one! One warning. The one-to-one teaching situation is intense. Try to stay positive, relaxed and cheerful. Enjoy this precious time together! However, don't worry about slimming down the course. If you panic when you see all the areas covered, try sticking to the essentials at first. Bible reading/narration/discussion; English and literature; Math, and at least one good book being read aloud. When you're into the swing of the basics, you'll probably find you can add a science project, go for a nature walk regularly, read a history book, etc. But don't worry!

Alternatively, you may feel that with housework, libraries and bookstores far away, and a feeling that "I'm not sure if I'm *able* to actually teach my child . . ." you need more detailed help than this guide can give you.

That's exactly what I've needed myself! And there is an excellent provision for this need: a private school in Baltimore that will give you packaged home school requirements. You receive all the basic books needed to teach each grade, and clear instructions about *how* to teach. Better still, the philosophy behind Calvert is very similar to the Child Light one. The exception is that it has no directly Christian teaching, but you give this by starting each day with the daily Bible reading and adding missionary projects, discussions, and extra family reading times out of school. You can use this guide and *Books Children Love* to give you material and ideas so that the Calvert-educated child has everything Charlotte Mason hoped for! Although the pattern of history topics is different, the overall plan has a similar educational philosophy as the one Child Light stems from: a structured teaching of the three R's, a love of literature and history, a teaching of the history of art (painting, sculpture, architecture), and an emphasis on the development of good composition. Further, the day-by-day instructions to the parent teach you to teach! Excellent habits in study are fostered, and enough time is spent for the child to *really* learn.

The package you buy is a very good value. If it seems expensive, price separate learning to read materials, for instance. It is sometimes expensive or difficult to make up your own package of materials! Another consideration: although there are many home study programs to choose from, Calvert is the only one with over eighty years of responsible experience. Hundreds of thousands of children and parents have proved that Calvert works. Secondly, if you're convinced that you want the Child Light approach—Calvert is the *only* program I know of that uses the kinds of books we've been talking about.

Calvert's complete service is not only useful as a time-saver (no separate books to buy, a teaching manual for each grade), but it also provides a teaching service (optional). Lastly, the lessons are scheduled so that the child has only the morning filled with "school." This is *truly* Charlotte Mason! In fact, in the lower grades, an hour or two of lessons sees it done.

Calvert's "all-in" service saves time as everything is mailed in a package, and teaching training is provided "on the job" as you follow directions. The program has other benefits as well. For instance, you can subscribe to an extra service for teaching help. Children send in a monthly test, and a teacher will guide you in practical ways. This may not be necessary, but some children aim to do especially well for an outside authority, a *real* teacher!

You can rearrange the course if you like: leave out reading workbooks, go slower in arithmetic, use easier spelling if the one set of words seems too advanced, etc. You will also have to be very careful that the child is really ready for first grade work. Some five-year-olds are ready, while other seven-year-olds may just be nearing readiness.

• For more information write to: Calvert School
Tuscany Rd.
Grades K-8 available   Baltimore, MD 21210

However, you may not be able to afford Calvert, or you may opt for the Child Light curriculum in all its richness. For instance, you may find plenty of books in your library from those suggested in this guide and *Books Children Love*. Maybe you even picked up a good set of math books discarded by your local school. So, all you need is information about where to buy a package of reading instruction and books. Also, you want to add art supplies.

You'll find that the resource book *The NEW Big Book of Home Learning* by Mary Pride (published by Crossway Books) will tell you what is available, and where to send for it. This information, of course, would be helpful to parents sending children to schools and children's programs as well as to home schoolers.

Cassettes on Home Schooling

There is lots and lots more to say about home schooling. "How do I know it's a good idea for our family? How do I find time? Won't children be social misfits if they don't go to school?" and much more! Child Light has a set of cassettes available as a course on home schooling. It covers ideas, "how to" questions, etc. Many teachers attending the sessions also found them directly relevant to school situations. The tapes cover:

Understanding Life—Education (Number CL1)

Educating at Home—How?(Number CL2)

Living Education at Home—(Number CL3)

The Child Light Approach and Selecting Textbooks (Number CL4)

Contributors were Susan Macaulay, Diane Lopez, and Elizabeth Wilson. Tapes are available directly by mail from:
Sound Word Associates
P.O. Box 2035
430 Boyd Circle
Michigan City, IN 46360
USA
(219) 879-7753

Susan Schaeffer Macaulay

Appendix V:
Reading Shakespeare
with Children

Y ou will have noticed that in the English guides, grades 4-6, in the list of books that is given at the end of each chapter for "listening, reading and narrating" are several plays by Shakespeare. This is very unusual material for grade school children. We often only meet Shakespeare in high school or college.

The reading of Shakespeare was included in the Mason schools not to impress anybody, but because Charlotte Mason believed in leading children to a feast for the mind, the best source materials. She *didn't* make an examination subject out of it, prescribing what and how much the child should remember. This is rather like a marine biologist who observes and remembers more about a day on the beach than his three-year-old daughter. However, both of their experiences have value in response to the reality of the beach. Children and adults all find something rich in material such as Shakespeare's plays.

Children who are products of homes where not a book has been read aloud, whose minds have been dulled by constant TV viewing, who cannot listen to a whole story read through, shouldn't usually be immersed directly into listening to a Shakespeare play! There has to be a time when they begin to enjoy listening to whole books read chapter by chapter. After they are used to this, read a few books that use more and more literary language. Children won't notice that they are becoming familiar with a more structured language usage of another generation.

Perhaps, as has been remarked in another place in this guide, a good introduction to a Shakespeare play is to first have read aloud one of the stories Shakespeare used from the retelling in *Tales From*

Shakespeare by Charles and Mary Lamb. Then, as a special treat, view that same play in the original. PBS sometimes screens the excellent BBC Shakespeare productions.

Following this, or with only the reading of the story, each child has their own copy of the Shakespeare play being read. An act is read aloud once a week. Different children can read a character part, making this into a fun play-reading. No matter if every detail isn't picked up. Shakespeare is a treasure house, not least in the tales told, the vivid language used, and the ideas spawned. This should be an alive, interesting reading, not a dull flat lesson.

The next day, the children (or a selected child or two) tells back the story from the previous day's reading. Older children narrate their memory of it in writing.

Children often have lively discussions and arguments about the characters in the plays, the moral issues, etc. They also enjoy acting out a scene from the play (or even an entire play for experienced Shakespearians).

One other interesting resource is the excellent tapes of great actors reading through an entire Shakespeare play. Following the performed play in the written text is exciting. It is best if this follows the first reading session, so that the flow of the words has already been understood.

How many Shakespeare plays are taken on? In the original Mason schools, three plays a year were read. (One in the autumn, one in the winter, and one until the summer vacation.) With American timetables, one a semester might be better, or two a year. These can be covered with one Shakespeare reading a week.

Susan Schaeffer Macaulay

Appendix VI: Family (Sex) Education

The Christian worldview which Child Light has does not ignore the necessity of clear instruction and guidance in every area of life. This includes the communicating of the absolute moral standards of Christianity in a society which has abandoned the pretense of believing Christianity.

A warm family is the best place for family or sex education. From preschool age up, children turn to their parents with questions. "Where do babies come from?" is easy, but "How does the seed get there?" may cause some perplexity as the right answer is sought! Of course, the *"unspoken"* curricula is the most powerful. We communicate our loyalty to each other, warmth, respect, affection, and our priorities without words, by *living*.

This, rather like the other areas, puts the onus back on *us*. Are our marriages communicating the right things? Do we chose to serve the people in our families as our top priority? Do we take the time, have the discipline, make the effort to have the right family *life*? *Marriages*? A challenge? None of us does very well, I'm afraid. But this is where growth, change, effort *counts*. Our lives are powerful educational tools.

Secondly, our *ideas* in this area have to be straight. The Ten Commandments still work best as they are the working rules given by our Maker. Although cultural changes have been rapid, God's *laws* and therefore what works *hasn't* changed. God's Word is our instruction book in life.

Thirdly, as we see that all of life was created by God, and under the Lordship of Christ, we don't think that sex is lower, say, than a spiritual activity. All of life is good and positive when used the way God intended it. This gives us true liberation. We should not be ashamed to teach explicitly about sexual matters any more than anything else in life.

□ *291*

In a perfect world, a lot of the education would be done in the home situation. Each institutional situation (church, school, etc.) must, however, take the responsibility of seeing that children do receive clear teaching in all areas of family and sex education. In any case, if you're a school following this curriculum, you'll be encouraging a lot of questioning and discussion. Topics covering sexuality, family, etc., will crop up from readings in *any* area: literature, current events and news magazines, Bible readings, history, etc. Teachers must be prepared to communicate a Christian worldview in this area as well.

One of the greatest effects of a child following material from the Child Light curriculum and *Books Children Love* will be that they will *not* be totally influenced by the social standards, values and practices of today. For instance, children who have the Little House series read to them will deeply appreciate traditional family life at its best. The influence upon a child of this other way of living and seeing things is to me one of the most important benefits I have been able to share with my children. The beauty of it is that it works wherever you live! It doesn't happen merely because you read one book *about* family life to children! Deep understanding of the worth of each individual, justice, righteousness, the effects of wrong choices in life, marriage and tender care of the young can come from a childhood where book friends open a door of everyday experience and friendships with people of another age who lived in more human, Christian ways than they see all around today. I'd personally be frightened to try to bring up a child in this TV- and filth-saturated age without the clean, wholesome fresh air of families, marriages, parents, communities of yesterday actually *known* and *loved* by the child listener. In the end, history, science, understanding the flow of culture, all this is nothing compared to the building up of wholesome, whole people who accept their human worth and dignity, and accept God's primary aim in life, "Love the Lord your God with all your heart, and with all your soul and with all your strength and with all your mind, and your neighbor as yourself." We can't even begin to do this if we don't honor God's life rules, and encourage love amongst us, including serving and loving our families.

Note: Cassette tapes on subjects such as "Female and Male as Portrayed in the Bible," marriage and sex are available from the L'Abri cassette address given in Chapter 23. (For the adults!) Recommended material is also available from Focus on the Family, Pomona, CA 91799.

See, too, AIDS education suggestions in 6th grade social studies curriculum guide.

Susan Schaeffer Macaulay

Appendix VII: Homework

A n integral part of the Child Light philosophy is that children need time to be children—to play creatively, to run, to climb, to sit, and to do nothing. They need to have time for family interaction and activities, to be involved in church activities, and to participate in special interest activities—drama, art, music, sports, etc.

Any homework assigned should be meaningful and never homework for homework's sake. At the elementary level it should never be given daily or on weekends. Children do not complete work at the same rate and homework assignments need to be made with this in mind. Using the child who works the most quickly as a guide will not be giving due consideration to those who may need two or three times as long to complete the same assignment. In the lower grades ten to fifteen minutes, in the middle grades fifteen to thirty minutes, and in the upper grades forty-five minutes to one hour are reasonable guidelines. Book report reading and long-range projects could require additional time.

Any homework assigned should be clearly understood by the student. Sufficient classroom instruction must be given so that the student is thoroughly familiar with the procedures involved in the assignment. Assignments should be able to be completed independently by the student. Parents are responsible for providing an environment conducive to study, for showing interest in what the child is doing, and in offering some guidance if necessary. They should not have to teach or need to do extensive searching for materials to be utilized by the student in completing the work.

Homework should never be assigned as a disciplinary measure.

Homework can involve pre-teaching materials for a lesson—finding pictures, collecting leaves or seeds, looking up information, selecting a relevant article in a magazine or the newspaper, etc. It can also be reinforcement practice of a newly learned skill.

Appendix VIII: Discipline

T he goal of all discipline should be to assist children in becoming self-disciplined individuals. Self-discipline and not external discipline is the ultimate goal. Children should decide to do what is right because it is the right thing to do, and not because there will be discipline administered if the wrong decision is made.

In order for learning to take place in a classroom there must be an atmosphere of order. Behavioral expectations need to be clearly understood and preventative discipline employed.

Students should be dealt with consistently and fairly. Each child should learn to accept responsibility for his or her own actions. When a situation arises, the teacher needs to deal separately with each child and lead him or her step-by-step through the occurrence. It is important to have the child repeat exactly what he or she said and did and not what might have been said or thought, or what someone else did that contributed to the problem. After each child has gone through this process, all the individuals involved should come together and a solution be reached. A child should never automatically be suspect. The teacher needs to listen to all parties involved and to any witnesses, ask questions, and then carefully process the information. A child needs to know that he or she is not automatically condemned. The fact that love is unconditional but approval is not, should be a concept that children understand. It is vital that they fully comprehend that it is what they did wrong that is not accepted. The disciplinary action taken should be administered in a firm, loving, positive manner. The child or children involved need to be helped to change attitudes and behavior.

The teacher should never insult or knowingly humiliate a child. Care also needs to be taken to never label a particular child or class—

loud, lazy, rough, dumb, bad, etc. Because a child or group of children responds in a certain way at a certain time does not mean they will always respond or behave in a certain manner. The Holy Spirit works in children's lives to cause them to grow, mature, and change.

Teachers need to be creative in their disciplinary actions and to reward positive responses. Good guidelines to follow are to be sure that the disciplinary action fits the seriousness of the offense, that the type of discipline for similar situations does not vary too much, and that consistency in expectations and corrective measures is exercised.

Notes

Chapter One: The Child Light Curriculum Guide: Philosophy and Use

1. Susan Schaeffer Macaulay, *For The Children's Sake* (Westchester, IL: Crossway Books, 1984).

Chapter Three: Language Arts Overview

1. A very small proportion of children have actual physiological or psychological problems which require medical diagnosis and special instruction. Such cases should have individualized analysis and are outside the scope of this program.

Chapter Four: Reading

1. A well-written book, fiction or nonfiction, classic or contemporary.
2. Susan Schaeffer Macaulay, *For the Children's Sake* (Westchester, IL: Crossway Books, 1984), pp. 29-30.
3. The best approach for a child with a diagnosed "learning difference" or "learning disability" should be discussed with a specialist.
4. Available from the Paternoster Press, Paternoster House, 3 Mount Radford Crescent, Exeter, Devon, England.
5. See note 4 above.
6. See note 4 above.
7. See note 4 above.
8. See note 4 above.
9. See note 4 above.
10. See note 4 above.
11. See note 4 above.
12. See note 4 above.

Chapter Seven: English

1. Susan Schaeffer Macaulay, *For the Chilren's Sake* (Westchester, Il: Crossway Books, 1984), pp. 111, 112.

Chapter Thirteen: Science

1. Charlotte Mason, *School Education* (London: Kegan Paul, Trench, Trubner and Co., Ltd., 1929), p. 156.
2. Susan Schaeffer Macaulay, *For the Children's Sake* (Westchester, IL: Crossway Books, 1984), p. 133.

Chapter Fifteen: Bible

1. Charlotte Mason, *An Essay Toward a Philosophy of Education* (London: J. M. Dent and Sons, Ltd., 1931), p. 272.
2. *Ibid.*
3. *Ibid.*
4. *Ibid.*, pp. 272-273.
5. Barry Seagren, *What Does It Mean to be Spiritual?* L'Abri Fellowship tape. (See Chapter 23 for more information on L'Abri Fellowship Tapes.)
6. Charlotte Mason, *Home Education,* 17th ed. (Oxford: The Scrivener Press, 1955).

Chapter Eighteen: Art

1. Charlotte Mason, *School Education,* 5th ed. (London: Kegan Paul, Trench, Trubner and Co., Ltd., 1929), p. 239.
2. Charlotte Mason, *An Essay Towards a Philosophy of Education* (London: J. M. Dent and Sons, Ltd., 1931), p. 214.
3. *Ibid.*
4. Susan Schaeffer Macaulay, *For the Children's Sake* (Westchester, IL: Crossway Books, 1984), p. 128.

Chapter Twenty-one: Textbooks

1. Charlotte Mason, *School Education* (London: Kegan Paul, Trench, Trubner and Co., Ltd., 1929), p. 180.

Chapter Twenty-three: Developing a Christian Mind and a Christian Worldview

1. *What in the World Is Real?* (Champaign, IL: Communication Institute, 1982), chapter by R. C. Macaulay, p. 122.
2. *Ibid.*, p. 123.

3. From "Jungleland" by Bruce Springsteen. All selections © 1975 Laurel-Canyon Music Ltd. (ASCAP).
4. Francis A. Schaeffer, *The Great Evangelical Disaster* (Westchester, IL: Crossway Books, 1984), p. 44.
5. *Ibid.*, pp. 11, 12.
6. Recommended: a set of *The Complete Works of Francis A. Schaeffer* (Westchester, IL: Crossway Books, 1982). An important wide-reaching resource for any Christian school staff or church.
7. Francis A. Schaeffer, *He Is There and He Is Not Silent* in *The Complete Works of Francis A. Schaeffer,* Vol. 1 (Westchester, IL: Crossway Books, 1982), pp. 275, 276.
8. Other materials relating a sound Biblical worldview to every area are available from: Probe Ministries, 1900 Firman Dr., Suite 100, Richardson, TX 75081. (214) 480-0240.
9. Francis A. Schaeffer, *How Should We Then Live?* (Westchester, IL: Crossway Books, 1983), pp. 19, 20.

Appendix I: Alternate Social Studies Overview

1. E. D. Hirsch, Jr., *Cultural Literacy* (Boston: Houghton, Mifflin Co., 1987).
2. Francis A. Schaeffer, *How Should We Then Live?* (Westchester, IL: Crossway Books, 1983).
3. Allan Bloom, *The Closing of the American Mind* (New York: Simon and Schuster, 1988).
4. Concepts and Inquiry Series (Newton, MA: Allyn and Bacon). Books are out of print but are widely available. See Chapter 21.
5. The *How Should We Then Live?* film series is available in 16mm film and various videotape formats. To purchase or rent contact Gospel Films National Film Library, P.O. Box 455, Muskegon, MI 49443.

Appendix III: Alternate Social Studies Curriculum, Grades Five and Six

1. *Time,* 25 Jan. 1988, p. 38.